"Phil Moore's new commentaries are outstanding: biblical and passionate, clear and well-illustrated, simple and profound. God's Word comes to life as you read them, and the wonder of God shines through every page."

– Andrew Wilson, Author of Incomparable and If God Then What?

"Want to understand the Bible better? Don't have the time or energy to read complicated commentaries? The book you have in your hand could be the answer. Allow Phil Moore to explain and then apply God's message to your life. Think of this book as the Bible's message distilled for everyone."

– Adrian Warnock, Christian blogger

"Phil Moore presents Scripture in a dynamic, accessible and relevant way. The bite-size chunks – set in context and grounded in contemporary life – really make the make the Word become flesh and dwell among us."

– Dr David Landrum, The Bible Society

"Through a relevant, very readable, up to date storying approach, Phil Moore sets the big picture, relates God's Word to today and gives us fresh insights to increase our vision, deepen our worship, know our identity and fire our imagination. Highly recommended!"

– Geoff Knott, former CEO of Wycliffe Bible Translators UK

"What an exciting project Phil has embarked upon! These accessible and insightful books will ignite the hearts of believers, inspire the minds of preachers and help shape a new generation of men and women who are seeking to learn from God's Word."

– David Stroud, Newfrontiers and ChristChurch London

For more information about the Straight to the Heart series, please go to **www.philmoorebooks.com**.
You can also receive daily messages from Phil Moore on Twitter by following **@PhilMooreLondon**.

STRAIGHT TO
THE HEART OF

Galatians
to
Colossians

60 BITE-SIZED INSIGHTS

Phil Moore

MONARCH
BOOKS

Oxford, UK & Grand Rapids, Michigan, USA

Published by Monarch Books
an imprint of
Lion Hudson plc
Wilkinson House, Jordan Hill Road,
Oxford OX2 8DR, England
Email: monarch@lionhudson.com
www.lionhudson.com/monarch

ISBN 978 0 85721 546 8
e-ISBN 978 0 85721 547 5

First edition 2014

Acknowledgments
Scripture quotations taken from the *Holy Bible, New International Version* Anglicised. Copyright © 1979, 1984, 2011 Biblica, formerly International Bible Society. Used by permission of Hodder & Stoughton Ltd, an Hachette UK company. All rights reserved. "NIV" is a registered trademark of Biblica. UK trademark number 1448790. Both 1984 and 2011 versions are quoted in this commentary.
Scripture quotations listed as English Standard Version are from The Holy Bible, English Standard Version® (ESV®) copyright © 2001 by Crossway, a publishing ministry of Good News Publishers. All rights reserved.
Scripture quotations listed as King James Version as from The Authorized (King James) Version. Rights in the Authorized Version are vested in the Crown. Reproduced by permission of the Crown's patentee, Cambridge University Press.
p. 29: Extract taken from "Why Don't They Listen?", *Christianity Today*, September 2003. Copyright © 2003 John R. W. Stott. Courtesy of the John Stott Literary Executors.
p. 63: Extract from *The New Man* by Martyn Lloyd Jones copyright © Martyn Lloyd Jones, 1972. Used by permission of The Banner of Truth Trust.
pp. 146–47: Extract from *For the Glory of God* by Rodney Stark copyright © 2003 Princeton University Press. Reprinted by permission of Princeton University Press.

A catalogue record for this book is available from the British Library.

Printed and bound in the UK, April 2014, LH26

This book is for any church
which dares to believe that the
Gospel means we can have
God on the inside.

CONTENTS

PART THREE – COLOSSIANS: STRONG ON THE INSIDE

PART FOUR – PHILIPPIANS: JOYFUL ON THE INSIDE

About the *Straight to the Heart* Series

On his eightieth birthday, Sir Winston Churchill dismissed the compliment that he was the "lion" who had defeated Nazi Germany in World War Two. He told the Houses of Parliament that *"It was a nation and race dwelling all around the globe that had the lion's heart. I had the luck to be called upon to give the roar."*

I hope that God speaks to you very powerfully through the "roar" of the books in the *Straight to the Heart* series. I hope they help you to understand the books of the Bible and the message which the Holy Spirit inspired their authors to write. I hope that they help you to hear God's voice challenging you, and that they provide you with a springboard for further journeys into each book of Scripture for yourself.

But when you hear my "roar", I want you to know that it comes from the heart of a much bigger "lion" than me. I have been shaped by a whole host of great Christian thinkers and preachers from around the world, and I want to give due credit to at least some of them here:

Terry Virgo, David Stroud, Dave Holden, John Hosier, Adrian Holloway, Greg Haslam, Lex Loizides and all those who lead the Newfrontiers family of churches. Friends and encouragers, such as Stef Liston, Joel Virgo, Stuart Gibbs, Scott Taylor, Nick Sharp, Nick Derbridge, Phil Whittall, and Kevin and Sarah Aires. Tony Collins, Jenny Ward and Simon Cox at Monarch Books. Malcolm Kayes and all the elders of The Coign Church, Woking.

My fellow elders and church members here at Everyday Church in Southwest London. My great friend Andrew Wilson – without your friendship, encouragement and example, this series would never have happened.

I would like to thank my parents, my brother Jonathan, and my in-laws, Clive and Sue Jackson. Dad – your example birthed in my heart the passion which brought this series into being. I didn't listen to all you said when I was a child, but I couldn't ignore the way you got up at five o' clock every morning to pray, read the Bible and worship, because of your radical love for God and for his Word. I'd like to thank my children – Isaac, Noah, Esther and Ethan – for keeping me sane when publishing deadlines were looming. But most of all, I'm grateful to my incredible wife, Ruth – my friend, encourager, corrector and helper.

You all have the lion's heart, and you have all developed the lion's heart in me. I count it an enormous privilege to be the one who was chosen to sound the lion's roar.

So welcome to the *Straight to the Heart* series. My prayer is that you will let this roar grip your own heart too – for the glory of the great Lion of the Tribe of Judah, the Lord Jesus Christ!

Introduction: God on the Inside

> *I plead with you, brothers and sisters, become like me, for I became like you.*
>
> (Galatians 4:12)

If Paul hadn't written letters to the churches which he planted, we would have to assume he was like a superhuman movie hero: brilliant to admire from a distance but not a person we can copy.

Paul's ministry results were deeply impressive. When he and his friend Barnabas visited Galatia in 48 AD, they planted four churches in almost as many months. They were so effective in spreading the Christian faith that the Galatians afforded them godlike status. Paul needed to rebuke them in Acts 14:15: *"Why are you doing this? We too are only men, human like you."*

When Paul moved on to Philippi in 50 AD, he speeded up instead of slowing down. We are told in Acts 16:12 that he planted a vibrant church in the city because he *"stayed there several days."* Modern-day church planters can spend decades in a city and only leave behind a fragile work, but not Paul. It only took him a few days to establish a church in Philippi that was strong enough to transform an entire region.

Paul made a much longer visit to Ephesus. He found a dozen confused believers in the city in 53 AD and he turned them into a megachurch of tens of thousands of radical disciples by the end of 55 AD.[1] He was so successful in his preaching that *"all the Jews and*

---

[1] We can tell the size of the church from the cost of the items burnt by the Ephesians in Acts 19:19. The haul was worth 100,000 days' wages for an

Greeks who lived in the province of Asia heard the word of the Lord" and his enemies complained that *"this fellow Paul has convinced and led astray large numbers of people here in Ephesus and in practically the whole province of Asia."*[2] The church which Paul planted at Ephesus was so strong that it went on to plant many more churches across the entire region. Paul was able to write to Colossae, a city 120 miles east of Ephesus, and tell his readers that he was praying *"for you and for those at Laodicea, and for all who have not met me personally."*[3] Judged on results alone, Paul jumps out from the pages of Church history like a superhuman titan.

That's why I am so grateful that we have copies of the letters which Paul wrote to the churches which he planted. Without them, we would feel like we were watching the efforts of an unreal movie hero. There is a scene at the beginning of *Terminator 2* where Arnold Schwarzenegger saves the life of a young boy.[4] He hugs the boy close to his chest and turns his back on the would-be assassin, receiving bullet after bullet in his back to protect the boy. After enduring enough firepower to kill an elephant, he walks away unscathed because, we discover later, his body isn't at all like yours or mine. He is a robot from another world with a titanium endoskeleton. He is a fictional hero we can admire, not a real person we can copy. He is like the apostle Paul would be if we didn't have his letters. We might put him on a pedestal, we might name churches after him, but we wouldn't believe it is God's will for us to be like him. We would preserve his memory in

---

unskilled labourer. It is quite feasible that a church could number tens of thousands of people in a city of 250,000 freemen and women and 400,000 slaves, although they would have needed to meet at multiple times and in multiple locations.

[2] Acts 19:10, 26.

[3] Colossians 2:1. Revelation 2–3 lists five churches in the region of Asia beyond those at Colossae and Laodicea. The church at Ephesus evidently went on to plant a great many other churches.

[4] *Terminator 2: Judgment Day* (TriStar Pictures, 1991).

the history books of a distant apostolic age, but we wouldn't drag him into the present and expect to be as fruitful as he was.

Paul's letters to his churches stop us from making this error. They reveal that Paul was a flesh-and-blood believer like us. Far from presenting himself as a unique exception, Paul pleads with the Galatians to *"become like me, for I became like you."* Paul makes it clear that his superhuman strength does not come from any virtue of his own. He tells the Colossians that *"I strenuously contend with all the energy Christ so powerfully works in me,"* and he tells the Philippians that *"I can do all this through him who gives me strength."*[5] Paul tore his clothes in grief when the Galatians tried to worship him as a superhuman hero in Acts 14:15, and he would tear his clothes in far greater grief today to see the hero worship which is bestowed on him by Christians who should know better because of his letters. Paul wrote these letters to teach us how to follow his example. He wrote them to show us what it means for us to have God on the inside.

Paul taught the people in the churches he planted that God had saved them in order to come and live inside them through his Holy Spirit. He didn't treat this as an add-on to the message of Christianity. He taught in Galatians 3:14 that God *"redeemed us in order that... by faith we might receive the promise of the Spirit."* He taught that following Jesus means having God on the inside – being strengthened by the same Holy Spirit who made Paul fruitful in the early days of Church history.

In 49 AD, Paul wrote his letter to the **Galatians** to teach them how the Holy Spirit makes people **free on the inside**. In 60 AD, he wrote to the **Ephesians** to explain how the Holy Spirit makes people **new on the inside**, and to the **Colossians** to teach them how the Spirit makes people **strong on the inside** too. In 61 AD, he wrote to the **Philippians** to teach them how the Holy Spirit makes people **joyful on the inside**.[6] He wrote each of these

13

---

[5] Galatians 4:12; Philippians 4:13; Colossians 1:29.

[6] Paul also wrote other letters, but these have been covered separately in *Straight to the Heart of Romans, Straight to the Heart of 1 and 2 Corinthians*

four letters to stop people from placing him on a pedestal as a superhuman hero. He wrote to teach us that, if we have God on the inside, then we can be every bit as fruitful as he was.

The posters for one of the *Terminator* movies proclaimed: *"Same make. Same model. New mission."* That's a pretty good summary of what God wants to speak over your own life as you read these four letters. In a world where 60 per cent of people groups are still considered unreached or only nominally reached with the Gospel, and where some of these people groups are over 50 million people strong, it is vital that we take Paul's message seriously. In a world where 2.7 billion individuals have no indigenous church which can tell them the good news about Jesus, we can't afford to honour Paul by putting him high upon a pedestal. We can only honour him by reading the letters which he wrote to equip us to continue his work long after he was gone.[7]

So get ready to respond to the message which Paul wrote to these four churches. Get ready to believe that God can use people like you and me. Get ready to understand what the Bible means when it promises that we can have God on the inside.

and *Straight to the Heart of 1 Thessalonians to Titus*.

[7] This data was taken from the website of the Joshua Project in 2013.

Part One – Galatians:

Free on the Inside

One Staple (1:1–9)

If we or an angel from heaven should preach a gospel other than the one we preached to you, let them be under God's curse!

(Galatians 1:8)

David Nowitz had tried very hard. The Society for Family Health in Johannesburg had never had such a conscientious marketing manager. He had managed to secure government funding for a mass distribution of pamphlets throughout the city to warn people of the dangers of sexually transmitted infections. He had the pamphlets translated into Zulu, Xhosa, Sotho and Afrikaans. He had paid a distribution company to deliver the pamphlets throughout the city along with a free condom to help people to respond to his warnings. It was only when he visited a home and saw one of his pamphlets that he realized with horror what had happened: the distribution company had stapled the condom to the pamphlet, putting two holes in every single condom.

David Nowitz admitted to reporters that *"We made a deal with a low-budget distribution company."* He had entrusted his message to people who thought a single staple wouldn't make any difference, when in reality those two tiny pinpricks undermined everything. His safe-sex campaign actually increased the danger of sexually transmitted infections and unwanted pregnancies across Johannesburg.[1] If you can imagine how David Nowitz felt when he saw his stapled pamphlet for the first time, then you

---

[1] This happened in February 1999, recounted by Stephen Pile in *The Ultimate Book of Heroic Failures* (2011).

can imagine the horror that stirred Paul to write his letter to the Galatians at the start of 49 AD.

Paul had spent part of 48 AD planting churches in Pisidian Antioch, Iconium, Lystra and Derbe – the cities of Galatia, which is now in southern Turkey.[2] We are told in Acts 14:3 that he went as God's missionary to preach *"the message of his grace,"* explaining that Jesus lived the perfect life which the Galatians had failed to live and that he had died the brutal death which the Galatians deserved to die. Paul's announcement that human sin provokes God's judgment wasn't news to the people of Galatia (the Jews and pagans were agreed on that), but what was news was Paul's announcement that religious rituals and good behaviour were not enough to atone for human sin. The Galatians tried to stone him to death for preaching that *"Through Jesus the forgiveness of sins is proclaimed to you. Through him everyone who believes is set free from every sin, a justification you were not able to obtain under the law of Moses."*[3] The essence of Paul's message to the Galatians was grace, which is why Acts 13:43 tells us that he *"urged them to continue in the grace of God."* Grace offers us *G*od's *R*iches *A*t *C*hrist's *E*xpense. If they forgot this, the Galatians were as foolish as a Johannesburg pamphlet distribution company.

Paul was very agitated when he wrote his first New Testament letter.[4] Since he does not mention the decisions that the apostles made in Jerusalem towards the end of 49 AD in Acts 15, he must have written to the Galatians earlier that same

---

[2] See Acts 13–14. *Galatia* had originally referred to the Celtic settlements to the north of these four cities, but by Paul's day the Roman province of Galatia stretched much further south.

[3] Acts 13:38–39. Tom Wright and other writers from the "new perspective" school point out that Paul's message was about more than individual salvation. Yes, but it wasn't about *less* than individual salvation.

[4] Paul's first letter was probably the second earliest letter in the New Testament, since James wrote his letter in about 48 AD. This early dating is not just based on Paul's failure to mention the pivotal rulings recorded in Acts 15, but also on the way he chides the Galatians in 1:6 for abandoning the Gospel *"so quickly."*

year while he was staying in Syrian Antioch.[5] We are told in Acts 15:1 that *"Certain people came down from Judea to Antioch and were teaching the believers: 'Unless you are circumcised, according to the custom taught by Moses, you cannot be saved.'"*[6] Evidently these same false teachers were making inroads into the churches which Paul had planted in Galatia, for he writes in 5:12, *"As for those agitators, I wish they would go the whole way and emasculate themselves!"* Circumcision, obedience to the Jewish Law and reliance on a few good works might seem like tiny pinpricks in the Gospel, but Paul could see that it undermined absolutely everything. He warns the Galatians not to be *"fools."* If Jesus' work of salvation is perfect, then adding anything to it obscures its saving power.

This background helps us understand the opening verses of Galatians. It's why Paul begins this letter with the phrase *"Grace and peace to you from God our Father and the Lord Jesus Christ."* He doesn't use this phrase out of habit to open all of his letters, but because the Gospel is about God's grace from start to finish. It tells us that Jesus has done everything to free us from God's judgment because we are powerless to free ourselves. We don't need God's reward for our best efforts. We need God's mercy (not punishing us as we deserve) and we need God's grace (blessing us even though we don't deserve it). We can never earn these things from God ourselves. We can only receive them as gifts because we believe in the perfect life that Jesus has already lived for us.

Paul wrote to the Galatians in their native Greek, and he uses three Greek words to show them just how serious these pinpricks of self-reliance are. The first word is *metatithēmi,* a

---

[5] Acts 14:26–28. Instead of appealing to decisions made in Jerusalem, Paul writes in 1:2 that his letter is endorsed by *"the brothers who are with me"* – the Antioch church, which sent him to Galatia the previous year.

[6] James, the leader of the church in Jerusalem, is at pains to clarify in Acts 15.24 that these teachers came out of the church he led but they in no way spoke for him.

word which was normally used for soldiers who switched sides before a battle (1:6). Paul tells the Galatians that switching to self-reliance instead of continuing in God's grace makes them turncoats who have sided with the people who attacked him. The second word is *heteros* (1:6). The Greeks had two words for *another*: the word *allos* meant *another of the same type* (Jesus uses this word to describe the Holy Spirit as *another* helper like himself in John 14:16), and the word *heteros* meant *another of a different type* (this is the root of the English word *heterosexual*). By describing the new message that was being preached in the Galatian churches as a *heteros* gospel, Paul emphasizes that Christian self-help is very different from the real Christian Gospel. Since the Gospel is perfect, adding to it is just as fatal as subtracting from it. These tiny pinpricks of self-reliance couldn't be more serious.

The third word that Paul uses is *anathema* (1:8 and 1:9). This is the word used throughout the Greek Old Testament to translate the Hebrew word *hērem*, or *handed over to the Lord for destruction*. It was the strongest curse which a first-century Jew could place on anyone, so Paul utters it twice in order to convey to his readers the seriousness of their situation.[7] By smuggling human works into the finished work of Jesus these false teachers had committed the same sin as Achan in the time of Joshua.[8] They must be cut off from God's People or the Galatians would be cut off with them.[9]

That's why Paul's letter to the Galatians is the Magna Carta

---

[7] The word *anathema* is also used in the solemn oaths in Mark 14:71, Acts 23:12, 14 and 1 Corinthians 16:22.

[8] The words *hērem* and *anathema* are used repeatedly in the Hebrew and Greek texts of Joshua 6:17–18 and 7:11–13. The Galatians understood Paul to be effectively saying *"To hell with them!"*

[9] Paul probably refers to an *angel from heaven* because the Galatians originally mistook him for Hermes, the messenger of the Greek gods (Acts 14:12), but it is also significant that Mormons and Muslims claim that their alternative gospels were given by angels to Joseph Smith and to Muhammad. See 2 Corinthians 11:14.

of the New Testament, the proclamation of God's freedom as a gift to sinful people who believe in Jesus Christ.[10] Paul tells us that this message of freedom cannot be earned. It is all about what Jesus has done for us and not about what we can do for him in return. Reliance on religious rituals or on our own good works isn't a different emphasis. It is an entirely different gospel.

---

[10] When Paul tells us in 1:2 that Jesus is *Christ* (the Greek translation of the Hebrew word *Messiah*) and *Lord* (the Greek translation of the Hebrew word *Yahweh*), he identifies Jesus both as Saviour and as God.

Good Ideas and God's Idea
(1:10–2:14)

I want you to know, brothers and sisters, that the
gospel I preached is not of human origin.

(Galatians 1:11)

Paul's message was deeply unpopular in Galatia. We tend to miss this because he was so successful in planting churches there. We tend to forget that the Jews forcibly expelled him from two cities because they hated his message that only Jesus' death on the cross could free them from God's judgment. We tend to forget that he fled from another city having almost been lynched for trying to persuade the pagans there that they needed to turn from the hero gods of Mount Olympus to the crucified God of Mount Zion.[1] Unless we grasp the full scandal of Paul's message in Galatia, we will fail to understand why the churches he planted there modified it very shortly after he sailed back to Syria.

We will also fail to understand why the first two chapters of this letter read like Paul's autobiography. He feels he needs to persuade the Galatians that the Gospel he preached in their cities wasn't just his own good idea but God's idea. It's why he begins the letter by stating that he is an apostle *"sent not from men nor by a man, but by Jesus Christ and God the Father,"* and it's why he spends much of these first two chapters listing his credentials as a Gospel preacher.

First, he tells the Galatians in 1:10–24 that they need to

---

[1] Paul explicitly links the unpopularity of his message to the cross of Jesus in 5:11 and 6:12. The idea that Jesus had to be punished in our place because of our sins is still deeply unpopular today.

take his Gospel seriously because *he received it directly from God*. They must not believe the propaganda of his critics, which he refers to in 1:10, that he is merely the lackey of influential Greek Christians in Syria.[2] He is more Jewish than any of the false teachers in Galatia, and he was once more tangled up than they are in Jewish traditions. But God freed him through the message of his grace. Jesus appeared to him personally on the road to Damascus and commissioned him to be a preacher of the very Gospel that he sought to destroy.[3] The good ideas preached by the false teachers might sound convincing, but they were no match for God's idea which he had entrusted to Paul. If the Galatians modified his message, they were rejecting the very words of Jesus.

Second, Paul tells the Galatians in 2:1–10 that they need to take his Gospel seriously because *it has been endorsed by all of the apostles*. Fourteen years after his conversion, in 47 AD, he responded to the words of the prophet Agabus in Acts 11:27–30 by going down to Jerusalem with a financial gift for the Christians in Judea. He took advantage of this opportunity to set out before the apostles the Gospel that he was preaching about *"the freedom we have in Christ Jesus."* These apostles – men like James, Peter and John[4] – fully endorsed Paul's Gospel message and *"recognised the grace given to me."* Paul ups the ante for the Galatian churches when he tells them that, if they modify his message, they are rejecting the collective teaching of Jesus' apostles.

Third, he tells the Galatians in 2:11–14 that they need

---

[2] Paul's refusal to seek human approval does not mean that he was careless or deliberately offensive. It means that he sought to please people only when it was also pleasing to God (1 Corinthians 10:32–33).

[3] The Greek word for church is *ekklēsia*, a word used throughout the Greek Old Testament for the *assembly* of Israel. As a voting member of the Jewish Sanhedrin (Acts 26:10), Paul had led the attack on this new assembly.

[4] Paul describes a very relaxed system of government during the first 20 years of Church history. He talks about *"those who seemed to be leaders"* and clearly views James and himself as apostles equal to the Twelve.

to take his Gospel seriously because it has been vindicated when challenged in the past. He tells them that he had a public confrontation with Peter, the leading apostle,[5] over the very same issue that was troubling the churches in Galatia – whether Gentiles needed to convert to Christ alone or convert to all the trappings of Judaism as well.[6] Historians refer to the false teachers in Galatia as "Judaizers" because they tried to force Greek converts to embrace these Jewish trappings, but Paul simply calls them "the circumcision group" in 2:13 because this was their most obvious demand. If the apostles had not forced Titus the Greek to be circumcised (2:3), and if Peter had backed down when Paul opposed him (2:11–14), then Paul warns the Galatians they are flying in the face of the past two decades of theological discussion if they believe the subtle lies of the Judaizers.

We live in an age that is full of good ideas, so these two chapters are far more than a lesson in Church history. They teach us how to respond to good ideas that promise us greater freedom if we adapt the Gospel to fit our culture. Paul warns us in 2:4 that such compromise always traps us into greater slavery instead.

These two chapters teach us to walk humbly whenever we discuss the Gospel. If even Peter and Barnabas could be led astray by false teaching, we must not be so proud as to imagine that we are immune to this danger ourselves.[7] It is far easier to point out flaws in the thinking of others than it is to admit that we may have succumbed to false teaching ourselves. If

[5] Paul refers to him by his Aramaic name *Cephas* in 1:18 and 2:9, 11 and 14. He refers to him by his Greek name *Peter* in 2:7 and 2:8. Both names mean *Rock* and he was evidently known by both names in Galatia.

[6] The Greek word *Ioudaïsmos*, or *Judaism*, only occurs in the New Testament here in 1:13 and 14. Whereas Acts stresses the continuity between Judaism and Christianity, Galatians stresses the discontinuity.

[7] These verses warn us not to treat the words of popes or denominational leaders as infallible. If even Peter made mistakes, no pope or church leader is completely free from error.

even Paul thought it was important to receive *"the right hand of fellowship"* from the other apostles, we ought to be accountable to other trusted Christians and willing to allow them to correct us.[8]

These two chapters also teach us to honour the conclusions of previous generations of believers. When Rob Bell was interviewed about his controversial statements about the nature of hell and about same-sex marriage, he was asked, *"Isn't the humility of orthodoxy to say, 'I'll stay where the church is unless I'm sure that the church has always been wrong about this?'"* His response was that *"This is why so many people don't want to be part of the church."* When he was challenged further – *"You're saying the world's moved on, God's going to get left behind... because it looks boring and retrograde and backward and intolerant"* – he simply replied, *"That's well said."*[9] Whatever you think about his conclusions, you should sense from these two chapters that his reasoning is very dangerous. Paul warns the Galatians that, whenever we compromise the Gospel to accommodate our culture, we do not sweeten the meaning of Jesus' death on the cross (5:11 and 6:12). We deny it.

God calls us to challenge the good ideas of men and women to their faces (2:11), and to do so publicly for the sake of others (2:14). He calls us to do so lovingly (1:11) but firmly (1:9) in order to save them from the Devil's trap. Good ideas always sound good, by definition, but they are no substitute for God's idea as he revealed it to the apostle Paul.

---

[8] We can tell from ancient Greek art that Paul's contemporaries shook hands with each other using their right hands – the hand in which they might hold a weapon – as a gesture of peace, trust and fellowship.

[9] Rob Bell, author of *Love Wins* (2011), took part in this interview on London's Premier Radio on 20th April 2013. His interviewer was Andrew Wilson, author of *If God, Then What?* (2012).

Inside-Out God (1:16, 24)

It pleased God, who separated me from my mother's womb, and called me by his grace, to reveal his Son in me... And they glorified God in me.

(Galatians 1:15–16, 24, *King James Version*)

If you want to understand the difference between Paul's Gospel and the false gospel that was being peddled in Galatia, look no further than the two words that Paul repeats in 1:16 and 1:24. The words only contain six letters between them, but they hold an eternity of meaning: *en emoi* is Greek for *inside me*.

Paul had been an expert at outside-in religion. He tells us in Acts 26:5 that *"I conformed to the strictest sect of our religion, living as a Pharisee."* The Pharisees were those who preached strict separation from the Gentiles and radical obedience to the Law of Moses, modernizing and categorizing it into 248 commands, 365 prohibitions and 1,521 amendments. Paul had been one of them, and he had done everything humanly possible to free his heart from sin and to win acceptance from God. But in doing so, he had discovered that outside-in religion always fails, as Jesus pointed out in Matthew 23: *"You clean the outside of the cup and dish, but inside they are full of greed and self-indulgence. Blind Pharisee! First clean the inside of the cup and dish, and then the outside also will be clean."* Paul didn't clash with the Judaizers in Galatia because he lacked sympathy for the Jewish Law. He opposed them because he had tried their outside-in religion and found it wanting.[1]

---

[1] "New perspective" writers argue that first-century Judaism was not an outside-in religion, but this is very hard to square with Jesus' words in Matthew

Paul had been mentored by Gamaliel, the famous Pharisee who argued in Acts 5:33–39 that the Christian faith would die out on its own if it were not of God. Paul had disagreed with his mentor on this point and had led the effort to hunt down and imprison anyone who followed Jesus. It was while he was travelling to Damascus to look for Christians that he saw a vision of Jesus and began to grasp the message of the inside-out God. Jesus asked him a very odd question in Acts 9:4: *"Saul, Saul, why do you persecute **me**?"* Persecute *me*. Not persecute my followers or my Church, but persecute *me*. Paul began to learn the message that dominates each of the four letters in this commentary: that God wants to live in the hearts of his followers and to change them from the inside out, as he lives in us and as we live in him.[2]

Paul wants the Galatians to understand that God-in-me is the only reason he has been *forgiven for his sins*. Far from earning God's approval, his outside-in religion turned him into a monster and an enemy of God's Church. He wasn't forgiven because he observed the Jewish Law but because God *"set me apart from my mother's womb and called me by his grace"* in order *"to reveal his Son in me."*[3] While he was still an enemy of God, the Lord broke into his heart and saved him from the inside out, convincing him to trade in *"a righteousness of my own that comes from the law"* for a righteousness *"which is through faith in Christ – the righteousness that comes from God on the basis of faith."*[4]

Paul wants the Galatians to understand that God-in-me is also the only reason why *his character has become more like*

27

23:23–28 or with the whole of Romans 1–3.

[2] He changed his name from Saul because he was tired of trying to be head-and-shoulders above his peers through outside-in religion (1 Samuel 9:2). He chose the name Paul because it was Greek for *The Little Guy*.

[3] God's sovereign choice in salvation is a key theme of Paul's letter to the Ephesians. Here in Galatians 1:15 it has profound implications for when human life begins.

[4] This quotation comes from Paul's salvation testimony in Philippians 3:2–9.

that of Jesus. He tells us that he was not discipled by Peter or by any of the apostles. He was simply led by the Holy Spirit to spend three years in Arabia and Damascus where he studied the Scriptures and learned how to let Jesus change him from the inside out. He tells us in 1:24 that, by the time he went up to Jerusalem for two weeks in 36 AD,[5] the Holy Spirit had changed his character so significantly that Peter and James could see it clearly and *"glorified God in me".*[6]

Paul wants the Galatians to understand that God-in-me is also the only reason *he is so fruitful in his ministry.* He doesn't want them to admire him for planting churches so successfully across their region. He wants them to imitate him by responding ever more deeply to his Gospel. He points out that, even though his background as a Pharisee made him a perfect missionary to the Jews, God sovereignly *"called me by his grace... so that I might preach him among the Gentiles."*[7] He also points out that, after his brief visit to Jerusalem, despite his desire to become a travelling preacher of the Gospel straightaway, God confined him for eleven years to Tarsus, the capital of Cilicia, and to Antioch, the capital of Syria.[8] Paul emphasizes in 2:9 that his fruitfulness in ministry is as much a gift of God's grace as his initial conversion.

Paul wants us to understand that the Gospel is fundamentally a promise that God will come and live inside us, making us righteous and holy and fruitful from the inside out.

---

[5] Paul had intended to stay longer than two weeks in Jerusalem but the church leaders there sent him to Tarsus when they discovered that the Grecian Jews in Jerusalem were plotting to kill him (Acts 9:26–30).

[6] Not every Bible translator understands what Paul is saying in 1:24, so some English Bibles render it *"they praised God because of me"*. However, this doesn't do justice to what Paul is actually saying in Greek.

[7] Acts 22:17–21 tells us Paul fought God over this illogical decision, before finally surrendering to his will.

[8] Paul lived in Arabia 33–36 AD, in Tarsus 36–42 AD and in Antioch in 42–48 AD. He made his second visit to Jerusalem fourteen years after his conversion, in 47 AD (Galatians 2:1).

The rule-keeping of the Pharisees and Judaizers cannot save anyone because it is more like the man-made religions of the world than it is the Christian Gospel. Paul is preparing us for his great statement in 3:14 that God *"redeemed us in order that... by faith we might receive the promise of the Spirit."* He wants us to see the Gospel as a promise from the invisible God to come and dwell inside us and to make himself visible in us by changing us from the inside out by his incomparable power. John Stott writes that

> *The invisibility of God is a great problem. It was already a problem to God's people in Old Testament days. Their pagan neighbours would taunt them, saying, "Where is now your God?" Their gods were visible and tangible, but Israel's God was neither. Today in our scientific culture young people are taught not to believe in anything which is not open to empirical investigation. How then has God solved the problem of his own invisibility? The first answer is of course "in Christ." Jesus Christ is the visible image of the invisible God. John 1:18: "No one has ever seen God, but God the only Son has made him known." "That's wonderful," people say, "but it was 2,000 years ago. Is there no way by which the invisible God makes himself visible today?" There is... "If we love one another, God dwells in us." In other words, the invisible God, who once made himself visible in Christ, now makes himself visible in Christians, if we love one another.*[9]

Visible in Paul. Visible in you and me. Visible in every single Christian. Let's not settle for an outside-in false gospel like the Galatians. Let's celebrate Paul's Gospel message that God wants to come and change us from the inside out.

---

[9] John Stott in an interview with *Christianity Today* magazine entitled "Why Don't They Listen?" (September 2003).

First Signs of Spring (2:10)

*All they asked was that we should continue to
remember the poor, the very thing I was eager to do.*

(Galatians 2:10)

I am writing this chapter during the second week of spring. I
don't need a calendar to tell you that. I just need to look out
of the window onto my garden. Two weeks ago my apple tree
looked dead and bare, but now it is in full leaf and covered with
beautiful white blossom. I can't see the life-giving sap at work
on the inside, but I can't miss the outward signs that spring has
come.

Paul wants us to understand that it's the same with the
Gospel. He wants to demonstrate practically what it means for
God to change believers from the inside out, so he homes in
on one of the first signs that God is at work in a person's soul.
When he went up to Jerusalem in 47 AD with an offering to help
the famine-stricken Christians in Judea (Acts 11:27–30), the
apostles asked him to guarantee one thing when they endorsed
his Gospel message. They asked him to remember that one of
the first signs a person has responded to the Gospel is that God
starts to change the way they feel towards the poor.

People who understand the Gospel *sense that they are
part of a bigger story*. The Pharisees and Judaizers were so self-
centred that they shunned the poor as something dirty, like
the priest and Levite who thought they were pleasing God by
leaving a man bleeding by the side of the road in Luke 10:25–

37.[1] Jesus exposed the futility of their short-sighted religion by touching lepers and corpses and by teaching his disciples to do the same. He filled them with the Holy Spirit and sent them out to show what happens when the power of God flows from the inside out. People who truly understand the Gospel stop thinking about how they can get to God and start thinking about how they can let God flow out of them to fulfil his purposes in the world. That's why Paul tells Gentile churches that *"they owe it to the Jews to share with them their material blessings."*[2] If anybody acts as if the message of God's salvation is all about them, they haven't understood it. If they understand that God has written them into a drama that began with Abraham and the Jewish race and now continues in every nation of the world, then this is one of the first signs of spring.

People who understand the Gospel *sense God's heart of compassion towards the poor*. They refuse to write off anyone as undeserving of God's mercy because they have a true view of themselves. They recognize that they too were entirely undeserving of God's mercy when he decided to lavish his unmerited grace upon their lives. I recently chatted with a Christian lady who told me how disgusted she was by a group of non-Christians and how much she felt they deserved God's judgment. I was forced to challenge her that her comments betrayed a forgetfulness of how much her own sins had offended God. When Catherine Booth triggered a revival among the prostitutes in the London dockyards, a reporter commented that *"She identified herself with them as a fellow sinner, showing that if they supposed her to be better than themselves it was a*

---

[1] Their disdain for the poor is seen by the way they treat a beggar in John 9:34. The Parable of the Good Samaritan describes how many first-century Jewish leaders thought and behaved.

[2] Paul writes this in Romans 15:25–28 while taking up another collection for the poor Judean Christians in 57 AD. He writes something similar in 55 AD in 1 Corinthians 16:1–4 and 2 Corinthians 8–9.

mistake, since all had sinned against God."[3] The reporter had witnessed another clear sign of spring.

People who understand the Gospel *believe that God's indwelling power can transform anyone.* Only this could have given Paul confidence to appoint some of his new converts as elders for the Galatian churches in Acts 14:23, even though none of them had been a Christian for more than a few months. People who believe discipleship takes place from the outside in tend to write off the poor and broken as too difficult for God to use, but people who believe discipleship is God's work from the inside out tend to write off nobody. They believe that Jesus delights to turn vagrants into vicars and prostitutes into preachers.[4] When the English middle classes sneered at William Booth's revival and asked him where he was going to find enough leaders to fulfil his grand plans to re-evangelize his nation, he replied that *"We shall get them from the public houses. Men who have felt the fire will be the best men to rescue others, and we shall never fail in getting the right men."* True to his word, he asked the notorious bare-knuckle fighter Peter Monk to manage his largest soup kitchen within two weeks of his conversion.

People who understand the Gospel *commit to pouring out their lives for Jesus' sake on behalf of the poor.* They understand that Jesus sacrificed the luxuries of heaven to pour out his blood for an undeserving world, so they share Paul's desire in Colossians 1:24 to *"fill up in my flesh what is still lacking in regard to Christ's afflictions, for the sake of his body, which is the church."* William Booth was by no means the most talented church leader in Victorian London, but he was convinced that God had come to live inside him to enable him to sacrifice his life for those in need. He explained in an interview shortly before he died:

---

[3] The reporter made this observation in *The Wesleyan Times* on 27th March 1865.

[4] While *"the poor"* refers primarily to the poor Christians in Judea in 2:10, Paul also makes it clear in 6:10 that God wants us to help poor Christians in general as well as poor unbelievers.

I will tell you the secret. God has had all there was of me. There have been men with greater opportunities; but from the day I got the poor of London on my heart, and a vision of what Jesus Christ could do with the poor of London, I made up my mind that God would have all of William Booth there was. And if there is anything of power in The Salvation Army today, it is because God has all the adoration of my heart, all the power of my will, and all the influence of my life.[5]

So don't be surprised that Paul insists that a desire to help the poor always accompanies the true preaching of the Gospel. It is easy to forget the poor if we succumb to the self-centred doctrines of outside-in religion, but when God comes to live inside us through the Holy Spirit, he helps us see the bigger picture, sense his passion for the poor, and believe in his power to transform sinners into saints. He makes us more like Jesus by motivating us to pour out our lives for the sake of those who are in need. Whenever we see these things in an individual or in a church, we are witnessing the fruit of the Gospel that was planted in their hearts. We are witnessing some of the first signs of spring.

---

[5] Quoted from Charles Bateman in *The Life of General Booth* (1912).

Moses Wasn't Wrong
(2:15–21)

We who are Jews by birth and not "Gentile sinners"
know that a man is not justified by observing the law.
(Galatians 2:15–16)

When I was a teenager, I came across an old copy of John Bunyan's classic seventeenth-century novel, *The Pilgrim's Progress*. I didn't know very much about the Bible, but I knew enough to get confused. I knew that Moses was meant to be one of the good guys, and yet John Bunyan places him on the other team.

> **Faithful:** *So soon as the man overtook me… down he knocked me, and laid me for dead… I cried him mercy; but he said, I know not how to show mercy; and with that he knocked me down again. He had doubtless made an end of me, but that one came by, and bid him forbear.*
>
> **Christian:** *Who was that that bid him forbear?*
>
> **Faithful:** *I did not know him at first; but as he went by I perceived the holes in his hands and his side; then I concluded that he was our Lord. So I went up the hill.*
>
> **Christian:** *That man that overtook you was Moses: He spareth none, neither knoweth he how to show mercy to those that transgress his Law.*[1]

---

[1] John Bunyan in *The Pilgrim's Progress* (1678).

I was confused and, since then, I have discovered that so are many people who read Galatians. They imagine Paul must be saying that Moses got things wrong in the Jewish Law and that Jesus died on the cross to undo his error. That's why we need to slow down as we read the final verses of chapter 2. They tell us that this isn't what Paul is saying at all.

Paul is saying that first-century Jews *knew they could not be saved through obedience to the Law*. Several times in these verses he uses the technical word "justified", which means being declared righteous in God's sight. It means more than forgiveness (being spared punishment for our sins). It is a declaration of our innocence (that we don't deserve any punishment at all). Put that way, every first-century Jew knew that obedience to Moses' Law could not save them. The Law simply pointed out how far short of God's righteousness they had fallen. Paul states this uncontroversially in 2:16–17.[2]

Paul is also saying that first-century Jews *knew the Law showed them that they needed God's blood sacrifice for sin*. The Law of Moses was not just a long list of rules. It described so many lambs and goats and bulls being sacrificed to atone for human sin that it was bloodier than the complete works of Quentin Tarantino. Paul wasn't telling the Galatians that Moses had been wrong, but that he had been absolutely right. The Law had prophesied a day when God's Messiah would be crucified to pay the penalty for sin.

Paul is saying that first-century Jews *knew they were to obey the Law out of gratitude that God had made them his People*. They saw significance in the fact that God had not given the Law to Moses when he met him at Mount Sinai while the Israelites were still in Egypt. God had not given the Law to Moses as a list of dos and don'ts through which the Israelites could earn their freedom, but as a set of instructions about how to walk

---

[2] Paul begins by saying *"**we** who are Jews by birth"* in order to persuade the Galatians that he is not opposing the Judaizers because he lacks sympathy for Moses' Law, but because he truly understands it.

in the freedom he had already given them. It was only after they had trusted in the blood of the Passover lamb and been baptized in the Red Sea that they were given the Law at Mount Sinai.[3] Circumcision, food laws, Sabbath-keeping and all the other commands that Paul had once held dear were never given as a way through which a person could become part of God's People. They were given as outward signs that a person had been granted a place among God's People in spite of their sin.

But if this means I was right to consider Moses one of the good guys, why did John Bunyan cast him in the role of villain? He did so because he understood the message of Galatians. He was so affected by this letter and by Martin Luther's commentary on it that he exclaimed, *"I do prefer this book of Martin Luther upon the Galatians, excepting the Holy Bible, before all the books that ever I have seen, as most fit for a wounded conscience."*[4] Bunyan understood what Paul was saying in Galatians 2:15–21.

Paul accepted that every first-century Jew knew the purpose of the Law of Moses, but he pointed out that they also found it very easy to forget. Instead of treating the Law as a mirror that showed them their sinfulness and their need for God's blood sacrifice, they had started trusting in their own obedience to the Law to set them right with God. They had turned the Law into something it was never intended to be, a manual for outside-in righteousness, and in doing so they had turned Moses from friend into foe. Even after they converted to Christ, some Jewish believers still put so much faith in these ancient symbols that they tried to force the Greek believers to observe the Law of Moses too.

Paul tries to help the Galatians to rediscover Moses as their friend by telling them in 2:19 that *"through the law I died to the law so that I might live for God."* Paul was saved through the Law since Jesus completely obeyed the rulebook and became the

---

[3] Paul explains in 1 Corinthians 5:7 and 10:2 that these two events pointed to Jesus and to water baptism.

[4] Bunyan wrote this in *Grace Abounding to the Chief of Sinners* (1666).

ultimate blood sacrifice when he died on the cross to pay the penalty for sin. Paul died to the Law because Jesus' death in our place brings such complete forgiveness that God can fill us with his Holy Spirit and change us from the inside out to truly live for him. The sign that we are God's People isn't circumcision or Jewish food laws. It is whether or not we have God on the inside. Paul rejoices in 2:20 that *"I have been crucified with Christ and I no longer live, but Christ lives in me."*

Every generation of Christians is vulnerable to the error that Paul confronts in Galatians. If you are a Protestant, you can probably see clearly that many Catholics rely on external rituals. If you are a Catholic, you can probably see clearly that many Protestants rely on the external fruit of their own character. We can all be equally guilty of trying to smuggle our own good works into the finished work of Jesus. That's why John Bunyan cast Moses in the role of villain and why each one of us needs to take note of Jesus' warning in John 5:45–47 not to turn Moses into our foe:

> *Do not think I will accuse you before the Father. Your accuser is Moses, on whom your hopes are set. If you believed Moses, you would believe me, for he wrote about me. But since you do not believe what he wrote, how are you going to believe what I say?*

Rebels in Disguise (2:21)

I do not set aside the grace of God, for if righteousness could be gained through the law, Christ died for nothing!

(Galatians 2:21)

There are two different ways in which we can reject the Gospel. We can be like the Greek pagans of Galatia, whose obvious idolatry Paul confronted by telling them in Acts 14:15 to *"Turn from these worthless things to the living God."* But we can also be like the devout Jews of Galatia, who looked very different from their pagan neighbours but who were idolaters all the same. Paul warned them that they were simply rebels in disguise.

John and Charles Wesley, the brothers who went on to lead the Methodist revival which swept Britain and America during the eighteenth century, were obsessed as young men with pleasing God. While at Oxford University, they founded "the Holy Club", which encouraged students to commit themselves to a strict regime of Bible reading, prayer, fasting and self-reform. John wrote later that *"I resolved to dedicate all my life to God – all my thoughts and words and actions – being thoroughly convinced there was no medium, but that every part of my life (not some only) must either be a sacrifice to God or myself, that is, the devil."*[1] In short, if they had both been in our churches today, we would probably have viewed them as model Christians. Yet they looked back later on this period in their lives and concluded that they had not been Christians at all, but religious people

---

[1] John Wesley recalled this in his *Plain Account of Christian Perfection* (1766).

who relied on their own good works for their salvation. They concluded that their outward devotion masked the fact that they were rebels in disguise.

The mistake that John and Charles Wesley made is normally referred to as "legalism". Legalism can be defined as *trying to achieve forgiveness from God and acceptance by God through obedience to God.* Greek idolatry was obvious – you only had to visit one of their temples – but Paul explains that Jewish legalism was just as idolatrous. When we obey God because we hope to earn our own salvation instead of as an expression of gratitude that he has freely saved us by his grace, we are simply idolaters in disguise. Thomas Schreiner explains:

> *Legalism has its origin in self-worship. If people are justified through their obedience to the law, then they merit praise, honour, and glory. Legalism, in other words, means that the glory goes to people rather than God... The desire to obey the law, though it appears commendable, is actually an insidious way to try to gain recognition before God.*[2]

Legalism couldn't be more serious. It is the very opposite of the Gospel. It tries to steal glory from Jesus as the one and only Saviour, and to direct that stolen glory towards ourselves.

That's why Paul warns the Galatians so strongly in 2:21 that the Judaizers are not simply modifying the Gospel. They are doing away with it altogether. Faith in Jesus requires us to admit we can do nothing to save ourselves, and this is fatally undermined when we continue to place any lingering confidence in our own obedience to God. Faith in Jesus also requires us to believe that Jesus died on the cross to pay the just penalty for all our sin. This is also undermined if we keep half an eye on our own acts of obedience. Paul says that if we do so, *"Christ died for*

---

[2] Thomas Schreiner in *The Law and Its Fulfilment: A Pauline Theology of Law* (1993).

nothing!" If we can gain merit with God through obedience to his commands, Jesus' crucifixion was either *unnecessary* because we can save ourselves or *insufficient* because we still need to top it up with our own good deeds. Either way, it was unjust because in that case God has punished Jesus for sins that we are in the process of atoning for without him. Devoting ourselves to good works in order to impress God seems commendable and virtuous, but we mustn't forget Paul's strong language in 1:8–9. Adding a little bit of legalism to the Gospel is like making tiny pinpricks in a condom. It undermines absolutely everything.

Sinclair Ferguson observes that

> *The glory of the gospel is that God has declared Christians to be rightly related to him in spite of their sin. But our greatest temptation and mistake is to try and smuggle character into his work of grace. How easily we fall into the trap of assuming that we remain justified only so long as there are grounds in our character for justification. Paul's teaching is that nothing we do ever contributes to our justification.*[3]

Nothing we do. Absolutely nothing. In fact, Paul tells us in 2:21 that if we try to smuggle character into God's free gift of salvation then we *atheteō* the grace of God – we *set it aside* or we *reject it* – and we consequently forfeit any place among his People (4:30). It isn't humble. It is as sinful as outright pagan idolatry. Overt rebels play down the seriousness of sin in order to be very bad, but legalists play down the seriousness of sin by relying on the fact that they are very good. They are rebels in disguise, undermining the grace of God in order to steal some of his glory and award it to themselves.

John and Charles Wesley were only saved when Charles read a copy of Martin Luther's commentary on Galatians. When

---

[3] Sinclair Ferguson in *Know Your Christian Life* (1981).

Charles read aloud, *"What, have we then nothing to do? No, nothing!"*[4] he convinced one of his friends to give up on good works and surrender to the Gospel. *"There came such a power over me as I cannot well describe,"* the friend wrote. *"My great burden fell off in an instant; my heart was so filled with peace and love that I burst into tears... When I afterwards went into the street, I could scarcely feel the ground I trod upon."*[5]

Charles himself was saved shortly afterwards, writing in his diary,

> *Who would believe our Church had been founded on this important article of justification by faith alone? I am astonished I should ever think this a new doctrine... I spent some hours this evening in private with Martin Luther, who was greatly blessed to me, especially his conclusion of the second chapter. I laboured, waited, and prayed to feel "who loved **me**, and gave himself for **me**."*[6]

A week later, his brother John was also converted.

The revival that swept Britain and America in the 1700s began with two brothers recognizing that there are two ways we can reject the Gospel and not just one. When they confessed that their attempts to impress God through their good deeds were subtle acts of idolatry, their hearts were freed to lay hold of the Gospel. Paul encourages us to search our own hearts to see if we have been infected by such legalism ourselves. Revival begins whenever people start confessing that they are rebels in disguise.

---

[4] We only know that we have understood the Gospel of God's grace if we ask the same question, just as Paul does in 2:17 and in Romans 6:1–4. Good works can save no one (James 2:10); they are simply proof that God is on the inside of a person and that they have therefore already been saved (James 2:14–26).

[5] The friend was William Holland. Quoted from Arnold Dallimore *George Whitefield (Volume I)* (1970).

[6] Charles Wesley wrote this in his Journal on 17th May 1738.

God's Dirty Dishes (3:1–5)

I would like to learn just one thing from you: Did you receive the Spirit by observing the law, or by believing what you heard?

(Galatians 3:2)

I was converted to Christ because somebody told me Jesus had lived a perfect life so that I didn't have to. Given what a mess I had made of my own life, this sounded like very good news. What wasn't there to like about a message that Jesus had lived the sinless life I had failed to live and that he had died the death I deserved to die? Like Charles Wesley's friend in the previous chapter, I felt I had been set free on the inside.

The Christians who discipled me informed me that I needed to be filled with the Holy Spirit. Again, this sounded like very good news because I knew I wasn't going to make it as a Christian unless I had God on the inside. Then came the small print. *"The Holy Spirit only fills clean vessels,"* I was told. I needed to sort out my life and show God I was serious about following him before I was ready to be filled with the Holy Spirit. That didn't sound much like the Gospel that had saved me, and it is why I got so excited the first time I read the start of Galatians 3. Paul tells us that my friends were wrong, that we receive the Holy Spirit in exactly the same way that we are justified – as a gift of grace through faith in Jesus. Paul tells us that God fills dirty dishes just like you and me.

I had been told that being filled with the Holy Spirit was rather like trying to get into an exclusive nightclub. There was a strict dress code (I was told I needed to sort out my life first).

There was a long queue (I was told I needed to do something called "tarrying"). The bouncers were unpredictable (I was told I shouldn't be presumptuous). There was a VIP lounge (I was told that many of the gifts of the Spirit had died out with the apostles). This kind of thinking is why Paul calls the Galatians *fools* at the start of chapter 3. Legalism doesn't just stop us from receiving God's forgiveness; it also stops us from growing as Christians after we have been forgiven. Paul therefore shatters these four myths about how to be filled with the Holy Spirit in the opening verses of chapter 3.

Paul tells us that *no dress code is required*. My friends were well-meaning – they wanted to spur me on to deal with the many areas of sin in my life – but, by telling me that the Holy Spirit only fills clean vessels, they were inadvertently encouraging me to mix a little legalism with the Gospel. They were telling me that, now I had been forgiven, it was time for a little hard work if I wanted to capture God's attention and leave the little leagues of Christianity behind. Paul begins these verses with a strong rebuke: *"You foolish Galatians!... Does God give you his Spirit... because you observe the law, or because you believe what you heard?"* Having been forgiven by grace through faith in Jesus in spite of our sin, we need to continue in the same way we began. Knox Chamblin explains: *"The Spirit does not take his pupils beyond the cross, but ever more deeply into it."*[1]

I find the Old Testament example of Samson very helpful. While he is on the way to enter into a sinful marriage, God anoints him with the Holy Spirit. He falls out with his neighbours so badly that they tie him up and hand him over to the Philistines, but God anoints him with his Spirit again all the same. While he is sleeping with a prostitute, the Holy Spirit gives him supernatural strength to escape from the Philistines. Could there be a better proof that God's grace means much more than

---

[1] J. Knox Chamblin in *Paul and the Self: Apostolic Teaching for Personal Wholeness* (1993). God's grace also sanctifies us, brings us to maturity and makes us very fruitful (Acts 14:26; 20:32; 26:18).

forgiveness and the offer of a second chance?! It is *G*od's *R*iches *A*t *C*hrist's *E*xpense, and so it means the Father tells us in Jesus that *"Everything I have is yours"* (Luke 15:31). Yes, we can grieve away the Spirit as Samson eventually did, but we will receive him back again like Samson the moment we repent and ask God to fill us anew.[2] God fills dirty vessels so that he can clean them from the inside out. It's just as well. Dirty dishes are the only ones available.

Paul tells us that *no waiting is required*. I was told that I needed to "tarry" or wait for the Holy Spirit because of Jesus' command in Acts 1:4, but he gave this command to a specific group of people because the Day of Pentecost had not yet arrived. Paul does not tell the Galatians that they will receive the Holy Spirit if they wait prayerfully – prayer itself can become the object of legalism. *"Are you now trying to attain your goal by human effort?"* he asks them incredulously. All they need to do is simply believe that the gift of the Holy Spirit has now been given.

Paul tells us that *no false humility is required*. Presumption is expecting God to do things he hasn't promised he will do. Faith is taking him at his word and believing that he will do as he has promised. Since Jesus has told us in John 7:38 that *"Whoever believes in me, as Scripture has said, rivers of living water will flow from within them,"* we can never presume too much when it comes to being filled with the Holy Spirit. In case we struggle to believe this, Paul assures us in 3:14 that God *"redeemed us in order that... by faith we might receive the promise of the Spirit."*[3] It is the very reason why he saved us.

Paul tells us that *there is no VIP lounge*. You need to hear this if you are tempted to believe that miracles and many other gifts of the Spirit belong to Paul and the other apostles but not to us. When Paul healed a lame man in one of their cities, he told

---

[2] See Judges 14:1–7; 15:12–17; 16:1–3, 20, 28–30.

[3] Just like Jesus in Acts 1:4 and Peter in Acts 2:39, Paul doesn't just refer to being filled with the Holy Spirit as *a* promise of the Father, but as **the** promise.

the Galatians in Acts 14:15 that *"We too are only men, human like you,"* and he repeats this same message here in 3:5: *"Does God give you his Spirit and work miracles in you because you observe the law, or because you believe what you heard?"* There are no VIP restrictions over who gets to perform miracles in Jesus' name. They are simply part and parcel of what it means for us to have God on the inside.[4]

So don't be ashamed to admit that you are one of God's dirty dishes and that you don't deserve to be filled with the Holy Spirit, no matter how long or how obediently you wait. Simply believe that this promise is as much for you as it was for the apostle Paul and the Galatians. Ask God to fill you with his Holy Spirit because of all that Jesus has already done to make you perfectly clean.

---

[4] This echoes Paul's statement that he ministered by grace in 2:9, and Peter's similar statement in Acts 3:12.

Abraham's Seed (3:6–29)

The promises were spoken to Abraham and to his seed. Scripture does not say "and to seeds", meaning many people, but "and to your seed", meaning one person, who is Christ.

(Galatians 3:16)

Challenging Paul to an argument about the Law of Moses was like challenging Zorro to a swordfight or Robin Hood to an archery competition.

The Law was Paul's weapon of choice. He had studied it for many years as a Pharisee, and then in a new light after his discovery that Jesus was the long-awaited Messiah. The Judaizers who were spreading their false teaching across Galatia had made a massive miscalculation. Paul wouldn't fight their legalism by denying that the Law of Moses mattered. He would fight it by showing what the Law of Moses really said.

In 3:6–9, Paul goes back to the start of the five books of Moses, using the life of Abraham to demonstrate that his Gospel is the true fulfilment of the Law. He points out that the great Jewish patriarch was saved by grace through faith long before the Israelites ever received God's detailed instructions at Mount Sinai. In 3:6, he uses a quotation from Genesis 15:6 to point out that Abraham was not saved through works of obedience but because he *"believed God, and it was credited to him as righteousness."*[1] Abraham's true descendants are therefore not

---

[1] Paul also unpacks this important verse in Romans 4:3, and so does James 2:23. Paul always quotes from the Greek Septuagint translation in Galatians because he knows they are Greek rather than Hebrew speakers.

the Jews but anybody, Jew or Gentile, who shares the same faith which Abraham had in the Gospel of God. To defend this statement to his shocked Jewish readers, Paul argues in 3:8 that God *"announced the Gospel in advance to Abraham"* when he promised him that *"All nations will be blessed through you."*[2] The Gospel has always been a call for people in every nation to find salvation through faith in Abraham's God.[3]

In 3:10–14, Paul sheds light on the other four books of Moses. He points out in 3:11 that the Law cannot have been given to teach people how to be saved through their good works because Habakkuk 2:4 repeats the exact same Gospel message that God preached to Abraham 1,500 years before:[4] *"The righteous will live by faith."*[5] In 3:10, Paul quotes from Deuteronomy 27:26 to prove that the Law was given in order to make it clear to the Israelites that they were sinners cursed by God and in desperate need of a Saviour. He argues that when Leviticus 18:5 promised that *"**The man** who does these things will live by them,"* it was a prophecy that a perfect man would one day fulfil the Law on our behalf, and that when Deuteronomy 21:23 warned that *"Cursed is everyone who is hung on a tree,"* it was a prophecy that the perfect man would die on a wooden cross to set us free. Jesus would live a perfect life and die a guilty

---

[2] Paul is quoting from God's promise in Genesis 12:3, but he adds to this some of the language God uses in later promises to Abraham in 18:18 and 22:18.

[3] Paul's Jewish enemies in Galatia had sabotaged Paul's preaching because they were jealous that he offered salvation to the Gentiles (Acts 13:45; 14:19). Paul's summary of the Law shows just how wrong they were.

[4] Exodus 12:40 tells us that the Israelites were in Egypt for 430 years, so about 650 years passed between God's promise to Abraham and the Lawgiving at Mount Sinai. Paul knows that the Galatians use the Septuagint translation of the Old Testament so he humours its mistranslation of Exodus 12:40 in 3:17. He isn't interested in straightening out their time charts of the Bible, but in straightening out their Gospel.

[5] Paul quotes from Habakkuk 2:4 again in Romans 1:17, and so does Hebrews 10:38. He quotes from the Septuagint but drops one word to preserve the original meaning of the Hebrew text.

death in our place because he is the true fulfilment of the Gospel through which Abraham was saved. By quoting six times from the Old Testament in just nine verses, Paul hopes to convince us that his Gospel and his passion to see the Gentiles saved are not Christian innovations. They are simply a proper understanding of the Law.[6]

In 3:15–25, Paul returns to God's promises to Abraham. He justifies his claim that the Law was the continuation of Abraham's faith in the coming Saviour by highlighting the way that God promised things to Abraham and *"to your seed,"* not to Abraham and *"to your seeds."*[7] The Judaizers may have used these verses to argue that salvation was restricted to Isaac's race alone, even though God still refers to *"your seed"* in the singular when he makes promises to Isaac in Genesis 26:3–4 and to Jacob in Genesis 28:13–14. Paul explains that God was not primarily talking about Isaac. He was talking about Jesus as the true Seed of Abraham and prophesying that he would be the Saviour of the world. He tells the Galatians that God gave the Law to Israel so it could serve as their *paidagōgos*, the slave in a wealthy Greek household who was entrusted with taking his master's children to and from school. The Law was never intended to be a list of rules by which Israel could be saved, but a body of teaching which kept them on the right path towards faith in Jesus. It showed them their sin, taught them to rely on the blood sacrifices in the Temple, and prepared them to receive Jesus as Messiah when he finally came.[8] The false teachers in

---

[6] This is why David speaks so highly of the Law in Psalm 19. It was very good if read correctly, helping David to write psalms that celebrated the Gospel and which prophesied about the coming Messiah.

[7] God used the singular noun *zera'* (Hebrew) and *sperma* (Greek) rather than their plural equivalents when he made promises about Abraham's *seed* in Genesis 12:7, 13:15–16, 15:5, 17:7–8, 21:12, 22:17–18 and 24:7.

[8] Paul is not saying that we must use the Law of Moses to lead people to Christ today. He is saying that the Law served this function for the Jews. We seldom find him quoting from the Law when preaching to pagans.

Galatia were not honouring Moses' Law. They had distorted it into something God had never intended it to be.

In 3:26–29, Paul states his radical conclusion. Since Jesus is the true Seed of Abraham and no one can be saved unless they put their faith in him, the markers which God gave to Moses to distinguish the Jewish race from the world are now defunct and superseded when it comes to salvation. It does not matter whether a person is a Jew or Greek, circumcised or uncircumcised, an eater of kosher foods or of bacon sandwiches. If a person is in Christ and if Christ is in them, then they are the Seed of Abraham and therefore heirs to the promises God gave to his People in the Old Testament. Simply being born a Jew cannot make anyone a child of Abraham, much less a child of God. A Greek who believes the Gospel is a child of Abraham and a child of God because God has adopted and united them with Abraham's Seed, his own Son.[9]

This is the glorious Gospel. It has always been the Gospel, even when God preached it to Abraham at the dawn of history, and it has now been revealed with greater clarity through the death and resurrection of Jesus Christ.[10] Let its glory sink in as you watch Paul use a true understanding of the Law of Moses to leave the arguments of the Judaizers in tatters. Like Zorro wielding his sword or Robin Hood firing his arrows, Paul the former Pharisee beats the Judaizers at their own game. He uses the Law of Moses to show us that his Gospel is the only message that truly saves. Jesus is and always has been the only Saviour in world history.

---

[9] Radical though this is, Paul is simply repeating what Jesus taught in Matthew 3:9 and John 8:39–47.

[10] This is what Paul means by faith *coming* in 3:23 and 25. People have had faith in the Gospel in every generation, but the object of their saving faith has only been fully revealed in Jesus the Messiah.

What Adam Lost (3:26–29)

There is neither Jew nor Gentile, neither slave nor free, nor is there male and female, for you are all one in Christ Jesus.

(Galatians 3:28)

When Adam sinned in the Garden of Eden, he lost everything. When Jesus chose to obey God in the Garden of Gethsemane, he won it all back again. Paul is too excited about what Jesus' death and resurrection have achieved for us to focus solely on the promise of forgiveness. He ends chapter 3 by telling us that Jesus has achieved far more for us than that. He has recovered all that Adam lost.

Adam was created to enjoy a *very close relationship with God*. Genesis expresses this by telling us that he and Eve were unique among all creatures because they were made in the image of God, and the New Testament expresses it by telling us that Adam was *"the son of God"*. Whatever words we use to describe it, it meant that God and Adam walked together in the Garden of Eden as closest friends.[1] When Adam rebelled against God by eating fruit from the forbidden tree, he was expelled from the Garden and lost his intimacy with God. Genesis 5:1–3 underlines this tragedy by telling us that, whereas Adam was created in the likeness of God, his son was merely born in the likeness of his human father.

That's why Paul is so excited here in 3:26. He tells us that Jesus has regained for us what Adam lost: *"You are all sons of God through faith in Jesus Christ."* Nobody was a son of God, except

---

[1] Genesis 1:26–27; 3:8–9; 5:1; Luke 3:38.

in the loosest sense, from the time that Adam sinned until the coming of Jesus the Son of God.[2] But by living and dying in our place, the Son has made a way for those who believe in him to be united with him through faith and to be counted as sons of God through him.[3] Paul expands on this elsewhere in his letters by telling us that Jesus is *"the image of the invisible God"* and *"the last Adam."*[4]

Adam was created in *naked perfection*. Before he sinned, we read in Genesis 2:25 that *"the man and his wife were both naked, and they felt no shame,"* but as soon as they sinned everything changed. They grew conscious of their imperfection and tried to cover up their naked bodies in order to hide their shame. They made clothing for themselves out of fig leaves but they knew it hadn't covered their shame because the fully clothed Adam admitted to God in Genesis 3:10 that *"I heard you in the garden, and I was afraid because I was naked; so I hid."* The Lord responded by offering the first blood sacrifice in history in order to clothe them with the skin of a slaughtered animal, as a prophecy about one who would die to take away their shame.

Paul is therefore very excited when he reveals in 3:27 that Jesus is the answer to Adam's problem. Those who have expressed their faith in Jesus' death and resurrection by being baptized in water have done far more than get their clothes wet; they have been given a completely new set of clothes to wear.[5]

---

[2] Paul only agrees with the Greek philosophers in the loosest sense in Acts 17:28. John 1:12 clarifies that we do not *become* sons of God in a true sense until we put our trust in Jesus the Son of God.

[3] Although it is correct to refer to women believers as *daughters of God* (2 Corinthians 6:18), Paul is actually saying something even more radical here. In a world that prized sons more than daughters, he insists that God treats women believers equally as sons of God because they have been equally included in the Son (3:28).

[4] Colossians 1:15; 1 Corinthians 15:45; 2 Corinthians 4:4.

[5] Paul assumes that every believer in Galatia has been baptized because true believers always express their faith by obeying Jesus in this primary command (Matthew 28:19; Acts 2:38; 16:15, 33).

They have been clothed in Jesus Christ – when God looks at them all he sees is the naked perfection of his Son. Jesus hasn't simply carried away our guilt through his death on the cross; he has also carried away our shame. If you ever look at yourself and don't like what you see, this is very good news. When God looks at a Christian he sees the spotlessness of Jesus.

Third and finally, Adam was created *in perfect harmony with the world*. He and his wife never argued, they respected the earth, and there was no fear between them and the animals. When Adam sinned, all this changed in an instant. Within a few verses of his eating fruit from the forbidden tree in Genesis 3, we read that he and his wife started bickering and playing power games with each other, that they found themselves at odds with the animals and with nature, and that one of their two sons murdered the other. All of the problems in our contemporary world – hatred, greed, selfishness, world wars, cruelty towards animals and the rape of the environment – had begun.

That's why Paul gets so excited in 3:28–29. He tells us that the death and resurrection of Jesus is not just good news for individuals, but for the entire world. If God had made his covenant with Abraham's *seeds* (plural), individuals might be reconciled to God and yet remain in disharmony with one another. But since he made his covenant with Abraham's *seed* (singular), every division is done away with when people are made one with Christ. They still retain their diversity as men and women, slaves and masters, Jew and Greek (Paul makes it clear in Ephesians 5:22–6:9 that God redeems these distinctions for good), but our primary identity is now found in who we are in Jesus Christ. God has put an end to the battle of the sexes, the battle between races, and the battle between castes and classes, by uniting us all together as one new person in his Son.[6] All of us matter equally to God and to one another in a harmonious community which has not existed since the Garden of Eden. It's

---

[6] Paul will go on to unpack this in more detail in Ephesians 2:14–18.

why Jesus defended his decision to save a man who was hated by his neighbours, saying in Luke 19:9–10 that *"This man, too, is a son of Abraham. For the Son of Man came to save **what was lost**."*

If you live in a multiracial city like mine or in a context where prejudice runs free, this should strike you as very good news. It should encourage you to commit yourself to sharing the Gospel with people out of a conviction that it is the only way that sinful humans can ever truly learn to live in harmony. These verses were nothing short of revolutionary for the Jewish Christians in Galatia who were trying to force their Greek brothers and sisters to live according to Jewish traditions as the price of acceptance by God. They are still every bit as revolutionary for our divided world today.

Paul tells us that the sign that we have been included in God's People is not circumcision or Sabbath-keeping or refusing to eat pork or obedience to the Jewish Law. It is our answer to the question *"Do you know God?"* It is our assurance that through faith in God's Messiah we have been set free from our guilt and shame and been clothed with the naked perfection of Jesus. It is whether we are committed to loving and accepting other people, whoever they are and whatever their backgrounds, because Jesus has recovered everything that Adam lost.

Abraham's Other Son
(4:1–31)

What does Scripture say? "Get rid of the slave woman and her son, for the slave woman's son will never share in the inheritance with the free woman's son."

(Galatians 4:30)

One of the most ridiculous movies I have ever watched starred Christian Slater as Winston Churchill and claimed that the British Prime Minister was in fact a young American marine.[1] It's completely preposterous historically, and it's meant to be. But while the history lesson which Paul gives us in Galatians 4 is every bit as outrageous, nobody is laughing. He really means it: Greeks who put their trust in Jesus are the real Israelites and Jews who reject Jesus as God's Messiah are the real Gentiles. It's easy to see why Paul was attacked by angry Jewish mobs at almost every stop-off on his missionary journeys.

In 4:1–7, Paul tells us that the coming of Jesus has completely changed the situation for the Jews. They had long been heirs to all God's promises to Abraham, but until the coming of Jesus they acted more like slaves than sons. They were supposed to be guided by the Law to Jesus,[2] but they let

---

[1] *Churchill: The Hollywood Years* (Pathé Films, 2004).
[2] The reference to *guardians and trustees* in 4:2 links back to the way Paul described the Law as a *paidagōgos* for the Jewish race in 3:24 – a trusted slave who ushered his master's children wherever they needed to go.

their thinking be shaped by *"the basic principles of the world."*[3] The coming of Jesus had changed what it meant to be a Jew as much as the coming of Moses to Egypt had changed what it meant for their ancestors to be Hebrews. God redeemed them,[4] freed them, made them sons, filled them with the Spirit of Jesus, and enabled them to address him using the same Aramaic name which Jesus used: *Abba*, or *Daddy*.[5] Paul urges his Jewish readers to recognize that the coming of Jesus has changed everything.

In 4:8–11, Paul tells us that the coming of Jesus has completely changed the situation for non-Jews too. They did not know the real God when their souls were enslaved to pagan idols, but when they heard the Gospel message they were set free. They became sons of God, just like the Jewish believers, because Jesus died for all the world.[6] They mustn't let the Judaizers trick them into acting like Hebrew slaves. If they observed Jewish Sabbaths and feast days then they were acting as if Jesus had not come and as if God had not adopted them as his sons.

In 4:13–20, Paul warns everyone in the Galatian churches that they need to fight to protect this Gospel. Paul had acted like a Greek in Galatia to make this lesson very clear: if the Gospel meant Jews needed to observe their Jewish customs less, it couldn't mean that non-Jews needed to observe them *more!*[7] He

---

[3] In 2 Peter 3:10–12 this same Greek word is used to mean the *basic elements* of the periodic table. The Law was good but the Jews infected it with the principles of the fallen world and enslaved themselves to legalism.

[4] The Greek word *exagorazō* in 3:13 and 4:5 means to *redeem* a slave. When first-century Jews thought about slavery, their thoughts immediately turned to their nation's period of slavery in Egypt.

[5] No first-century Jew would ever dare to use this intimate name to address Yahweh, yet Jesus did so in Mark 14:36. Paul tells us in 4:6 and in Romans 8:15 that we can use this same name ourselves.

[6] This is perhaps why the word *Abba* is always followed by the Greek word *Patēr*, or *Father*, whenever it occurs in the New Testament. Jews and Gentiles can cry out with one breath together that God is their Dad.

[7] Paul was happy to observe his national customs (Acts 18:18; 20:6, 16; 21:26), but he did not do so while in Galatia for the sake of modelling something to his

reminds them how much they showed their love for him when they nursed him through an unsightly eye condition during his time in Galatia,[8] and how they recognized that he spoke with authority because he had God on the inside.[9] He asks them to continue to love and trust him as their friend, despite the lying propaganda which the false teachers are spreading about him. He still loves them like a mother and can't wait to be back with them so that he can help them to win this battle instead of simply scolding them from afar.[10]

In 4:21–31, Paul therefore calls the Galatians to make a choice. This is his Christian Slater moment, his shockingly different reading of history, but he is inspired by the Holy Spirit to bring out the true meaning of a familiar story.[11] Every Galatian believer knew that Abraham had been promised a son in his old age through Sarah, had grown impatient, had taken matters into his own hands, had slept with his wife's slave girl Hagar, and had become the father of Ishmael fourteen years before the birth of the promised son Isaac. Every Galatian knew the story and thought they knew the moral of the story too: the Jews were all descended from the child of promise and the non-Jews were descended from Ishmael.

Now Paul turns the story on its head, and it's more outrageous than claiming Winston Churchill was an American

---

new converts (1 Corinthians 9:19–22).

[8] Paul was evidently still suffering from this eye condition in 6:11, and Acts 23:2–5 suggests it may have permanently damaged his eyesight. Paul was a man just like us and didn't always enjoy automatic healing.

[9] Paul is not commending them for mistaking him for the messenger-god Hermes, since this upset him in Acts 14:12–15. He is praising them for accepting his message as the words of the true God (Acts 13:48).

[10] Paul uses a play on words in Greek to emphasize the difference between the Law and legalism. The Law *sunkleiō*, or *shut in*, the Jews to protect them before Jesus came (3:23), but legalism *ekkleiō*, or *shuts out*, people from salvation now that he has come (4:17).

[11] Paul isn't giving preachers free rein to interpret Old Testament stories as allegories for whatever they want to say! He received divine revelation about this story and wrote with the authority of the Holy Spirit.

marine. He points out that Hagar was an Egyptian slave girl and that Mount Sinai is in Egypt,[12] so anyone who relies on human effort or Lawkeeping is like Abraham when he slept with Hagar and is therefore just as much a slave as Hagar and Ishmael. On the other hand, anyone who places their faith entirely in Jesus is like Abraham when he trusted in God and is therefore just as much a miraculous child of promise as Isaac. It therefore shouldn't surprise the Galatians that they are being pressured by false teachers who want them to cling to the outdated detail of Sinai, because Ishmael persecuted Isaac in Genesis 21:9. Abraham and Sarah were forced to face up to the fact that these two children could not live together, so they drove Ishmael out of their community in Genesis 21:10. Paul tells the Galatians that the teaching of the Judaizers is just as incompatible with Gospel. They need to expel the false teachers from among them so that they can throw off the yoke of slavery and start enjoying their Gospel freedom.[13]

If you want an insight into just how controversial Paul's words must have been in Galatia, try explaining to a Jewish friend that many Palestinian Arabs are heirs of Abraham and that many Jewish settlers are not. You'll definitely get a reaction. It might look something like the violent reaction that greeted Paul in almost every Jewish community he visited when he told them that there is a true and false Jerusalem, a true and false Israel, and a true and false Jewish nation.[14] He didn't preach

---

[12] Even though the eastern portion of Egypt was at that time part of the Roman province of Arabia, the Galatians knew that she was known as *"Hagar the Egyptian"* (Genesis 21:9).

[13] Weak church leaders never dare to put anyone out of membership because they hope to win them over, but expelling them is actually the only way to save them (Genesis 21:14–20; 1 Corinthians 5:4–13).

[14] The Church has *not* replaced Old Testament Israel. It is the continuation of Old Testament Israel, made up of any Jew or non-Jew who is united through faith with Jesus, the Seed of Abraham (6:16; Hebrews 12:22–23). Paul's quotation from Isaiah 54:1 in 4:27 comes from a great Old Testament prophecy about Jerusalem.

this because he disliked the Jews. He explains in Romans 9–11 that he did so because it is the best way to provoke ethnic Jews towards faith in Jesus. He preached it because it is the Gospel and because this truth sets us free.

Hagar and Sarah. Ishmael and Isaac. Legalism and grace. They just don't mix. So tell the Lord that you are not offended by Paul's history lesson. Tell him that you will not try to add anything to the message of his grace. Tell him that you want to be free on the inside.

Emancipation Proclamation (5:1–12)

It is for freedom that Christ has set us free. Stand firm, then, and do not let yourselves be burdened again by a yoke of slavery.

(Galatians 5:1)

On 1st January 1863, President Abraham Lincoln freed over 3 million American slaves. His Emancipation Proclamation is one of the most famous announcements of freedom in history. But what most people tend to forget is that by nightfall only around 20,000 slaves had actually walked free. The Emancipation Proclamation had declared them legally free, but that was only the beginning of the story. Steps needed to be taken in order to lay hold of that declaration and apply it to millions of individual lives.

Galatians 1–4 served as Paul's great emancipation proclamation. It announced that God sets anyone who believes the Gospel free on the inside. Those four chapters of salvation doctrine end with a fanfare. Paul trumpets in 5:1 that *"It is for freedom that Christ has set us free."* This fanfare marks the point where Paul starts applying his emancipation proclamation to our daily lives. He completes 5:1 with a warning against being passive about our freedom, which launches into two chapters of practical application. Paul urges us: *"Stand firm, then, and do not let yourselves be burdened again by a yoke of slavery."*[1]

---

[1] Paul actually mixes up his metaphors in 5:1, telling the Galatians not to be *ensnared* by a yoke of slavery. His point is that legalism throttles believers in the same way that a hunter's snare chokes a rabbit.

Many of the 3 million American slaves could only be freed with the help of other people. They lived in the Confederate states and they needed the Union armies to drive back the forces that stopped them from applying Lincoln's proclamation to their lives. The same is true of us, which is why God has placed us in church communities where we can share our spiritual struggles with mature Christians who can challenge us and help us to apply the Gospel to our lives. Paul advances like a general at the head of a liberation army on behalf of the Galatians in 5:2–6. If you want to grow in your practical experience of the Gospel, find a church full of Christians who will fight for you as much as Paul.

Paul is not embarrassed to put his own neck on the line to help the Galatians to live out their freedom through the Gospel. He begins these two chapters of practical application by saying, *"Mark my words! I, Paul, tell you..."* He has risked his life to plant churches across Galatia and he is not about to shrink back from danger now. He launches a full-frontal attack on the Judaizers by telling the Galatians that if they allow themselves to be circumcised, they are tearing up God's emancipation proclamation. He shakes them out of their complacency by warning them that even a little reliance on good works such as circumcision means rejecting the Gospel and committing themselves to a lifetime of abject slavery. He drives the false teachers from the battlefield by insisting that, if the Galatians simply believe the Gospel, God will fill them with the Holy Spirit and help them to live righteously through faith from the inside out.

Other American slaves were able to free themselves simply by believing in their newfound freedom. One slave who was employed as a rich man's coachman *"went straight to his master's chamber, dressed himself in his best clothes, put on his best watch and chain... and insolently informed him that he might for the future drive his own coach."*[2] Paul urges the Galatians in 5:7–12 to assert their freedom through courageous faith in the Gospel. If you want to experience the freedom that is yours through the Gospel, simply read the Bible and accept by faith that everything it says about you is true.

Paul is very sensitive towards the Galatians, reminding us that the message of God's grace also needs to be shared with grace. Note Paul's pastoral skill. He lets them save face in 5:7 by blaming the false teachers for their error: *"You were running a good race. Who cut in on you to keep you from obeying the truth?"* He points out gently where they went wrong by quoting a first-century proverb in 5:9, warning them to expel these spiritual slave traders because *"A little yeast works through the whole batch of dough."*[3] He assures them in 5:10 that *"I am confident in the Lord that you will take no other view,"* and he reminds them in 5:11 that their enemies were his enemies long before.[4] He ends his appeal with a touch of humour, telling the Galatians that he wishes that these preachers of circumcision would go the whole hog and cut off their genitals entirely (5:12).[5] Like any good Christian friend, Paul uses empathy and humour to make it easy for the Galatians to repent and rediscover their Gospel freedom.

Booker T. Washington recalls in his autobiography that, even as a young boy, he understood that the Emancipation Proclamation had changed everything:

---

[2] Quoted by Eric Foner in *Reconstruction: America's Unfinished Revolution* (1988).

[3] Paul also quotes this proverb six years later in 1 Corinthians 5:6. Jesus likens false teaching to yeast in Matthew 16:12, Mark 8:15 and Luke 12:1.

[4] Paul makes a play on words here. He uses the Greek word *katargeō* in 5:4 to describe our being *cut off* from Christ and in 5:11 to describe the Judaizers trying to *cut out* the offensiveness of the cross.

[5] The Greek text could simply mean that Paul wishes they were cut off from God (see 1:8–9), but most English translations assume that he is wishing that they would cut off more than just their foreskins!

Some man who seemed to be a stranger (a United States officer, I presume) made a little speech and then read a rather long paper – the Emancipation Proclamation, I think. After the reading we were told that we were all free, and could go when and where we pleased. My mother, who was standing by my side, leaned over and kissed her children, while tears of joy ran down her cheeks. She explained to us what it all meant, that this was the day for which she had been so long praying, but fearing that she would never live to see. For some minutes there was great rejoicing, and thanksgiving, and wild scenes of ecstasy.[6]

Paul expects us to be just as excited about his emancipation proclamation. He expects us to understand that the announcement we are free on the inside is not the end, but the beginning of our Christian story. He encourages us, as he encouraged the Galatians, to lay hold of our blood-bought freedom with both hands. He warns us that this proclamation will make little difference to our lives unless we start to apply it in very practical ways every day.

It was for freedom that we have been set free. Let's not settle for a Christian life that still shows traces of our former lives as slaves to sin.

---

[6] Booker T. Washington in *Up From Slavery* (1901).

Licence (5:13–26)

You, my brothers and sisters, were called to be free.
But do not use your freedom to indulge the flesh;
rather, serve one another humbly in love.

(Galatians 5:13)

There is an easy way for you to tell if you have fully grasped the Gospel message. It will make you slightly concerned that some people might abuse this message of freedom by making it an excuse for immoral living. Doing good things in order to impress God is known as "legalism" but treating God's grace as an excuse for doing bad things is known as "licence". You can tell that you have fully grasped the Gospel if you start to wonder if God has made too much room for licence by promising to forgive sinners freely through Jesus' merits and not their own. Martyn Lloyd-Jones observes that

> *There is no better test as to whether a man is really preaching the New Testament gospel of salvation than this, that some people might misunderstand it and misinterpret it to mean that it really amounts to this, that because you are saved by grace alone it does not matter at all what you do; you can go on sinning as much as you like because it will redound all the more to the glory of grace. That is a very good test of gospel preaching. If my preaching and presentation of the gospel of salvation does not expose it to that misunderstanding, then it is not the gospel.*[1]

---

[1] Dr Martyn Lloyd-Jones in *The New Man* (1972).

Paul certainly recognizes that licence is as big a danger as legalism. He addressed this concern in 2:17, and he will do so again in Romans 6:1–4. He deals with the threat of licence in some detail in Galatians 5:13–26, warning us, *"Do not use your freedom to indulge the sinful flesh; rather serve one another humbly in love."* What I find really fascinating about this response is that Paul doesn't fight licence by backpedalling on grace or by plying the Galatians with a new list of rules. On the contrary, he simply restates the Gospel even more clearly. He tells us that licence will not be a problem for us if we truly understand the message about how God frees us on the inside.

Paul's first point is a warning that our sinful flesh is a foe and not a friend.[2] Paul uses the military word *aphormē* in 5:13 to warn us that our flesh can become *a base for military sorties* if we are not vigilant.[3] One of the biggest mistakes a Christian can make is to try to become more like Jesus by gritting their teeth and summoning up the willpower to embark on a programme of self-improvement, because our flesh has its own desires and they aren't godly (5:16–17). Trying to forge an alliance with our flesh to overcome sin is like arming a city's criminals in order to promote law and order.

Paul's second point is deliberately ironic, but it is nevertheless very true. He informs us in 5:13 that the only way to enjoy our newfound freedom is to enslave ourselves to a new master![4] We can only be sanctified (made more like Jesus) in the same way that we were justified (declared righteous in Jesus). We can only deal with sin by confessing our powerlessness to free ourselves, by believing in Jesus' death and resurrection,

[2] Paul used the Greek word *sarx*, or *flesh*, to mean *body* in 2:16, 2:20 and 4:13–14, and to mean *human effort* in 3:3, 4:23 and 4:29. He uses it throughout chapters 5–6 to mean our *old sinful nature*.

[3] Paul also uses this exact same word in Romans 7:8 and 11 and 1 Timothy 5:14 to warn that sin and the Devil are constantly looking for things they can use as *a base for military sorties* against our souls.

[4] The Greek word *douleuō*, or *to enslave*, in 5:13 is the same word Paul used negatively in 4:8, 9 and 25.

and by surrendering ourselves to his Holy Spirit. Sinful desires always flourish in spiritual no-man's-land, so we can only stop sinful desires from growing in our hearts by surrendering to the Holy Spirit. Paul urges us in 5:16 to *"walk by the Spirit, and you will not gratify the desires of the flesh."* Licence doesn't stem from people believing the Gospel too much, but believing it too little. The Gospel of grace, properly understood, makes us want to use our freedom to become God's slaves.

Paul's third point builds on this. He promises us that the Gospel that brought us freedom from sin's penalty will also grant us freedom from sin's power. The Gospel tells us that God has united us with Jesus through our faith (3:29), which means we have been crucified with him (2:20), so we simply need to keep our sinful flesh on the cross where it belongs (5:24).[5] Good works could not save us, but now that we are saved through Jesus' death and resurrection we are free to do good works out of love and gratitude to God. If you are worried that people will fall into licence, don't tone down the Gospel. Preach it in all its life-changing power.

Paul's fourth and final point is therefore that, since genuine believers have God on the inside through the Holy Spirit, they cannot keep on sinning. The Law of Moses cannot save us, but it makes it pretty clear what God is like: Paul quotes from Leviticus 19:18 to summarize the Law as *"Love your neighbour as yourself."*[6] The desires of the sinful flesh are fairly obvious – Paul lists them in 5:19–21 – and they are anything but love. When we are filled with the Holy Spirit, we find these things repulsive because the Spirit gives us a deep desire to be holy.[7]

[5] Since Paul says that our flesh has already been crucified with Jesus in 2:20 and 6:14, he must be telling us that Christians *count it crucified* in 5:24. Paul explains this further in Romans 6:5–7 and Colossians 2:20–3:4.

[6] Leviticus 19:18 is one of the most quoted Old Testament verses in the New Testament – in Matthew 5:43, 19:19 and 22:39, Mark 12:31, Luke 10:27, Romans 13:9, James 2:8 and here.

[7] Paul uses the Greek present participle *prassontes* in 5:21, which means literally that *those that **go on practising** these things will not inherit the*

As we believe the Gospel and count our sinful flesh dead on the cross, the Holy Spirit starts to yield godly fruit in our lives. We experience *love* and *joy*[8] and *peace* and *patience* and *kindness* and *goodness* and *faithfulness* and *gentleness* and *self-control*[9] – none of which is anything like licence![10] Paul refers to these nine attributes as *fruit* (singular) and not as *fruits* (plural) because together they are the mark of someone who has God on the inside. I don't have to shout at my apple tree to get apples. It simply yields apples because it is an apple tree. Nor do I have to give myself a list of rules to become more like Jesus. I simply need to believe the Gospel and tell God that I am willing to be the Holy Spirit's slave.[11]

Paul accepts that this may take time. Being filled with Jesus (1:16) and clothed with Jesus (3:27) doesn't mean that we instantly behave like Jesus (4:19). But it does mean that the Gospel of grace which justifies us through faith in Jesus will also sanctify us through faith in Jesus too.[12] A proper understanding of the Gospel cures us from legalism by telling us that we are saved through faith alone, and it cures us from licence by telling us that saving faith can never remain alone.

This is the Gospel. This is the glorious promise that the God who forgives us our sins also frees us from those sins on the inside.

Kingdom. He is talking about a lifestyle rather than occasional slip-ups.

[8] Paul told us in 4:15 that legalism kills our joy. Now he tells us that joy is a key sign we are filled with the Spirit.

[9] Paul told us in 4:24 that legalism makes us slaves. The Spirit grants us self-control, which is very different.

[10] When Paul tells us at the end of 5:23 that *"against such things there is no law,"* he is pointing out that people who are full of the Holy Spirit will be marked by godliness and not by licence, as promised in Ezekiel 36:27.

[11] Paul uses a second military term in these verses to emphasize that holy living is a lifestyle and a daily battle. The word he uses for *walking* in 5:25 is not the same as in 5:16. *Stoicheō* means literally *to march*.

[12] Acts 26:18; 1 Corinthians 1:30; Titus 2:11–12.

Freedom Is a Verb (6:1–10)

Let us not become weary in doing good, for at the proper time we will reap a harvest if we do not give up.

(Galatians 6:9)

Freedom is a verb. Yes, I know that it is technically a noun, but Paul is very clear as he moves into the final chapter of Galatians that freedom is in every way an action word. God has freed us on the inside through his Holy Spirit so that we can love and serve one another. This means taking daily risks to follow Jesus. It can be a little scary.

In the classic movie *The Shawshank Redemption*, one of the main characters is a long-term jailbird named Brooks Hatlen. He has been inside Shawshank State Penitentiary for so long that when he is finally released he does not know how to live in the outside world. He calls prison "home" and cannot adjust to the daily challenges of freedom. He writes to the friends he left behind in Shawshank and confesses,

> *I have trouble sleepin' at night. I have bad dreams like I'm fallin'. I wake up scared. Sometimes it takes me a while to remember where I am. Maybe I should get me a gun and rob the Foodway so they'd send me home. I could shoot the manager while I was at it, sort of like a bonus. I guess I'm too old for that sort of nonsense any more. I don't like it here. I'm tired of being afraid all the time.*

Eventually he hangs himself from the rafters in order to escape the daily challenges of living free.[1]

Paul is up front with us that it isn't easy to live out our newfound freedom in Jesus. It is easy to drift back into the habits of our former lives or to settle for passive, fruitless lives instead of taking daily risks to live out the freedom we have been given. That's why he gives us seven practical instructions in Galatians 6:1–10 about how to use the freedom that God has given us through the Gospel. He doesn't want us to struggle with our freedom like Brooks Hatlen. He wants us to make the most of being free on the inside.

In 6:1, Paul tells us to use our freedom *to challenge other people*. Perhaps he starts with this because it is just about the last thing any of us wants to do. Our former way of life was dog-eat-dog, looking out for ourselves and resenting people poking their nose into our affairs. We used to see it as a mark of respect to leave other people alone, but Paul tells us that what we called respect the Holy Spirit calls lack of love. Jesus tells us in Luke 15 that God is like a shepherd who goes looking for a lost sheep, like a woman who searches her house for a lost coin, and like a father who throws decorum aside and runs to greet his lost son, so we shouldn't be surprised that the Holy Spirit wants us to use our freedom to seek out sinners and draw them gently back to God. It may be dangerous work – Paul warns us that going after sinners can open us up to increased temptation ourselves[2] – but it is worth it. It's what it means to serve other people in love.

In 6:2, Paul tells us to use our freedom *to care for other people*. Everyone wants the Church to help them carry their own burdens, but Paul clarifies in 6:5 that this isn't what he means. He is telling us to bear our own burdens and to make space in

---

[1] *The Shawshank Redemption* (Colombia Pictures, 1994).

[2] Paul does not clarify whether the danger lies in going to places where sinners hang out or in becoming proud in the way that we correct them. Proverbs 13:20 suggests the former and Romans 2:1 the latter.

our lives to help other people carry their burdens too. Paul tells us that this fulfils *"the law of Christ,"* linking back to 5:14.[3] We are to use our freedom to love other people as ourselves.

In 6:3–4, Paul tells us to use our freedom *to walk humbly with other people*. We used to compare ourselves ambitiously with one another when we were governed by the sinful flesh (5:20, 26), but we have now been set free from our selfish pride through the Gospel. It simply isn't possible for us to kneel before the cross and confess that we are sinners while looking down on other people around us. The Gospel has freed us from our old delusions of grandeur so that we can walk in sober humility.

In 6:6, Paul tells us to use our freedom *to honour church leaders*. He does not specify which "good things" we should share with those who instruct us in the Scriptures, but it includes encouragement, friendship, affection, support and, if appropriate, a salary that enables them to enjoy a similar standard of living to those they lead. We have not been freed through the Gospel in order to freeload on the resources offered by a church or by its leaders. That comes from the evil desires of the flesh, and Paul warns in 1 Timothy 5:8 that it makes us *"worse than an unbeliever."*

In 6:7–8, Paul tells us to use our freedom *to make good choices*. Many people think that God's grace means there are no longer consequences to our foolish actions, so Paul warns us, *"Don't be deceived. God cannot be mocked. A man reaps what he sows."* If we ignore Paul's instructions in chapter 5 and try to forge an alliance with our sinful flesh, we will forfeit the blessings which can be ours through surrendering to the Holy Spirit. Chuck Swindoll puts it this way: *"Life is like a menu in the Grace Restaurant. In this new establishment you are free*

---

[3] The Law is also summarized as "love" in Romans 13:8–10, James 2:8, 1 John 3:23–24 and 1 Peter 4:8.

to choose whatever you want. But whatever you choose will be served to you, and you must eat it."[4]

In 6:9, Paul tells us to use our freedom *to persevere in doing good*. We live in a generation that expects instant results for minimal effort or else it simply moves on. Paul warns us that Christian fruitfulness is much more like the life of a Galatian farmer. It involves lots of hard work for very little visible return, and it requires lots of patient faith and prayer, before a bumper harvest finally appears.

In 6:10, Paul tells us to use our freedom *to serve other people*. This brings us back to Paul's command in 5:13 to *"use your freedom to... serve one another humbly in love."* We have not been saved by good works but we have been saved for good works, as Paul spells out later in Ephesians 2:8–10. We have been set free to pour out our time, our treasure and our talents on behalf of any believers who are in need, and then on behalf of any unbelievers who are in need too. We have been set free to do as John Wesley is reputed to have instructed his converts: *"Do all the good you can, by all the means you can, in all the ways you can, in all the places you can, at all the times you can, to all the people you can, as long as ever you can."*

These seven items are not an exhaustive list of what it means for us to live out our freedom as children of God, because no day ever looks the same as the Holy Spirit leads us. Paul simply gives these seven examples in order to help us understand how to be active and not passive with our newfound freedom.

Because freedom isn't easy. It is a verb, an action word.

---

[4] Charles Swindoll in *The Grace Awakening* (1990). Farmers expect to receive back much more of what they sow, as is highlighted in a similar Old Testament warning in Hosea 8:7.

The Second Letter to the Galatians (6:11–18)

The grace of our Lord Jesus Christ be with your spirit, brothers and sisters. Amen.

(Galatians 6:18)

We have reached the end of Galatians, but we haven't reached the end of the story. Paul's letter was very successful and the churches responded very favourably to his passionate defence of the Gospel. It helped that when he visited their churches early the following year he came bearing a second letter to the Galatians.

Paul signs off this first letter with a clue in 6:11 which indicates that he wrote it early on in 49 AD. We can already tell this from his reference to things changing *"so quickly"* in 1:6 and from the fact he makes no mention of the discussions that were to take place in Jerusalem in Acts 15. Paul confirms it by apologizing for writing with such large letters as he takes over from his scribe to write the final verses of the letter in his own handwriting as a proof of its authenticity.[1] Paul's apology suggests that he was still suffering from the eye condition which 4:13–15 tells us he contracted in Galatia.[2]

Paul ends with a final plea in 6:12–17 for the Galatians to reject the false teaching of the Judaizers and to reaffirm their commitment and love for him. He accuses the false teachers

---

[1] See 2 Thessalonians 3:17.

[2] It is possible that 6:11 is a Greek metaphor that means *"See how emphatically I have written to you,"* but the simplest reading of the verse is that Paul was still suffering from the eye condition described in 4:13–15.

of wanting to be able to boast that they have convinced the Gentile Christians to be circumcised, because it will win them favour with the wider Jewish community. They are not really passionate about the Law of Moses or else they would obey it a bit more themselves! They want to boast in human externals, whereas Paul refuses to boast in anything but Jesus' death on the cross to set us free. It is amazing how much summary of the message of Galatians Paul is able to squeeze into these few final verses. He talks about having been crucified with Jesus (6:14), having been made a new creation in Jesus (6:15), having been made part of the true Israel of God through Jesus (6:16),[3] and having been called to march as a soldier of Jesus (6:16).[4] He argues one final time that all this means that the old Jewish rite of circumcision has ceased to matter (6:15). What matters now is whether we are willing to die with Jesus and to suffer for the Gospel of his grace (6:17).[5] It is evident from Paul's repetition that he is concerned as he signs off this letter that the Galatians may not listen to his warnings.

Therefore Paul ends the letter in 6:18 by turning the spotlight back onto *"the grace of our Lord Jesus Christ."* He calls the Galatians his *brothers and sisters*, convinced that they are true believers who will repent of the two extremes of legalism and licence, and he ends with a similar phrase to the one that began the letter in 1:3. The grace of God through Jesus Christ is all we need, without any top-up of our own through good works

---

[3] The Greek text of 6:16 can either read *"to all who follow this rule **and** to the Israel of God"* or *"to all who follow this rule, **even** to the Israel of God."* The flow of Paul's argument in chapters 3–4 forces the second reading.

[4] Paul deliberately echoes 5:25 by using the same military word *stoicheō*, or *to march*, in 6:16.

[5] The Greek word which Paul uses for the *marks* of Jesus in 6:17 is *stigmata*, which was normally used for a brand burnt on a slave's skin. Paul is not referring to literal nail marks in his hands. He is either saying he has been crucified with Jesus or that his body still bears the wounds from being stoned almost to death in Galatia in Acts 14:19. These are like brands burnt on his body to testify that he is a slave of Jesus.

or circumcision or Sabbath-keeping or Law-abiding. God's grace alone can make us free on the inside. Paul signs off, seals and sends his first New Testament letter.

Here's what happened next.

Only a few weeks after he sent his letter from Syrian Antioch, the issue he addressed came to a head in the church there. Luke was a member of the church at Antioch and he tells us in Acts 15:1–2 that some Judaizers arrived and started preaching that Greek converts needed to be circumcised like Jews if they wanted to be saved. Paul immediately turned from letter-writer into hand-to-hand fighter. When the church at Antioch saw his clear understanding of the issue and his passionate desire to expose this teaching as a lie, they appointed him to head up a team of representatives who would go to the apostles in Jerusalem in mid-49 AD to receive a definitive ruling on the matter.

In Acts 15, Luke describes the discussion, which has become known as the Council of Jerusalem. He tells us that Paul described the way in which God had saved many pagan Galatians during his first missionary journey, and then he let the other apostles do the talking. Peter agreed entirely with the message of Galatians, telling the assembly that salvation only comes by grace through faith in Jesus Christ and not by obedience to the Law, and arguing that the true mark of whether or not a person has been saved is not whether or not they have been circumcised but whether or not they have received the Holy Spirit. Paul interjected to describe some of the amazing miracles that had accompanied the pagan conversions in Galatia, then he let James do the rest of the talking. James also agreed entirely with Paul's letter to the Galatians, quoting one of God's great prophecies to Israel in Amos 9:11–12 and applying it to the Church as the true Israel of God. James pointed out that if the Law of Moses had not saved the Greeks before Jesus came then it was unlikely to start saving them now.

As a result, the Council of Jerusalem wrote a second letter

to the Galatians.[6] Luke records it for us in Acts 15:23–29 and, though much shorter, it completely supports Paul's first letter. It tells the Greek believers in Galatia that Paul is their friend, that the Judaizers are troublemakers who do not speak for the apostles, and that they should listen to Paul's insistence that there is no need for them to follow the detail of the Jewish Law. This second letter made Paul's first letter entirely successful. When Paul arrived back in Galatia, Acts 16:4–5 tells us that *"as they travelled from town to town, they delivered the decisions reached by the apostles and elders in Jerusalem for the people to obey. So the churches were strengthened in the faith and grew daily in numbers."*

Paul had succeeded in defining and defending the Gospel of freedom. He had protected the message that God justifies us, comes to live inside us, sanctifies us and frees us from the inside out through his grace towards us in Jesus alone. Paul left the cities of Galatia in early 50 AD and moved on to other unreached cities. His work was done among the Galatians. They had learned what it meant to believe in the Gospel and to be set free through Jesus on the inside.

---

[6] It was addressed to the Gentile believers in Antioch and Cilicia, but this included the Galatians because their churches had been planted by a missionary who came from Cilicia and had been sent out from Antioch.

Part Two – Ephesians:

New on the Inside

Eleven Years Later (1:1–2)

To God's holy people in Ephesus, the faithful in Christ Jesus.

(Ephesians 1:1)

A lot of things had changed during the eleven years that passed between Paul sending his letter to the Galatians and sitting down to write his letter to the Ephesians.

For a start, Paul was eleven years older and wiser. When he wrote to the Galatians in 49 AD, he was still very new to Christian leadership, with only a few months of missionary work under his belt. By the time he wrote to the Ephesians in around 60 AD, he had completed three missionary journeys and planted churches all across the Eastern Mediterranean. He looked around at the cities of Cyprus, Turkey, Macedonia and Greece in 57 AD and told the Romans it was time for him to move west because *"there is no more place for me to work in these regions."*[1]

Another big thing that had changed was the conditions under which Paul was writing. He had written to the Galatians from his home at Syrian Antioch, surrounded by the church family to which he had ministered for several years. He wrote to the Ephesians while under house arrest in Rome and about to stand trial for his life before the highest court in the Roman Empire. Paul had been right that it was time for him to head west and to start planting churches on the other side of the Mediterranean, but he hadn't anticipated how it would happen.

---

[1] Romans 15:23. Paul wrote 1 and 2 Thessalonians, 1 and 2 Corinthians and Romans during these eleven intervening years. Those letters are covered by other volumes in the *Straight to the Heart* series.

He was arrested on a visit to Jerusalem in 57 AD, kept in the main prison at Caesarea until 59 AD and then shipped in chains to Rome.[2] The Jews had been so infuriated by the Gospel message that he described to the Galatians that they attacked him as *"the man who teaches everyone everywhere against our people and our law."* The only way Paul could escape their clutches was to appeal to Caesar and ask the imperial governor to protect his route to Rome.[3] Yes, a lot of things had changed in the eleven years which passed between the writing of Galatians and Ephesians.

But one thing hadn't changed at all. Paul's Gospel message still remained the same. If anything, he is able to lay it out even more clearly in Ephesians than in Galatians because this is the only New Testament letter which he wrote to a church on his own terms instead of in response to local problems on the ground. He simply wrote it to lay out all the glories of the Gospel. He did not need to expose false teaching or confront sin or ask for money, as in his other church letters. In fact, what is striking is how little of what he writes is specific to the church at Ephesus at all. Paul keeps his message general, perhaps so that the letter can also be circulated to the other churches in Asia,[4] which makes Ephesians an even pithier summary of the Gospel than Romans. Having told the Galatians that the grace of God makes us *free on the inside*, Paul now explains in even greater detail to the Ephesians that the grace of God also makes us *new on the inside*.

Paul begins his letter with the very same greeting that he used to start his letter to the Galatians eleven years earlier:

---

[2] In theory, Paul's references to being in prison in 3:1, 4:1 and 6:20 could refer to his time in Caesarea rather than in Rome. It is the similarity between Ephesians and Colossians which confirms he was in Rome.

[3] Acts 21:28; 25:11; 28:16–31.

[4] This idea is supported by the fact that a few Greek manuscripts of Ephesians do not contain the words *"in Ephesus"* in 1:1. The church at Ephesus had been extremely successful at planting churches across the whole of Asia, so Paul may have wanted this letter to be relevant to any of those other churches too.

"Grace and peace to you from God our Father and the Lord Jesus Christ." His message is still all about God's grace which reconciles us to God and one another in Jesus, in spite of all our sin. He calls the Ephesians *hagioi*, which means *saints* or *holy ones* or *people set apart for God*, even though they started out as anything but holy. Their city was very pagan, famous all across the world for its Temple of Artemis, one of the Seven Wonders of the Ancient World. They were so polluted by their city's idolatry that, when they made a bonfire of their sinful books, Acts 19:19 tells us it was worth about £10,000,000 in today's money. Yet despite their sin, Paul insists that every one of them is now a saint through faith in Jesus Christ. If they are *pistoi – believers* or *faithful ones* – then they must also be *hagioi*, or *saints* of God. Their sinful past and their struggles with sin in the present do not change the fact that, through faith in Jesus, they have been made holy because the Gospel makes us new on the inside.

If I told you that a few weeks ago I flew at 600 miles per hour for a whole night at 40,000 feet in the air, I wouldn't have to tell you how I did so. It would be obvious to you that I must have been inside a plane. Bear that in mind as you read Ephesians 1:1 slowly. Paul tells the Ephesians that they have two addresses, not just one. They live *"in Ephesus"* but they also live *"in Christ Jesus."* This is the same Gospel message that so excited Paul in Galatians. God has somehow placed us *in Jesus* through our faith, just as I was inside a plane (Galatians 3:28–29). He has clothed us with Jesus' holiness and power (Galatians 3:27). He has filled us with the Spirit of Jesus (Galatians 4:6) and has afforded us the same status in his sight as Jesus (Galatians 3:26). He has hidden us in Jesus, so we are a new creation (Galatians 6:15). The Gospel has made us new on the inside.

This is the message of Ephesians, and it is a message that we desperately need to hear. Only this can stop us from treating Paul like a superhuman movie hero, brilliant to admire from a distance but impossible to copy. Only this can teach us to fly quickly behind him as people who have been made new on the inside through the Gospel.

At the height of his boxing career, Muhammad Ali told a flight attendant who asked him to fasten his seatbelt, *"Hey, Superman don't need no seatbelt."* The flight attendant immediately snapped back, *"Superman don't need no airplane either."* Paul's letter to the Ephesians stops us from being proud (it tells us to do things we know we cannot do) and it stops us from being falsely humble (pretending that Paul's experience of God was an exception to the rule). It teaches us how to fly high and fast and for long distances in God. The Ephesians had two addresses: *in Ephesus* and *in Jesus*. So do we.

So let's pick up Paul's story again eleven years after he wrote his letter to the Galatians. Let's sit beside him in his prison cell in Rome and discover how the Gospel makes us new on the inside.

Under the Skin (1:3–14)

You also were included in Christ when you heard the message of truth, the gospel of your salvation.

(Ephesians 1:13)

We began this commentary by likening Paul to Arnold Schwarzenegger in the *Terminator* movies. When we read the book of Acts, he can seem so superhuman that we are tempted to put him in a separate category to ourselves and to conclude that we can never copy him. But Paul did not plant a megachurch in Ephesus by acting as a one-man army. He taught the Ephesians to live the same way as he did through the Gospel. He begins this letter by taking us under the skin of his ministry to show us how we can be renewed like him on the inside too.

Paul had found only a dozen ragtag believers to start a church with when he arrived at Ephesus in 53 AD at the start of Acts 19. They understood little about Jesus and even less about the Holy Spirit, so they were hardly very likely to convert a city of over half a million people. Ephesus was the capital of the Roman province of Asia and the fourth or fifth largest city in the world. Paul had to help these dozen believers to allow the Gospel to change them from the inside out before they were ready to help him reach the rest of the city. He stayed for three years in Ephesus, investing his time in helping ordinary people to become new on the inside through the Gospel. As a result, even though he did not personally visit any other town in Asia, he planted churches all across the region by training and releasing an army of missionaries.[1] We are told in Acts 19 that *"All the Jews and Greeks who lived in the province of Asia heard the word of the Lord"* and that *"the word of the Lord spread widely and grew in power,"* resulting in the conversion of *"large numbers of people here in Ephesus and in practically the whole province of Asia."*[2]

That's why I love Ephesians 1:3–14. They are like the moment in *Terminator 2* when the cyborg Arnold Schwarzenegger peels back his skin to show his shocked companions the titanium skeleton inside. Paul is so excited about showing us the hidden power behind his fruitfulness that he writes all of these twelve verses as a single sentence in Greek, so eager to pour out his secrets that he does not stop to catch his breath. Most English translations add some punctuation because we need to read these verses slowly. They show us how we can be as fruitful as Paul and his Ephesian friends.

Paul tells us in 1:3 that the Gospel gives us *a new power supply*. Because we are in Jesus, we are plugged into every spiritual blessing in the heavenlies. Paul uses the phrase *"in Christ"* or *"in him"* ten times in these opening verses, and he uses the phrase *"in the heavenly realms"* five times in this letter, because the two phrases go together. If we are in Jesus then, by definition, we are wherever he is now. We live in Ephesus or London or Los Angeles or wherever, but we also live in heaven. From there we have already received all the power we need to live like Paul. He tells us that God *has* blessed us – not that he *will* bless us – because we simply have to lay hold of heaven's

---

[1] A single convert named Epaphras appears to have planted churches in Colossae, Hierapolis and Laodicea (Colossians 1:6–7; 2:1; 4:12–13).

[2] Acts 19:10, 20, 26.

power supply through the Holy Spirit each day[3] by praying *"Your kingdom come, your will be done on earth as it is in heaven."*[4]

Paul tells us in 1:4–6 that the Gospel gives us *a new status*. We have been adopted as children of God through Jesus the Son.[5] This makes us part of a great destiny, which is new to us but has been in God's heart towards us since before the dawn of time. Though we are sinful and rebellious, we have been counted holy and blameless through Jesus' perfect life, and God has even made something positive out of our past sins by using them to showcase the glory of his grace.[6] This is why Paul is confident that we can be every bit as fruitful in our Christian lives as he is. We have been chosen by God and saved into an amazing destiny.

Paul tells us in 1:7–8 that the Gospel gives us *a new freedom*. We are like slaves who have been redeemed from their masters, like guilty criminals who have been pardoned for their crimes, like paupers who have been made princes and like brute beasts who have been granted the wisdom of God.

Paul tells us in 1:9–12 that the Gospel gives us *a new purpose*. The Greek word *mustērion* was a technical religious word that meant far more than just a *mystery*. The mystery religions of the pagan Roman Empire promised to initiate a chosen few into the secret knowledge of the gods. Paul takes this word from the pagan phrasebook and applies it to the Gospel. He tells us that

---

[3] The Greek phrase *"every spiritual blessing"* can just as easily be translated *"every blessing of the Spirit."*

[4] This is what Jesus meant when he told us to pray these words in Matthew 6:10.

[5] The Greek word *huiothesia* means *adoption as sons* and it therefore echoes the teaching of Galatians 3:26–28. In a world that valued sons more than daughters, Paul insists that women are also adopted as sons of God through inclusion in the Son of God. The Father values them just as much as their brothers.

[6] The reference to Jesus as *the Beloved One* in 1:6 is a deliberate link back to the Father's words over him at his baptism and transfiguration in Matthew 3:17 and 17:5. Now God speaks those same words over you and me.

God has initiated us into his secret purpose for world history – he has made us part of his plan to use everything which happens in the world as part of his overarching plan to unite Jews and Gentiles together in the Church as one new body of believers under the headship of Jesus.[7] The Gospel isn't just the announcement that God makes individuals new on the inside. It is also an invitation to become part of the new community that he is creating to display his glory.

Paul tells us in 1:3–14 that the Gospel gives us *a new experience of God*. The Old Testament promised a time was coming when the Holy Spirit would fill more than just a few select individuals. This is such a constant theme of the Old Testament that even though it contains 8,000 promises – that's one promise for every three verses – the New Testament refers to this one as *the* promise.[8] Paul tells us that this promise is now ours through the Gospel. We aren't just in Jesus; he is also now in us. Paul compares this to the wax seal on an ancient letter: being filled with the Spirit authenticates that our salvation is a genuine work of God. Our experience of God on the inside acts as a deposit that guarantees that we are heirs of God's eternal Kingdom which will be fully revealed at the end of time.[9]

I'm very glad that the English translators added extra punctuation to Paul's very long sentence. There is a lot of truth crammed into these twelve verses. They show us what went on under the skin of Paul's walk with Jesus. They show us how he trained the Ephesians to walk the same way too.

So let's not put Paul on a pedestal. Let's listen to what he says instead. Let's expect to experience God in the same way that he did by allowing this Gospel to get under our own skin too.

---

[7] Paul uses the word *mustērion* again when he talks about this same plan in 3:3–9, 5:32 and 6:19.

[8] It does so in Greek in Luke 24:49, Acts 1:4 and 2:39. See also Galatians 3:14.

[9] The Greek word which Paul uses for *deposit* is *arrabōn*, a word which is still used in modern Greek to refer to a woman's engagement ring.

Let's Get Personal (1:3–14)

For he chose us in him before the creation of the world to be holy and blameless in his sight. In love he predestined us to be adopted as his sons through Jesus Christ.

(Ephesians 1:4–5)

One of our biggest dangers when we read these verses is to let the Gospel go into our heads without dropping into our hearts. Accepting these doctrines is not the same thing as letting them get under the skin of how we live our daily lives. So let's not rush on from these opening verses. Let's get personal about what they really mean.

One of my friends was conceived by mistake. Her parents were not married and didn't want her. When I met her in her early twenties she was still very affected by the feeling that her life was all one big mistake. Then she believed the Gospel. I don't mean she became a Christian – she had given her life to Jesus as a child – I mean that she believed the Gospel message as Paul describes it in 1:4. She actually took to heart Paul's statement that God chose her in Jesus before the creation of the world, and it turned her entire life around.

We are more affected by our thought life than we know. We become who we think we are deep down. When my friend's self-perception changed through the Gospel, it changed everything else as well. Her parents might not have planned her life, but God planned it long before he ever said, *"Let there be light."* Add to this Paul's statement in 1:14 that God chose her to be part of his *peripoiēsis* – a jewel in his *royal treasure collection*[1] – and it isn't too hard to see why she is a completely different woman today. These verses changed her sense of identity, and then everything else changed as well.

Another of my friends was adopted as a baby. His new parents were amazing but, like many adopted children, he felt a deep sense of rejection that his birth mother had given him away. He felt like a second-rate person with second-rate parents until he took to heart what Paul teaches in 1:5. An adopted baby in the Roman Empire was not second-rate at all, which is why God uses adoption as a picture of our becoming children through a father's free choice and delight rather than simply through nature. Add to this Paul's statement in 1:14 that adopted sons are *heirs*, and it isn't too hard to see why this friend's life was turned around by the Gospel as well. There had only been five Roman emperors by the time Paul wrote his letter to the Ephesians, and four of them, including the current one, became emperor because the previous emperor chose to adopt them as his heir.[2] Paul's teaching about God's election and our adoption enabled my friend to see his life with completely different eyes.

Another of my friends is gay. In the run-up to his fortieth birthday he confessed that he feels he has nothing to look forward to but death. He knows that pursuing his gay feelings would be wrong (Paul is very clear about that in passages such as Romans 1:24–27, 1 Corinthians 6:9–11 and 1 Timothy 1:9–11), but in struggling to be celibate he feels guilty and confused that this temptation hasn't gone away. Sometimes he wonders if he can carry on with his Christian faith at all. That's why he has to keep on turning back to these verses. Paul assures us in 1:7 that Jesus died to set us free from slavery to all of our sinful

[1] This is the Greek word which God uses when he promises to turn people into his *royal treasure collection* in Malachi 3:17. The Gospel makes us heirs to all of God's Old Testament promises to Israel.

[2] Augustus was adopted by Julius Caesar, Tiberius was adopted by Augustus, Caligula was adopted by Tiberius, and Nero was adopted by Claudius.

desires, not just to some of them,[3] and he promises us in 1:6 that our sinfulness does not disqualify us. It makes the grace of God shine even more brightly in the dirty mire of our lives. Perhaps being a new creation in Christ will change my friend's desires so that he can marry a woman and have children, but if this change proves slower than he hopes then he has Paul's promise that the Holy Spirit will enable him to work out his struggle with his sexuality each day.[4]

One of the few things that offends people as much as Paul's teaching on homosexuality is his teaching about God's election and predestination, yet Paul is absolutely clear that God has chosen who he is going to save and has predestined their salvation since before he made the world. Rather than being offended by this (Paul never teaches the flipside of this, that God has chosen not to save others), I find it far more helpful to stand back and watch what happens to people who take this teaching to heart. There are basically three scenarios: God chooses who is saved, the Devil chooses who is saved or we choose who is saved. If we strike the Devil off the list because he does not possess that much power, we are left with only two scenarios. Either we chose God and therefore have to carry the burden of keeping on choosing him every day, or God chose us and therefore promises to carry the burden of keeping us in his salvation every day. Paul's teaching about predestination may be offensive to many, but I can tell you it's a sweet breath of life to my struggling gay friend.

Another friend of mine has suffered from depression ever since she discovered that her mother tried several times to abort her. She is just beginning to apply these verses to her heart, but she is already finding that Paul's Gospel is the

---

[3] Paul deliberately links forgiveness and freedom in 1:7 and in Colossians 1:14. Having forgiven us for our sins, God also promises to free us from our sins. We can no more doubt the one promise than the other.

[4] If you are living out this struggle, a great book is *Washed and Waiting* by Wesley Hill (2010).

answer to her own troubled background too. She is learning to believe Paul when he says in 1:11 that God has a perfect plan for each one of our lives. She is beginning to focus less on her mother's attempts to abort her and more on the Lord's gracious intervention to save her each time. Your situation may be less dramatic. You may simply be stuck in a dead-end job, frustrated with church or struggling to cope with the demands of a young family – whatever the details, the fact is that we all need to know that God is working out his perfect plan in our lives. It gives life meaning and it makes us new on the inside. The Gospel always does that when it gets personal.

Jerry Bridges reminds us that

> *The gospel is not only the most important message in all of history; it is the **only** essential message in all of history. Yet we allow thousands of professing Christians to live their entire lives without clearly understanding it and experiencing the joy of living by it... Every day of our Christian experience should be a day of relating to God on the basis of His grace alone. We are not only saved by grace, but we also live by grace every day.*[5]

---

[5] Jerry Bridges in *The Discipline of Grace* (1994).

How to Dive for Treasure (1:15–23)

I pray that the eyes of your heart may be enlightened in order that you may know the hope to which he has called you, the riches of his glorious inheritance in his holy people.

(Ephesians 1:18)

Everybody dreams of finding buried treasure, but the problem is not that there is too little of it around. We know where lots of treasure is buried. We just don't know how to retrieve it.

On 16th February 1941, the British merchant ship the SS *Gairsoppa* was almost at the end of her journey back from India when she was spotted by a German U-boat and torpedoed in the side. Within twenty minutes she had sunk with £150 million of silver bullion on board. She still lies there on the ocean bed today, 300 miles off the coast of Ireland and three miles under water. The problem isn't finding buried treasure. It's knowing how to dive for treasure which we know is there.

Paul catches his breath after the very long sentence of 1:3–14, but he only does so to encourage us to dive with him again. He wants to help us to recover all the treasure that he has pointed out in the ocean of God's grace. He gives us four ways in which we can move these doctrines from our heads into our hearts.

First, Paul teaches us in 1:15–16 to *pray prayers of thanks*. There is no better way to make doctrine come alive than to repeat it back to God in worship and thanksgiving. God knew what he was doing when he decided to teach the Gospel to the

Israelites by giving them a songbook containing 150 psalms. Christoph Barth argues that Psalms is divided into five books because they are *"the five-fold answer of the congregation to the word of God in the five books of Moses."*[1] God speaks and we answer, and as we answer we find that our hearts are changed. If you want to believe the Gospel, the answer isn't just to study apologetics. It is also to exercise your tongue in praise. If you want the doctrines of grace to slip eighteen inches from your head down into your heart, take note of the fact that God has nestled your heart in between your lungs. Paul models how we should use our voices to offer prayers of thanksgiving, because this is the first way we can dive to retrieve all the treasure buried in the Gospel.[2]

Second, Paul teaches us in 1:17 to *pray for help from the Holy Spirit*. He reminds us that the Old Testament calls the third person of the Trinity *the Spirit of wisdom and revelation*.[3] Diving for treasures in the Gospel therefore begins with us responding to the treasures we have already found in the Gospel! We will only succeed if we accept God's invitation to let him come and dwell inside us by grace through faith. When Jesus promised to give us the Holy Spirit, he said in John 14:18 that *"I will come to you,"* and when Paul talked about the promise in 1 Corinthians 2:9–16 he told us that it means *"we have the mind of Christ."* We are not in the same situation as the British government in 1989 when it tried in vain to find a salvage company that knew how to recover the silver bullion from the SS *Gairsoppa*. We have a retrieval expert on the inside, because Jesus lives in us to help us understand all that he has done.

Third, Paul teaches us in 1:18 to *pray that God will help us to take to heart what we see and read*. Wisdom does not simply

---

[1] Christoph Barth in his *Introduction to the Psalms* (1966).

[2] Paul's rich and worshipful prayer life is evident elsewhere in his letters too – in 3:14–21, in Romans 1:8–10, in Philippians 1:3–11, in Colossians 1:9–12, in 1 Thessalonians 1:2–3 and in Philemon 4–6.

[3] Deuteronomy 34:9; Isaiah 11:2.

come through praying for it. It comes through reading Scripture and Christian books, it comes from listening to sermons, it comes from conversations with godly friends and it comes from studying the world around us. Paul won't let us become super-spiritual and mystic about understanding the Gospel. Study alone cannot retrieve Gospel treasures from God's Word unless God enlightens the eyes of our hearts to see it (John 5:39), but nor can our hearts retrieve Gospel treasures unless they have something to look at with their enlightened eyes (Mark 12:24)! When the theologian B. B. Warfield overheard one of his students boasting that ten minutes on his knees would give him deeper knowledge of God than ten hours over his books, he exclaimed: *"What! than ten hours over your books on your knees?"*[4] That's the right kind of balance Paul wants us to aim for in order to experience the treasures of the Gospel.

Paul tells us in 1:18–21 that if we actively study the Gospel, we make room for the Holy Spirit to open our eyes to many more things. It provides a way for him to show us the *hope* contained in the Gospel, the *riches* contained in the Gospel and the amazing *power* contained in the Gospel – a power which when unleashed through the Holy Spirit raised Jesus' corpse from the dead and raised him to heaven where he now reigns over the whole universe. Eugene Peterson describes this kind of Holy Spirit inspired study when he tells us that *"We read Scripture in order to listen again to the word of God **spoken**, and when we do, we hear him **speak**. Somehow or other these words **live**."*[5]

Fourth, Paul teaches us in 1:22–23 to *look for help from other people in the church*. He reminds us that God's purpose through world history is to gather a new and holy community of people led by his Son. He tells us that the ascension and glorification of Jesus were not ends in themselves; they took place *"for the church, which is his body, the fullness of him who fills*

---

[4] B. B. Warfield in "The Religious Life of Theological Students", published by Mark Noll as part of *The Princeton Theology* (1983).

[5] Eugene Peterson in *Working the Angles* (1987).

everything in every way."[6] If Jesus is this devoted to the Church and if the Church is truly at the centre of God's purposes for humanity, we are very foolish if we neglect the Church ourselves. Solo divers are in grave danger. We will only go deeper into the Gospel if we learn to dive with others. God has promised us that we will discover greater Gospel treasures if we devote ourselves to diving with other Christians on his team.

In 2012, the Florida-based salvage company Odyssey Marine Exploration finally reached the wreck of the SS *Gairsoppa* and retrieved the silver bullion inside. More than seventy years after she was sunk by the Germans, someone had finally learned how to retrieve the £150 million of silver deep inside her hold. Paul wants us to be equally determined to lay hold of the riches of the Gospel. As we offer prayers of thanksgiving and prayers to receive more of the Holy Spirit, God will enlighten the eyes of our hearts and those of the other Christians with whom we dive, so that we can rejoice together over the riches of the Gospel.[7]

---

[6] The Greek text is deliberately ambiguous in 1:23. It can mean either that Jesus is seen in his completeness through the Church, or that Jesus' work only finds its true completion in the Church.

[7] Paul tells us in 3:8 that the riches of God's grace are *unsearchable* – in other words, they are so great that we can never retrieve all of them in a lifetime. We must never get tired of diving.

The Portrait of Our Salvation (2:1–10)

*For it is by grace you have been saved, through faith
– and this is not from yourselves, it is the gift of God
– not by works, so that no one can boast.*

(Ephesians 2:8–9)

In my family photo album there are two different types of picture. There are portrait photos and landscape photos. The portrait photos tend to be close-up shots of a single individual, whereas the landscape photos tend to be wide-angle shots of a group of people all together. I find it helpful to see Ephesians 2 as a kind of photo album of salvation. The first ten verses offer us a portrait shot of what the grace of God means for an individual. The final twelve verses offer us a landscape shot of what the grace of God means for humanity as a whole.[1]

Ephesians 2:1–10 is one of the best-loved and most preached-upon passages in the entire Bible, and rightly so. It is an amazing summary of what the grace of God means for us as individuals. It is so jam-packed full of truth that we need to read it slowly and with a willingness to dive for treasure yet again. Let's try to draw out each of the colours that Paul uses in his portrait shot of our salvation.

In 2:1, Paul tells us we were *dead* before Jesus saved us. Not many of us tell our salvation testimony that way, but Paul insists that it is true. We were not drowning people who needed

---

[1] The "new perspective" writers such as N. T. Wright are correct to argue that we have overemphasized 2:1–10 at the expense of 2:11–22. However, they are in danger of overemphasizing 2:11–22 at the expense of 2:1–10.

to be thrown a life belt. We were not sick people who needed rehabilitation. We were not sleepy people who needed to be awoken. We were dead; not so much in need of medicine as of a miracle. That's why Paul talks so much about God's election and predestination when he explains the Gospel. We don't get to play the leading role in the story of our salvation. That role belongs to Jesus alone.

In 2:2–3, the colours are even darker. Paul tells us that we used to be subject to the thinking of the world, to the cravings of our sinful flesh and to the authority of the Devil. Not being adopted as God's children or filled with the Holy Spirit did not mean that we were fatherless and empty before we were saved. We were by nature *"children of wrath"*[2] and filled with a satanic spirit of disobedience.[3] We were not cut off from God's promises because we sinned and therefore became sinners; we were born sinners and therefore sinned. We did not choose to be saved, because the Gospel was completely at odds with who we were until the Holy Spirit shone the light of truth into our hearts and taught us to run to God as Father.[4] The background in this portrait picture is one of powerlessness and desperate need of God's unsolicited grace and mercy.

The picture suddenly changes in 2:4–5, as God makes dead sinners alive *"because of his great love for us."* Only love could have made him do this because we had nothing to offer him except for the sin which made salvation necessary. Sending his Son Jesus to become a corpse so that we might be raised from

---

[2] Although some English translations talk about our being *"objects of wrath,"* the Greek text actually says we were *"sons of disobedience"* (2:2) and *"children of wrath"* (2:3).

[3] Paul refers to Satan literally as *"the ruler of the authority of the air."* His lingering authority in this present age will soon vanish into thin air. The Greek word that Paul uses to describe Satan *working in* the hearts of unbelievers is *energeō* – the same word he uses for the inworking of the Holy Spirit in 1:11, 1:20 and 3:20.

[4] Paul stresses this complete change of direction by using the same Greek word *peripateō*, or *to walk*, first negatively in 2:2 and then positively in 2:10.

the dead was entirely an act of mercy (not punishing us as our sins deserved) and entirely an act of grace (giving us blessings we did nothing to deserve). If Paul stopped his portrait picture of salvation here then it would be breathtaking enough, but he is only halfway through.

In 2:6–7, he tells us that God's grace has not merely united us with Jesus in his death and resurrection. It has also united us with him in his ascension. Even though we still live bodily on earth, we have ascended with Jesus spiritually to sit at the right hand of the Father in heaven. This is what Paul meant when he began his letter by telling his readers that they live both *"in Ephesus"* and *"in Christ Jesus,"* and its implications are mind-blowing. It means that we now have a share in the authority given to Jesus in Psalm 110, since in him we now sit on the throne of the universe. It means we now have immediate access to God the Father,[5] and it means we can be certain that all our prayers are heard because we have the ear of God and he therefore cannot fail to hear us. Forget all the silver on the SS *Gairsoppa*. It is nothing compared to what Paul calls *"the incomparable riches of his grace."*

In 2:8–10, Paul therefore finishes off our portrait picture of salvation by underlining that all of this is about the glory of God's grace. We are saved by faith alone and not by any good works of our own. In fact, Paul tells us in 2:8 that we cannot even boast about our faith because even this was granted to us as a gift from God because he chose us before the beginning of time! Our salvation is entirely God's work, enabling us to start the good works that he has prepared for us to do. We must not fool ourselves that our good works make any contribution to our salvation.[6]

---

[5] Staggering though this is, we are also told this in Hebrews 10:19–23. See also 1 Kings 2:19 and Psalm 45:9.

[6] 2:8–10 states the same thing as James 2:24. We are saved by faith alone but the faith which saves will never remain alone. We are not saved *by* good works but we are saved *for* good works.

Paul is writing to the believers in the church at Ephesus so he naturally talks as if all of his readers have experienced this salvation. I am writing, on the other hand, for anyone who wants to understand the message of Ephesians, so I don't want to assume that Paul is describing everyone who reads these pages. If you are unsure that you have experienced the salvation Paul is describing (and he tells us in 1:13–14 that saved people are usually sure), don't move on before getting down on your knees and telling God that you believe this Gospel. Admit that you are as dead in sin as Paul says you are in 2:1–3. Believe that Jesus died and rose again for you as Paul promises in 2:4–7. Tell God that you commit your life to him through faith from this day forwards to do the good works he has prepared for you to do.

And if you know that you are saved, gaze long and hard at this portrait picture of your salvation.[7] Since you contributed nothing to this portrait other than your sin, you can rest in the fact that it is utterly finished in Jesus. Paul was never more saved than you. The Ephesians were never more saved than you. There has never been anyone in Church history who has been more saved than you. It is finished, which is why we mustn't try to smuggle our own good works into this portrait. As Paul points out in 2:9, this is a portrait that allows no room for human boasting. It reserves all of the glory for our salvation to God alone. It is a portrait picture of his amazing grace.

---

[7] The Greek word for *handiwork* in 2:10 is *poiēma*, the root of the English word *poem*. These are not simply doctrines for us to assent to. They are a beautiful work of art which should stir our hearts to worship.

The Landscape of Our Salvation (2:11–22)

His purpose was to create in himself one new humanity out of the two, thus making peace, and in one body to reconcile both of them to God.

(Ephesians 2:15–16)

To understand the message of Ephesians, it helps to remember why Paul wrote the letter from prison. He was there because he painted a landscape picture of the Gospel for a Greek friend who came from Ephesus.

Trophimus was one of the leaders of the church at Ephesus. The church had grown so much in the four years since Paul left the city that he needed to begin this letter by telling newcomers he was an apostle, but Trophimus needed no such introduction. Everybody knew him and knew what Paul had sacrificed for him. Paul had been arrested in Jerusalem in 57 AD because the Jews *"had previously seen Trophimus the Ephesian in the city with Paul and assumed that Paul had brought him into the temple area."*[1] A riot started against Paul because he was *"the man who teaches everyone everywhere against our people and our law and this place. And besides, he has brought Greeks into the temple area and defiled this holy place."* Not everybody liked Paul's landscape picture of salvation. It told them that the Gospel was far more than a life-changing message for individuals. It had changed everything for the nations of the world.

In 2:11–12, Paul describes for his non-Jewish readers just

---

[1] Acts 20:4; 21:27–29.

how bleak things were for the nations before Jesus came. They were not part of Israel, they had no share in God's promises to Abraham and the fact that they were not circumcised was simply an outward sign of their inward hostility towards God's covenant with Abraham. The nations were devoid of hope. They were as dead as their lifeless idols.[2]

In 2:13, Paul begins to paint with much happier colours. The coming of Jesus altered everything for the nations. The angry Jewish mob was right about one thing: a non-Jew was not allowed to enter the inner courtyards of the Temple. The first-century Jewish historian Josephus tells us that a large wall kept them out with a sign that warned them that if they crossed the threshold, they would be executed.[3] Paul wrote this letter from prison because he preached that the Gospel destroyed this wall: *"You who once were far away have been brought near by the blood of Christ."* As Paul explained to the Galatians, Jesus is the true Seed of Abraham and Jews can therefore only be saved if they are united with him through faith. It stands to reason that non-Jews can also become the Seed of Abraham if they are united with Jesus. Jesus was Jewish and circumcised and heir to God's promises to Abraham, so anyone who is counted as being in Jesus, regardless of their race, is all of those things too.

In 2:14–18, Paul unpacks what this means. The Ephesian church was largely Gentile, which is why he quotes far less from the Old Testament in this letter than he did in his letter to the Galatians, so Paul tells them that the Gospel has renewed God's true definition of Israel.[4] The wall that divided Jew from Gentile in the Temple has been done away with once and

[2] Paul calls them *atheists* in 2:12, even though they worshipped many gods, because the pagans called Christians *atheists* for rejecting their idols. Paul uses the pagan word to say that they are the real atheists.

[3] Josephus records this in *Antiquities of the Jews* (15.11.5).

[4] Israel has not been "replaced". Jesus is the true Israel, and he now invites both Jew and Gentile to continue Israel's story by being united with him. See Acts 26:6–8 and 28:20.

for all through Jesus. Non-Jews excluded by the Law are now welcomed inside by faith, because their faith means they have died and been raised with Jesus to become part of the true Israel. The nations of the world all came from one man but sin divided them (Acts 17:26), so God restored all that Adam lost by uniting the nations together as *"one new humanity"* in Jesus Christ. They have access to the same Father through the same Holy Spirit and through the same Gospel message about God's Son. They are therefore not simply reconciled to God through the Gospel; they are also reconciled to one another. The fierce battle that has raged between the nations throughout world history has been turned to peace through the Church, God's new multiracial community.

In 2:19–22, Paul helps his non-Jewish readers to grasp how revolutionary this is by using several Old Testament pictures. When God created the Jewish nation, he commanded them not to intermarry with foreigners, so Paul tells the Ephesians that they are no longer foreigners but fellow Jews (2:19a). When God chose Abraham's family, he commanded them to remain separate from their Canaanite neighbours, so Paul tells the Ephesians that they have now become part of the family too (2:19b). The Gospel was founded on the words of the Jewish prophets, the Jewish apostles and the Jewish Messiah, so Paul assures the Ephesians that these have now become their own apostles and prophets and Messiah too (2:20).[5] The Temple was so precious to the Jews that Paul caused a riot by challenging its rules, so he tells the Ephesians that they are now part of a new and far better flesh-and-blood Temple in Jesus (2:21). God wants to fill them with his Holy Spirit like the Most Holy Place at the Temple in Jerusalem (2:22). This message, which angered Paul's Jewish enemies, is breathtakingly good news for the world.

It is good news if you are Jewish, because it means that

---

[5] Unlike in 3:5, it is unclear in 2:20 whether Paul is talking about first-century Christian prophets or about the Old Testament prophets. He is probably being deliberately ambiguous in order to include both.

God has fulfilled his ancient promise to Abraham in Genesis 12:3, that *"all peoples on earth will be blessed through you."*[6] The black-and-white sketches in Moses' Law were simply shadows of this glorious landscape picture which God has now painted for Abraham's children. Chopping off foreskins, refusing to marry Canaanites and visiting a man-made Temple are worth nothing now that God has established a new community through Jesus which completely fulfils the hopes of Abraham in Jesus.

It is also very good news if you are not Jewish, because it means that the Gospel does more than simply make individuals new on the inside. It has also renewed the human race in Jesus. God loved our divided multiracial and multicultural world so much that he gave his only Son to unite all the people groups of the world together in him.

So don't let your enjoyment of the portrait picture of your own salvation distract you from enjoying this amazing landscape group picture of the world's salvation too. God has glorified himself by painting a Technicolor landscape portrait, which includes all the different colours of the world.

---

[6] The Jews should have celebrated the fulfilment of prophecies such as the one in Isaiah 66:20–21. Paul's reference to Jesus being the *chief cornerstone* links back to the prophecy in Isaiah 28:16.

Chickens and Pigs (3:1–13)

I ask you, therefore, not to be discouraged because of my sufferings for you, which are your glory.

(Ephesians 3:13)

There is a famous story about a chicken and a pig who wanted to do something kind to help their farmer celebrate his birthday. They decided to make him breakfast in bed, and the chicken suggested they should treat him to a plate of eggs and bacon. *"Hold on a minute,"* the pig objected. *"You only have to make a contribution to eggs and bacon. I have to make a total commitment!"*

Paul is still recovering from describing the two pictures of God's grace in chapter 2. He tries to pray in 3:1, but he feels he needs to break off into more teaching in 3:2–13 before he can resume his prayer in 3:14. He feels that he has to add some encouragement before he can close his teaching with a prayer. He tells us to respond to this Gospel with total commitment, like a pig and not a chicken.

In 3:1, Paul expresses his own total commitment to *this new message*. He points out what proclaiming this Gospel has cost him personally. Most of the persecution that came Paul's way from the Jews was not provoked by his teaching about sin and judgment, but by his landscape picture of God's salvation. He tells his Ephesian readers that he is in prison *"for the sake of you Gentiles."*

Paul fled Jerusalem in 37 AD because the Grecian Jews tried to kill him (Acts 9:29). It was the Jews who came from Gentile lands who took the greatest objection to this landscape picture.

Paul was chased across Galatia in 48 AD by Grecian Jews who were jealous that he included the Gentiles in God's promises (Acts 13:45; 14:19). He was attacked and pursued by Grecian Jews across Macedonia in 50 AD because they were jealous he was telling the Gentiles they could be saved (Acts 17:4–5; 17:12–13). So when Jews from the province of Asia attacked Paul for including his Ephesian friend Trophimus in God's work of salvation, it wasn't anything new. Paul had always been a pig and not a chicken. He was totally committed to God's desire to save people from all nations.

In 3:2–6, Paul expresses his total commitment to *this new understanding*. As a former expert in the Jewish Law, his thinking had been completely turned around by his encounter with Jesus. His visions and his fresh study of the Old Testament in the light of Jesus' coming[1] had convinced him that the Christian apostles and prophets were right and that the Jewish rabbis were wrong.[2] In 3:2, he calls the understanding that God gave him an *oikonomia*, the Greek word for *something entrusted to us as stewards*. Paul wants to emphasize that God will hold us responsible for what we do with the revelation of the Gospel he has given us. Paul refused to play chicken, simply paying lip service to the full implications of the Gospel. The former Jewish rabbi became like an unkosher pig, totally committed to living out his new understanding.[3]

Sadly, many Christians are much more like chickens than pigs when it comes to facing up to what the landscape picture of

---

[1] Paul's *revelation* did not simply come through the visions recorded in Acts 9:3–6, 22:17–21 and 2 Corinthians 12:1–4. The sheer number of Old Testament quotations in his letters shows that he also received much of this revelation through studying the Scriptures.

[2] Paul must be referring in 3:5 to first-century Christian prophets rather than the Old Testament prophets. He also stresses the ongoing importance of Christian prophecy in 4:11.

[3] In 3:6, Paul uses three compound words in Greek to tell us that the Gospel means the Gentiles are now *joint-heirs* with the Jews in a *joint-body* and have a *joint-share* with them in God's promises to Abraham.

God's grace really means. In the past, Europeans shut their eyes to what the Gospel meant for the nations that they colonized. Today, many non-Europeans who settle in Europe shut their eyes to what the Gospel means by planting churches that are decidedly non-European and very unlikely to connect with people in the cities where God has sent them to live. The rich ruling classes can shut their eyes to what the Gospel means for the poor, and those whom they oppress can talk more about how to right wrongs than about how to become a new humanity together. Chickens embrace only those aspects of the Gospel that advance their interests, but Paul tells us to be like pigs and lay down everything to apply what we have learned.

In 3:7–9, Paul expresses his total commitment to *this new power*. There was no way that an out-of-towner like him could plant a thriving church in a metropolis like Ephesus.[4] His only hope was to remember that God has entrusted us with divine power through the Gospel, which is why he uses the word *oikonomia* again in 3:9. The grace that saved us through the Gospel is also able to make us fruitful as we share the Gospel. In 3:7, Paul describes himself as a *diakonos*, the Greek word that is used for the *servants* or *errand boys* who brought water to Jesus at the wedding in Cana in John 2:1–9. Chicken Christians never dare to step out in God's power because their focus is on playing it safe. Paul gambled everything in Ephesus because he believed that if he offered everything to God then he would set the scene for a miracle like the one when Jesus turned water into wine. The miracle at Cana displayed God's power to the disciples, and Paul expects our miracles to display God's power *"to the rulers and authorities in the heavenly realms."*[5]

---

[4] Paul actually makes up the Greek word *elachistoteros* in 3:8 in order to emphasize just how feeble he is personally. He literally calls himself *"the leastest"* of them all!

[5] Paul deliberately links his fruitfulness to the fact that he is seated with Jesus in heaven (2:6). He fully devoted his life to glorifying Jesus, both on the earth and in the spiritual realms beyond.

In 3:10–13, Paul expresses his total commitment to *this new focus*. He sees the Church as the culmination of God's eternal plan, displaying the many different facets of his glory through the many different people groups of the world. God is glorified by allowing people from every nation to approach God together freely in Jesus, as one new humanity, so Paul makes this the entire focus of his life. Chicken Christians give Sunday mornings to God and then go home reflecting on whether the worship helped them, whether the preaching entertained them, whether the congregation were friendly to them and why their own Christian lives appear so dull. Mature Christians sacrifice everything to use the few short years they have on earth to play a part in this landscape picture of salvation. Paul ends these few verses by encouraging the Ephesians not to grow discouraged that he is still in prison. He is committed to suffering far more than this if it grants a few more Gentiles a share in God's glory.

We live in a world where 340 million people are still without the Bible in their own language.[6] Those aren't just people who are kept from worshipping God freely in their heart language; they are people through whom God cannot yet display some of the different facets of his glory. They are unreached because Christians have embraced the Gospel like chickens instead of like pigs. Paul encourages us to sacrifice everything for the sake of God's plan to display his glory by creating one new humanity out of the many tribes and nations of the world.

---

[6] This is 2011 data from the website of Wycliffe Bible Translators.

Five Iron Rods (3:14–21)

I pray that out of his glorious riches he may strengthen you with power through his Spirit in your inner being.

(Ephesians 3:16)

A few weeks ago I demolished a brick wall at the rear of my property using a sledgehammer. It was hard work but a lot of fun. A few hard knocks with the sledgehammer and it shattered into rubble. All except for one stubborn concrete post, that is. I discovered after a lot of effort that it was made of reinforced concrete. It had five iron rods running through it on the inside, and as a result it defeated my sledgehammer. I can still see it from my window as I write, laughing up at me.

In 3:14, Paul restarts the prayer that he tried to pray in 3:1. Paul's letters give us a wonderful insight into his active prayer life and into which things he prayed for. He ends these three chapters of doctrine by praying about five different ways in which his readers can apply what he has taught them.[1] They are like five iron rods which can give us fresh strength on the inside. Paul tells us: *"I pray that out of his glorious riches he may strengthen you with power through his Spirit in your inner being."*

The first way Paul wants us to be strengthened, in 3:14–15, is through a proper understanding of God the Father. He starts by telling us that he prays *"for this reason"* – in other words, in response to the Gospel he has described. A proper

---

[1] This should be a challenge to any preacher. We are to be diligent in praying for our hearers, both before and especially after we preach.

understanding of Paul's teaching strengthens us on the inside to withstand whatever sledgehammer blows life may hurl against us. Paul tells us that *Father* is not simply a human metaphor to help us grasp what God is like: God is the original Father and every human dad is a reflection of him, not the other way around. God can no more cease to be our loving Father than renege on his own character. The Gospel strengthens us on the inside by telling us that God is as much a faithful Father towards us as he was towards Paul and the Ephesians.

The second way Paul wants us to be strengthened, in 3:16–17, is through a proper understanding of what it means to be filled with the Holy Spirit. Paul began his church plant in Ephesus with a dozen ignorant believers who confessed to him, *"We have not even heard that there is a Holy Spirit."*[2] As somebody who travels round lots of churches, I am amazed how ignorant many Christians are about how to be filled with the Spirit. Paul homes in on this, telling us that it is not an optional extra to the Christian life. When God's Spirit lives in our inner being, it means that Jesus lives in our hearts through faith and it changes everything.

The young Billy Graham was a very ordinary preacher. As he read the Scriptures he knew what he was missing. When he heard Stephen Olford preach on God's promise to fill believers with his Holy Spirit, he took the man aside and begged him: *"You've spoken of something that I don't have. I want the fullness of the Holy Spirit in my life too."*

Olford remembers spending time with Billy Graham, helping him to read the Scriptures and to pray:

> *I gave him my testimony of how God completely turned my life inside out – an experience of the Holy Spirit in his fullness and anointing. As I talked, and I can see him now,*

---

[2] This must be shorthand for their not having heard there is a *baptism in* the Holy Spirit, since the Spirit of God gets a mention as early on as the second verse of the Old Testament!

EPHESIANS: NEW ON THE INSIDE

those marvellous eyes glistened with tears, and he said,
"Stephen, I see it. That's what I want. That's what I need
in my life"... I can still hear Billy pouring out his heart in
a prayer of total dedication to the Lord. Finally, he said,
"My heart is so flooded with the Holy Spirit! I have it!
I'm filled. This is a turning point in my life." And he was
a new man.[3]

Sure enough, Billy Graham looked back on that experience as one that completely changed him on the inside.

We have already read enough of Paul's letters for you to know for sure that God wants to fill you with his Holy Spirit. It is what he saved you for (Galatians 3:14), and it is how he wants to put a seal on your salvation (Ephesians 1:13–14). When the Holy Spirit comes to live inside you in all his fullness, he will help you to know God better (Ephesians 1:17; 2:18), and he will change you from the inside out (Galatians 5:16–25). He will strengthen you on the inside like an iron bar in a fragile piece of concrete (Ephesians 3:16). You may find it helpful to ask a mature Christian friend to help you, like Paul with the Ephesians or like Stephen Olford with Billy Graham, but if you do not have a friend to help you, you still have God's promise that he will fill you if you simply believe that this is the Christian Gospel (Galatians 3:5; Ephesians 3:17).

The third way Paul wants us to be strengthened, in 3:17–19, is through a proper understanding of Jesus' love for us. He describes it as a *"love that surpasses knowledge"* because it is so vast that nobody can ever stray outside its boundaries. Paul uses two technical terms in Greek when he prays that we may be *rooted* and *established* in God's love.[4] The first word was used for the way a massive oak tree is grounded deep into the earth,

---

[3] Harold Myra and Marshall Shelley in *The Leadership Secrets of Billy Graham* (2005).

[4] The only other place where Paul uses these two Greek verbs is in Colossians 1:23 and 2:7.

and the second word was used for the way a solid building was held firm by its deep foundations. Occasionally the earth may give way to allow an oak tree to fall or a building to wobble, but the love of Jesus will never let you go.

The fourth way Paul wants us to be strengthened, in 3:20, is through a proper understanding of the power of prayer. When Tennyson wrote in one of his most famous poems that *"more things are wrought by prayer than this world dreams of,"* he may have been referring to Paul's great promise here that the Holy Spirit will help us to pray and receive answers which are *"immeasurably more than all we ask or imagine."*[5]

The fifth and final way Paul wants us to be strengthened, in 3:21, is through a proper confidence in God's plan for the Church. If you live in Europe or North America, you might think it is very normal for the Church to be in terminal decline. You might even have started to believe those who claim that the Church will be wiped out in a generation. Don't listen to them. Paul tells us that the sledgehammer blows of the Devil can do nothing to stop God's plan to glorify himself through the Church in every single generation. God the Father can no more renounce his faithfulness to the Church than he can renounce Jesus as his Son.

Life is not easy. Life as a Christian can be even harder. But we have these five iron rods to strengthen us on the inside. My concrete post is still standing outside my window, no longer laughing at me but encouraging me: nothing can topple us when we have God on the inside.

---

[5] Alfred, Lord Tennyson in *Morte d'Arthur*, published in 1842.

Sit, Walk, Stand (4:1–6)

I therefore, a prisoner for the Lord, urge you to walk in a manner worthy of the calling to which you have been called.

(Ephesians 4:1, *English Standard Version*)

One of the most helpful books I have ever read on the message of Ephesians is a slim volume by Watchman Nee entitled *Sit, Walk, Stand*. Watchman Nee was a Chinese church leader who spent the last twenty years of his life in one of Mao Zedong's prison labour camps, but who was one of the pioneers who prepared the ground for the great move of God which has swept China in the past thirty years. Nee takes three key verses in Ephesians and uses them to give us a very helpful structure, which highlights the turning point that we have now reached in Paul's letter.

The key verse in the first three chapters of Ephesians is 2:6: *"God raised us up with Christ and **seated** us with him in the heavenly realms in Christ Jesus."* Ephesians 1–3 is bursting with life-changing teaching about how to sit with Christ and rest in all that he has done for us. It echoes the message of Galatians by telling us that we can do nothing to save ourselves. If we try to do so, we are actually trying to steal the glory for our salvation away from God so that we can award it to ourselves. Watchman Nee writes:

> *Most Christians make the mistake of trying to walk in order to be able to sit, but that is a reversal of the true order. Our natural reason says, If we do not walk, how can we ever reach the goal? What can we attain without*

*effort? How can we ever get anywhere if we do not move? But Christianity is a queer business! If at the outset we try to do anything, we get nothing; if we seek to attain something, we miss everything. For Christianity begins not with a big DO, but with a big DONE. Thus Ephesians opens with the statement that God **has** "blessed us with every spiritual blessing in the heavenly places in Christ" (1:3) and we are invited at the very outset to sit down and enjoy what God has done for us; not to set out to try and attain it for ourselves.[1]*

The key verse in Ephesians 4:1–6:9 is Paul's statement in 4:1: *"I therefore, a prisoner for the Lord, urge you to **walk** in a manner worthy of the calling to which you have been called."*[2] We can only start walking when we have learned to sit, because living out the Christian life is only possible when we have responded fully to the Gospel. Paul starts this new section with *therefore* because walking is impossible unless we have first learned to sit. If we accept Paul's message that in Jesus we have been crucified, raised and exalted to heaven to sit at God's right hand, then walking like Jesus comes naturally.

That's what Paul means when he tells us in 4:1 to live a life *worthy* of our calling. He isn't like Tom Hanks in *Saving Private Ryan*, telling the young soldier for whom he is dying that he must now *"Deserve it!"* Quite the opposite. Paul has spent the first half of this letter persuading us that we can never earn our salvation, pay God back for our salvation or live up to our salvation in any way. He is simply telling us that the life we live must be *in keeping with* our calling.[3] If we are seated with Jesus

---

[1] *Sit, Walk, Stand* (1957) was originally a sermon series on Ephesians, published after his imprisonment.

[2] The Greek word for walking is *peripateō*, the same word which Paul used in 2:2 and 10. He uses it six times in 4:1–6:9.

[3] We can see the normal day-to-day meaning of this Greek word *axios* from the way Paul uses it in 2 Thessalonians 1:3 to tell people to do something

in the holy throne room of heaven, it makes no sense for us to carry on walking in filthy sin on earth! Having our doctrine right does not guarantee that our lifestyle will be right (otherwise Paul wouldn't have needed to write this section at all), but it is only natural that what is in our hearts should be expressed by the way we live our lives.

Make sure you notice the subtle change that Paul makes to his vocabulary in 4:1. He talked repeatedly about our being *"in Jesus"* in the first three chapters of this letter when he was focused on our relationship with God, but now he starts to talk instead throughout this second section about our being *"in the Lord."* If we are seated in Jesus in the heavenlies, it is only natural that we should make him our Lord on the earth. We do not have to strain hard to live with the humility, gentleness, patience and love that are described in 4:2. The more we let our new life in Jesus sink into our hearts, the more the character of Jesus will spill out.

That's why Paul does not tell us in 4:3–6 to be united with one another. He tells us that love and unity require a bit of effort – we all know that! – but he tells us that the effort is to *"**keep** the unity of the Spirit,"* which we already have with one another. Since Christians have been united together as a new humanity in Jesus, we do not need to aim at church unity as some sentimental goal. We simply have to live out *"the bond of peace,"* which Paul told us is already ours in 2:11–22.[4] We simply need to remember that we all have one hope and one faith, which have granted us adoption by one Father. We simply need to recognize that we have been saved through one Lord and filled with one Spirit, and that we have all been baptized

---

because *it is only fitting*.

[4] The Greek word that Paul uses for *bond* in 4:3 is a sister word to the one he uses for his being a *prisoner* in 4:1. He wants love to chain the Ephesians together as much as he is chained to his prison guards.

with one water baptism into one Church body.[5] We simply need to grasp that we are already as united as it is possible to be. We can rest in who we are in Jesus in heaven and walk it out on earth with the help of the Holy Spirit.

This helps us when we come to the third and final section of the letter in 6:10–24. The key verse in that section is 6:11: *"Put on the full armour of God so that you can take your* **stand** *against the devil's schemes."* If we believe the Gospel and enjoy sitting with Jesus in the heavenlies, and if we walk out our new identity in Jesus on the earth through the Gospel and with the help of the Holy Spirit, then of course we will be able to stand against the Devil. What can he do to people who are in Christ Jesus and who are fully submitted to his Lordship every day?

Watchman Nee died in a communist labour camp in 1972 after almost two decades in prison. His understanding of Ephesians had been tested to the limit as he walked out his faith that Jesus is Lord in a country that told him Mao Zedong was Lord, and as he stood against the Devil in a filthy prison which made a mockery of the faith that told him he was seated in the heavenlies with Jesus. However, when his grand-niece went to the labour camp to collect his remains, one of the prison guards furtively handed her a piece of paper he had found under Watchman Nee's pillow. Nee had scribbled a few words on it just before he died. It read: *"Christ is the Son of God who died for the redemption of sinners and was raised after three days. This is the greatest truth in the universe. I die because of my belief in Christ."*[6]

Sit, walk, stand. Because, if we believe chapters 1–3, God will enable us to live out the instructions of chapters 4–6, no matter what may lie ahead.

---

[5] Some people twist Paul's words in 4:5 to deny the reality of the baptism in the Holy Spirit. Hopefully it is obvious to you that Paul is simply emphasizing that we all share in the same water baptism.

[6] Witness Lee describes this final message in *Watchman Nee: A Seer of the Divine Revelation in the Present Age* (1991).

Blown Away (4:7–16)

Then we will no longer be infants, tossed back and forth by the waves, and blown here and there by every wind of teaching.

(Ephesians 4:14)

A terrible tragedy occurred a few weeks ago in my part of London. My neighbourhood is still in shock and mourning. As the father of four young children, it chills me to the bone, but Paul is concerned that something similar might happen to the Ephesian Christians or to you and me.

One of my neighbours was leaving her house a few Monday mornings ago. She strapped her three-year-old daughter into her buggy and stepped onto the pavement, when she suddenly remembered she had left something inside the house. She only left her daughter for a few seconds, but it was a few seconds too long. A gust of wind hit the buggy and propelled it into the road in front of a van. Her three-year-old daughter was dead by the time the ambulance arrived at our local hospital.[1]

My neighbourhood is still in shock. One of my neighbours told the BBC News that *"I'm gripping onto my son's pram now every moment."* That's what Paul wants us to do after we read his warning in 4:14 not to let go of his teaching. He tells us he has written these verses so that we will *"no longer be infants, tossed back and forth by the waves, and blown here and there by every wind of teaching."* Having outlined the Gospel in great

---

[1] This tragic incident is still so raw that I have not named the mother or daughter. For the full story, see the newspaper reports in every British newspaper on Tuesday 26th March 2013.

detail in chapters 1 to 3, Paul now warns us what will happen if we let our guard down to false teaching, even for a moment.

Paul tells us in 4:7–10 that our first safeguard against the winds of false teaching is to walk together in *humble unity*.[2] People get blown away when Satan gets them on their own. I discovered this as a young Christian when I was targeted by members of a cult.[3] What struck me powerfully was just how many of their number were once radical young Christians who had grown disillusioned with the half-hearted apathy they found in churches. Their road towards deception had begun with a conviction that they had all the answers and that the rest of the people in their church had all the problems. *"To each one of us grace has been given as Christ apportioned it,"* Paul warns us. Don't be too proud, too self-confident or too busy to devote yourself to fellowship with other Christians. Their faults may be obvious to you but that also means that your faults are obvious to them. Don't let your passion for Jesus isolate you and put you at risk of being blown away.

Paul tells us in 4:11 that our second safeguard against the winds of false teaching is to walk in *humble submission* to anointed church leaders. He quotes from the Old Testament for the first time in this letter because his readers need to understand what David prophesied in Psalm 68:18. He helps us to see that David's joyful celebration of the journey that the Ark of the Covenant made from Mount Sinai to Mount Zion was a picture of a far greater ascension: it prefigured Jesus returning to heaven and receiving the gift of the Holy Spirit to pour out on all believers.[4] Paul lists four groups of church leaders, all

---

[2] The *unity* Paul describes in 4:1–6 goes hand in hand with the *diversity* he describes in 4:7–16.

[3] The word Paul uses for *cunning* in 4:14 means literally *dice-playing* and therefore *cheating sleight of hand*. He warns us that false teachers and cult leaders are like shady dice-players in the casino.

[4] The Hebrew text of Psalm 68:18 can either mean that Jesus received gifts *from* men or *for* men. Paul's interpretation follows the Aramaic translation of the

of them stronger than us in different ways, and he promises that we will not be blown away by false teaching if we submit ourselves to their lead.[5]

Jesus appointed *apostles* such as Peter and Paul to lay foundations of Gospel truth for the Church (2:20). Nobody possesses the same authority for shaping Christian doctrine today as they did, but Paul seems to give us no sense in these verses that he expects Jesus to stop anointing apostles for his Church. He does not hesitate in his letters to call James, Silas, Epaphroditus, Andronicus and Junias apostles, as if the title belonged only to the Twelve.[6] He expects Jesus to continue to protect his Church by anointing certain leaders with the gift of apostleship to safeguard New Testament teaching and to keep the Church pushing ever forwards to take new ground in fulfilment of its promises.[7]

Jesus also appointed *prophets*, like Agabus in Acts 11:27–30, who speak messages from God and train others to do so.[8] While Acts 21:10–14 warns us that their words are certainly not infallible, Acts 15:32 shows us that their words can strengthen us to stand against the winds of false teaching. Jesus also appointed *evangelists* to preach the Gospel effectively and to *"equip his people for works of service"* as Gospel witnesses

---

Old Testament. The reference to Jesus *descending* is a reference to his leaving heaven and becoming a man on earth (John 3:13; 8:23).

[5] These four groups of people are not officers created by the Church. They are gifts given to us by Jesus and merely recognized by the Church.

[6] Galatians 1:19; 1 Thessalonians 1:1; 2:6; Philippians 2:25; Romans 16:7. Translators who believe there are no modern-day apostles tone down the Greek word *apostolos* unjustifiably to mean *messenger* in these verses, but Paul did not oppose the false apostles in Corinth by claiming the number of apostles was limited. He believed it wasn't.

[7] *Apostle* comes from the Greek verb *to send*, so advance is intrinsic to apostleship. Even James, an apostle who stayed behind to lead the church in Jerusalem, wrote a letter to Jewish Christians around the world.

[8] Paul tells us in 4:12 that the main difference between a prophet and somebody who simply prophesies is that the Holy Spirit enables prophets to teach other people to prophesy too.

themselves.[9] He hasn't given us these leaders to do the work of ministry for us. In 4:13, we are told that true maturity means submitting to apostles and prophets and evangelists as they equip us to live out Jesus' mission every day.

Jesus also appointed *pastor–teachers*. We can tell from the Greek text that this is one group of people rather than two, and this is actually very important.[10] Whenever pastoral care descends into tea and sympathy or a Christianized form of psychology, people are in danger of being blown away. The same is true whenever teaching becomes purely academic. Paul tells us that true shepherds of God's flock feed his sheep on the Scriptures, helping them to feast on the answers which the Word of God gives to all the issues in their lives.

That's why Paul tells us in 4:15 that our third safeguard against the winds of false teaching is to *speak the truth to one another in love*. Truth spoken without love can hurt people because it is too hard, but love spoken without truth can hurt people because it is too soft. Only truth and love together can protect us from the fatal gusts which blow.[11]

My neighbourhood is still in mourning because a mother let her little daughter get blown away. Paul is determined to protect us from a similar spiritual tragedy in our own lives and in our churches. So let's be alert to the winds of false teaching all around us. Let's do as Paul says and let's not allow ourselves to be blown away.

---

[9] The only person the New Testament specifically names as an evangelist is Philip (Acts 21:8), but Paul also tells Timothy that he should *"do the work of an evangelist"* (2 Timothy 4:5).

[10] The Greek text says literally that Jesus *"gave **some** to be apostles, **some** to be prophets, **some** to be evangelists, and **some** to be pastors and teachers."*

[11] "Submissive" is a very unpopular word in Western culture. It was unpopular in the first-century Roman Empire too, but Paul insists in 5:21 that it is vital we submit to one another.

No Pressure (4:11–16)

From him the whole body, joined and held together by every supporting ligament, grows and builds itself up in love, as each part does its work.

(Ephesians 4:16)

I can't even begin to imagine what kind of pressure Paul must have felt under when he arrived at Ephesus in 53 AD. There was plenty to intimidate a would-be church planter about the proud city that controlled the busy trade routes into Asia. The Roman travel writer Strabo observed that *"the city, because of its advantageous situation, grows daily and is the largest emporium in Asia."*[1] Antipater of Sidon exclaimed that the city's great temple overshadowed the Pyramids of Giza: *"Those other marvels lost their brilliance, and I said, 'Look! Apart from Mount Olympus the sun has never gazed on anything so grand!'"*[2] Planting a city-changing church in Ephesus was not going to be easy.

Nor can I begin to imagine what kind of pressure the newly appointed elders of the church in Ephesus must have felt under when they waved goodbye to Paul in 55 AD. He had managed to plant a megachurch in two and a half years, and now he had entrusted its future to them. So let's not treat these verses in Ephesians 4 as a piece of abstract theology. This is Paul's very practical teaching on how we can cope with the overwhelming pressure of continuing Jesus' mission in the world. He tells us

---

[1] Strabo wrote this in his *Geography* (14.1.24), which he completed in about 20 AD.

[2] Antipater of Sidon wrote this in about 140 BC in his *Greek Anthology* (9.58).

that the pressure instantly subsides when we understand what it means for a church to have God on the inside.

First, Paul takes the pressure off *church leaders* by telling them that Jesus builds great churches, not them. He tells them that the ability to lead a church is a gift that Jesus gives to people by his grace (4:7), and that he has deliberately shared the necessary gifting across several individuals so that they can share the burden of leadership with one another (4:11). Acts 20 tells us that Paul appointed a team of elders rather than a single leader for the church in Ephesus, because Jesus alone is the true Senior Pastor, the true Apostle, the true Prophet, the true Evangelist and the true Pastor–Teacher.[3] He has shared the gifts required to lead a church across several individuals in order that the glory, and the pressure, is shifted away from us and onto him.[4]

Next, Paul takes the pressure off *church members* by telling them that Jesus will equip them to achieve all he has called them to do. The same Jesus who promised his first disciples, *"Come, follow me and **I will make you** fishers of men,"* still makes the same promise to you and me.[5] He has given us anointed leaders who can equip us to live out what it means to be children of God. Together, these leaders can build us up in the truth, unite us in the faith[6] and bring us to a mature knowledge of Jesus. Jesus is not like Pharaoh, who told his Hebrew slaves to make

[3] A healthy eldership team is therefore not simply a team of great elders. It is a team of elders whose complementary gifting enables them to lead the church to Christian maturity in all areas.

[4] Paul modelled this by planting the church at Ephesus through a diverse team of individuals. Acts 18–19 mentions Priscilla, Aquila, Timothy, Erastus, Gaius, Aristarchus and Alexander.

[5] Mark 1:17–19 tells us that the disciples were *mending* their nets (*katartizō*), and Ephesians 4:12 uses the same word to tell us that Jesus enables church leaders to *mend* God's People for works of service (*katartismos*).

[6] Paul told us in 4:3 that we are already united together in Christ, so he is telling us in 4:13 that Spirit-filled church leaders help us to live out this unity in practice. We *attain* unity by *maintaining* the unity we have.

bricks without giving them any straw. Whenever Jesus tells us to do anything, he also gives us everything we need in order to obey.[7]

Paul therefore takes the pressure off *the hardworking few*. Many churches are a bit like a football stadium: a few individuals work very hard while being watched by a crowd who could really do with a bit of exercise! Paul says this isn't what the Church should be like at all. He insists that Jesus has given grace *"to each one of us"* (4:7) because every church member has a role which is uniquely theirs to play.[8] He emphasizes that the role of church leaders is not to work hard so that those they lead don't have to – on the contrary, it is *"to equip his people for works of service"* (4:12).[9] Apostles and prophets ensure that churches keep pressing forwards through a proper understanding of God's Word. Evangelists equip every believer to share their faith with those around them. Pastor–teachers disciple those who are saved and help them to find their place in Jesus' mission. A few years ago I was invited to speak to a group of Christians who described themselves as "mature but declining in number". It didn't take me long to discover that their basic problem was that they were not mature at all. They had been Christians for decades, but they had not understood that true maturity means taking responsibility (4:13). It means leaving the comforts of the spectator seats and running onto the pitch to join in the game. John Piper writes:

> *According to the New Testament, "ministry" is what all Christians do. Pastors have the job of equipping the saints for the work of ministry. But ordinary Christians*

---

[7] Paul's play on words is lost in most English translations. He says that Jesus apportions his grace *according to the measure of the gift of Christ* (4:7) in order to build us up *according to the measure of the fullness of Christ* (4:13).

[8] Insecure leaders monopolize ministry. Secure leaders multiply ministry.

[9] When Paul writes these words in 4:12, he appears to be making a deliberate link back to 2:10.

do the ministry. What ministry looks like is as varied as Christians are varied... Whether we are bankers or bricklayers, it means that we aim at advancing other people's faith and holiness.[10]

In saying this, Paul takes the pressure off *the Church as a whole*. He points out that the Head of the Church is Jesus (4:15) and that he takes full responsibility for the health of his body (4:12). So long as we are willing to let him fill us with his Holy Spirit and to speak the truth to one another in love, he promises to join us together as one body, to build us up through his love and to make us very fruitful as every member of the body does its work.[11] Paul tells us literally in 4:13 that Jesus is making us into *"a mature man"* or *"a perfect man,"* which appears to be a deliberate reference back to his teaching in 2:15 that God has made us *"one new man"* in Christ. The Gospel that saved us from sin is also the Gospel that saves us from crushing pressure. What Jesus has started, Jesus will finish. The pressure is all on him.

That's how Paul coped with planting a church in Ephesus, and it's how the new team of elders coped with leading the church he left behind. They were confident that the God who had made them into a new man in Jesus would also make them into a mature man in Jesus too. They understood the Gospel as Jesus describes it, in all its pressure-bursting glory, in Matthew 11:28–30:

Come to me, all you who are weary and burdened, and I will give you rest. Take my yoke upon you and learn from me, for I am gentle and humble in heart, and you will find rest for your souls. For my yoke is easy and my burden is light.

---

[10] John Piper in *Future Grace* (1995).

[11] These verses in Ephesians 4 echo those in 1 Corinthians 12. God has deliberately set up the Church to prosper through humble unity and to flounder through pride and disunity.

Be Who You Are
(4:17–5:20)

You were once darkness, but now you are light in the Lord. Live as children of light.

(Ephesians 5:8)

Ephesus was one of the great port cities of the ancient world. It was full of drunken sailors and greedy traders, so it isn't surprising that Paul needed to devote much of the second half of this letter to teaching Christians how to live godly lives at the heart of an ungodly city.

But what is surprising, very surprising indeed, is the way in which he tells them to live godly lives. It is nothing short of revolutionary. He doesn't give them a Christianized version of the Ten Commandments or encourage them to make a series of spiritual resolutions about how they are going to improve their lives.[1] He doesn't actually tell them to become godly at all. He tells them that they are already godly through the Gospel and that their challenge is simply to live out who they already are. Since they already sit in the heavenlies with Jesus and since Jesus already dwells in them on earth, they merely need to let their heavenly identity transform their earthly lifestyle.[2]

Make sure you don't miss this. It follows on from Paul's

---

[1] Although Paul quotes the Fifth Commandment in 6:2–3, he does so to remind us of God's gracious promise. He tells us in 6:1 that we should honour our parents because *"this is right"* for God's People.

[2] Paul repeatedly uses the phrase *"in Christ"* in Ephesians 1–3, but he repeatedly uses the phrase *"in the Lord"* in Ephesians 4–6. Since we live in Jesus and he lives in us, it follows that he must be Lord of our lives. Paul uses very strong language in 4:17 to *"insist on it in the Lord."*

great "therefore" in 4:1. He tells the Ephesians to speak the truth to one another, not because it is the Ninth Commandment, but because *"we are all members of one body"* (4:25). He tells them to guard their hearts against anger, not because it is the Sixth Commandment, but because the Devil must not be given any opportunity to launch a counterattack on their redeemed souls (4:27).[3] He tells them to love and forgive one another, not so that they might become something they are not, but so as not to *"grieve the Holy Spirit of God, with whom you were sealed for the day of redemption,"* and out of gratitude that *"in Christ God forgave you"* (4:30, 32).

The first three chapters of Ephesians explained how we are justified (declared holy) through the Gospel. Now these verses explain how we are sanctified (made holy) through that same Gospel too. It was revolutionary news for a city in which both Jews and pagans tried hard to improve their behaviour in order to gain the favour of their gods. It is still just as revolutionary for us today, since many Christians have been taught that God saves us by grace but then expects us to work very hard to become like him. If the Devil can't trick us into trying to earn forgiveness from God through our own effort, he will resort to Plan B and attempt to trick us into trying to grow in godliness through our own effort. Legalism has many different faces.

That's why Paul constantly repeats this message throughout these verses. He tells us to act like God because we have already become his children through the Gospel (5:1) and to love others because Jesus has first loved us (5:2). He tells us to repent of all impurity because such things are *"out of place"* and *"improper for God's holy people"* (5:3–4). We have been saved out of the sinful world and into God's glorious Kingdom, so we must not partner ourselves with the other team through what we say and do (5:7). In all of this, Paul teaches us that the Gospel is as much

---

[3] The Devil is a defeated foe, but he can still use sin to gain a foothold for a counterattack against our souls. Jesus guarded his own heart and was able to say in John 14:30 that the Devil had no such foothold in his life.

the key to how we are sanctified as it is to how we are justified: *"You were once darkness, but now you are light in the Lord. Live as children of light... and find out what pleases the Lord"* (5:8–10).[4]

Becoming a child of light affects *the way we think* far more powerfully than mere commands or spiritual resolutions. It means we can cooperate with the Holy Spirit to put to death impure, greedy and lustful thoughts on the inside (5:3–7). It means we can replace bitter, spiteful and selfish thoughts (4:31) with kind, compassionate, worshipful and forgiving ones instead (4:32; 5:19).[5] It means the Holy Spirit starts to make us angry about what angers Jesus (such as injustice, hypocrisy and the Devil's destructive work in the world), while at the same time freeing us from the sinful anger that used to grip our souls (4:26, 31).[6] When I power down my computer at night, it sometimes detects and deals with a virus. People who are full of the Holy Spirit also find that bedtime serves as a God-given opportunity to power down from the day. If our hearts refuse to switch off from dangerous emotions such as anger, it is a warning sign that we need to spend time asking the Holy Spirit to deal afresh with the virus of sin in our hearts.

Becoming a child of light affects *the way we speak*. Before Jesus saved us, we used our mouths for filthy talk, foolish banter and coarse joking (4:29; 5:4), but this is no longer fitting for who we have become. We are full of God's Holy Spirit so we

---

[4] We have not simply believed in the Light of the World. Paul tells us in 5:8 that we have *become* the light of the world (see Matthew 5:14–16). It is therefore only natural that we should bear *"the fruit of the light"* in 5:9.

[5] We will look at how we cooperate with the Holy Spirit to do this in a few pages' time in the chapter "Filled Is Not Full". We will also do so in the chapter "What Not to Wear" when we reach Colossians 3:1–14.

[6] In 4:26, Paul states that anger is not always sinful by quoting from Psalm 4:4, telling us literally: *"Be angry and do not sin."* However, since anger can very easily lead to sin, he reminds us that Psalm 4 also tells us to go to bed peacefully before acting in our anger. This is precisely what Jesus did in Mark 11:11.

must speak only truth (4:25) and words that build up other people in God (4:29; 5:19). We point out areas of sin (5:11) and we give thanks to God as he delivers us from each one of them (5:4, 20).[7] When revival swept Wales in 1905, the pit-ponies in the coalmines stopped obeying their masters because they didn't recognize commands that were no longer filled with expletives. That's a great picture of what happens when our hearts are changed through the Gospel. God on the inside is always evidenced by very different chatter on the outside.

Becoming a child of light affects *the way we act*. When we used to live in darkness, we naturally performed *"the fruitless deeds of darkness"* (5:11). We stole from others and sucked all that we could from society like the selfish little parasites we were (4:28). Now that we have been saved through Jesus' love, we live lives of love (5:1–2), work hard so that we can meet the needs of others (4:28)[8] and *"redeem the time"* – that is, we seize every opportunity to partner with the Holy Spirit to make up for the time which we wasted in our former lives (5:16).[9]

No amount of religious willpower can bring about this radical change in a person's thoughts, speech and action. Such radical change requires nothing less than the Gospel: *"You were taught... to put off your old self... and to put on the new self"* (4:22–24). It can only flow from the Gospel message, which made the eighteenth-century Scottish preacher Ralph Erskine write a hymn of celebration:

> *A rigid matter was the law, demanding brick, denying straw.*

---

[7] Paul is not quoting from the Old Testament in 5:14, yet he expects the Ephesians to know these words well. He is therefore probably quoting from one of their early worship songs, tying in with 5:19–20.

[8] 1 Corinthians 12:28 and Romans 12:8 tell us that earning money to help Christians in need is as much a charismatic gift as prophecy, healing or tongues.

[9] The parallel verses in Colossians 4:5–6 suggest this includes seizing chances to share the Gospel with others.

But when with gospel tongue it sings, it bids me fly and gives me wings.[10]

---

[10] *The Sermons and Practical Works of Ralph Erskine, Volume 10* (1778). A version of this poem is often attributed to John Bunyan, but it does not actually appear in any of his surviving works.

One Another (4:32)

Be kind and compassionate to one another, forgiving each other, just as in Christ God forgave you.

(Ephesians 4:32)

The tourists who visit the ruins of Roman Ephesus always do one thing. They have their photo taken sitting on one of the municipal toilets of the ancient city. That may sound strange, but it's because the city's latrines appear so strange to our modern eyes: ten toilets to a room and not so much as a cubicle wall for privacy. When I had my own photo taken at the latrines of Ephesus a few years ago, it was a very helpful insight into the culture of the city to which Paul wrote this letter.

Very few of the homes in Ephesus had its own toilet. The city's residents had to leave their homes and go to the communal latrines together. Nor did most of the homes in Ephesus have a bathroom. Residents left their homes and washed with their neighbours in the city's public baths. In the evenings, they could not stay at home to watch television or surf the internet. They had to find their entertainment in the city's 25,000-seater theatre or in one of the city's crowded taverns. Day-to-day life was a community project in every way at Ephesus.

It can't have been surprising for the Ephesians, therefore, when Paul taught them to live out their Christian lives in the same way. He hired a lecture hall in the city and gathered the believers together every lunch break. In the evenings he went *"from house to house"* to encourage them more personally as they gathered together in smaller groups. As a result, he was able to tell the Ephesians when he left them that *"You know how*

I lived the whole time I was with you."[1] He had shared his life with them, so it made sense when he told them that growing in godliness meant *"bearing with **one another**"* (4:2), *"building **others** up"* (4:29), being *"kind and compassionate to **one another**"* (4:32), *"forgiving **each other**"* (4:32), encouraging *"**one another** with psalms, hymns and songs from the Spirit"* (5:19), and submitting *"to **one another** out of reverence for Christ"* (5:21).[2] Sanctification, like everything else at Ephesus, was to be a community project. The Ephesians could hardly have imagined going about it in any other way.

For us, it is very different. I have four toilets in my house and locks on all the bathroom doors. The people who live in my house own four computers and three smartphones. We don't always do life with one another, let alone with the people who live on our street, in our community or in our city. We do not live in a culture of community like ancient Ephesus. We live, instead, in a culture of individualism, which Ayn Rand describes in one of her novels:

> *The word "We" is as lime poured over men, which sets and hardens to stone, and crushes all beneath it... I am done with the monster of "We," the word of serfdom, of plunder, of misery, falsehood and shame. And now I see the face of god, and I raise this god over the earth, this god whom men have sought since men came into being, this god who will grant them joy and peace and pride. This god, this one word: "I."*[3]

---

[1] Acts 19:9–10; 20:18, 20. A few Greek manuscripts tell us that Paul hired the Lecture Hall of Tyrannus *"from the fifth hour to the tenth."* This was from 11 a.m. to 4 p.m., gathering the believers during their daily siesta.

[2] Paul also tells us literally in 4:25 that *"we are members of one another."*

[3] Ayn Rand in *Anthem* (1938). We need to recognize that Western culture has been heavily influenced by her thinking in this novel and in *The Virtue of Selfishness* (1964).

Paul was chased out of Ephesus for confronting the city's goddess, and he is just as determined to confront the god of our culture too. Having told us that justification is about whole communities in chapter 2, he insists that sanctification is also worked out in community in chapters 4 and 5. We must not let our upbringing blind our eyes to this deliberate emphasis as we read these verses. Paul is telling us that the Ephesians got something right which we get wrong. We can only learn to live out who we are in Jesus if we devote ourselves to doing life together.

Sharing our lives with other Christians *reveals how sinful we are*. I used to think I was a very easygoing person until I got married. I didn't become more self-centred when I started to share my life with another person; I simply discovered how self-centred I had always been. I used to think I was a very patient person until I became father to four children, and they revealed to me just how impatient I actually was. I used to think I was a humble person before I got a job in a highly competitive business environment. When some of my new colleagues took credit for my work and trod on me to get a leg-up for promotion, I discovered just how self-assertive my heart had been all along. That's why Jesus called his twelve disciples to do life together, it's why Paul told the Ephesians to do life together, and it's why we need to do life with other Christians too. Sin makes us put ourselves at the centre. It is only through sharing our lives with others that we discover those areas of our lives where sin still reigns.

The individualism of our culture is why Christian commitment to gathering for Sunday services is at an all-time low and why commitment to midweek fellowship groups is even lower still.[4] It isn't just that we are too busy or that we dislike organized religion. It's that we naturally shrink away

---

[4] 1 Peter 2:17 tells us this is a mark of spiritual immaturity. Mature Christians *"love the family of believers."*

from community because we know that in it our deepest secrets will be revealed. Paul's teaching in these verses replies to the question in Jeremiah 17:9: *"The heart is deceitful above all things and beyond cure. Who can understand it?"* Paul tells us that the way to understand our hearts is to share our lives with other people who are not like us and who can point out our blind spots towards sin. Even choosing Christian friends who are like us is not enough. Paul insists that we will only learn to live out our new identity in Jesus if we devote ourselves to sharing life with other Christians who are not like us at all.

Sharing our lives with other Christians also *helps us to put our godliness into practice*. Paul deliberately describes godliness in these two chapters in a way that makes no sense outside of our relationships with one another. How can we learn to share, to forgive or to be unselfish on our own? How can we learn to speak the truth and words that build up others if we attempt to live out our Christian lives in isolation? How can we learn to give instead of taking when our diaries are built around ourselves? When Peter told Jesus in John 21:15–17 that he loved him, Jesus replied with a concrete command to *"Feed my lambs,"* *"Take care of my sheep"* and *"Feed my sheep."* His command has not changed.[5]

So don't rush over these verses and miss the heart of Paul's teaching on how we can grow in godly character. Grasp what he taught his converts in 2 Corinthians 8:5: *"They gave themselves first of all to the Lord, and then by the will of God also to us."*

---

[5] Peter put this into practice in Acts 2:41–47 by telling his converts to be *"added to their number"* and by teaching them to gather in the Temple courtyards and in smaller fellowship groups which broke bread together in each other's homes. As a result, *"All the believers were together and had everything in common."*

Demetrius and His Partners (5:5)

For of this you can be sure: no immoral, impure or greedy person – such a person is an idolater – has any inheritance in the kingdom of Christ and of God.

(Ephesians 5:5)

The final days of Paul's three-year stay at Ephesus were not happy ones. He told the Corinthians that *"I fought wild beasts in Ephesus"* and that *"We were under great pressure, far beyond our ability to endure, so that we despaired of life itself."*[1] Paul had made some powerful enemies at Ephesus who almost succeeded in killing him at the end of Acts 19. Those enemies were Demetrius and his partners.

Demetrius was one of the chief idol-makers at Ephesus. He was a silversmith at the world-famous temple of Artemis, which housed an image of the goddess that most Ephesians believed had fallen to earth from heaven. Demetrius sold miniature silver replicas of the image to pilgrims from all across the empire, persuading them to take one home to add to the collection of gods in their household shrine. Although Paul never attacked Artemis directly,[2] he warned his listeners that they needed to *"turn from these worthless idols to serve the living and true God."*[3]

---

[1] Paul wrote this in 55 AD, the year he left Ephesus, in 1 Corinthians 15:32 and 2 Corinthians 1:8.

[2] Acts 19:37 shows us how to topple idols. Instead of preaching *against* an idol, we should preach *for* Jesus. Whenever people truly fall in love with Jesus, they willingly renounce their former idols.

[3] This is an amalgamation of Paul's words to the Galatians and Macedonians in Acts 14:15 and 1 Thessalonians 1:9. We can tell from Acts 19:26 that he also

Demetrius and his fellow silversmiths were businessmen and they were furious about what Paul's message threatened to do to their bottom line. They stirred up a riot that forced Paul to flee Ephesus in a hurry.

Knowing this background helps us to understand Paul's startling words in Ephesians 5:5. When Paul tells us that immorality, impurity and greed are forms of idolatry, he is making a deliberate link back to the way in which he left Ephesus. His original readers must have expected him to warn them to stay away from Demetrius and his partners, but instead he tells them that some of them are idol-makers themselves! He tells them that not all of the idols in Ephesus are made with silver. If they are greedy or immoral, they are partners with Demetrius too.

Paul may have been inspired by Ezekiel 14:3, where God issued a similar warning to the elders of Israel. He was not pleased with the way they patted themselves on the back for not worshipping in the temples of Babylon, so he told his prophet that *"these men have set up idols in their hearts."* Paul reminds the Ephesians that an idol is not simply a graven image of a false god. It is anything to which we turn in our hearts for satisfaction and fulfilment instead of to God. John Calvin gave a similar warning to Protestants during the Reformation when he saw that they despised the Roman Catholics for praying to images of saints in their churches: *"The human mind is, so to speak, a perpetual idol factory... The human mind, stuffed as it is with presumptuous rashness, dares to imagine a god suited to its own capacity... It substitutes vanity and an empty phantom in the place of God."*[4] We don't have to be skilled in fashioning idols out of silver to become partners with Demetrius.

Paul points out that idolatry lies behind all human sin because he knows it is the best way *to convict people of their*

---

preached something very similar in Ephesus.

[4] John Calvin wrote this in 1536 in his *Institutes of the Christian Religion* (1.11.8).

sin. If he had simply quoted commandments from the Jewish Law, the Ephesians might have responded in the same way as Westerners today. They might have told him, "That's simply your way of seeing the world, Paul, but we take a different view." If you have ever been laughed at and told that the Christian perspective on sex or capitalism is outdated, you need to listen to what Paul is saying. He doesn't counter the promiscuity and greed in Ephesus by pointing out that it contravenes the Seventh and Tenth Commandments, but by pointing out that they are proof that the city has rejected the real God. The Ephesians can see clearly, whether they claim to be Christians or not, that worshipping sex and money is short-sighted and dehumanizing.[5] Alexis de Tocqueville followed Paul's example when he warned in the nineteenth century that the American dream was an empty idol and that *"the imperfect joys of this world will never satisfy [the human] heart."*[6]

Paul also points out that idolatry lies behind all human sin because he knows it is the best way *to deal with the root of sin*. When I chop down the brambles in my garden, they grow back very quickly. I can only rid my garden of brambles by digging deep into the earth and dragging them out by their roots. In the same way, Paul does not target our sinful actions alone, since they are only symptoms of idolatry buried deep within our hearts. If you struggle with lust, you will not cure it by throwing out your pornographic magazines; you will just find other images online instead. You cannot change your heart by going one step further and giving away your computer; you will simply find yourself creating fantasies in your head. You can only change your heart by confessing to God that you are worshipping sex as an idol, and by believing that you have died to your old idolatrous way

---

[5] Paul's argument in 5:5 is not that greedy and immoral Christians will lose their salvation, but that their greed and immorality show they are not Christians at all. No one who is new on the inside can ever stay the same on the outside.

[6] Alexis de Tocqueville issued this prophetic warning in *Democracy in America* (1835).

of living and been raised to a new life in Jesus.[7] Only faith in Jesus' resurrection can deal with the fundamental problem of idolatry of which lust is merely an outward symptom. Don Carson captures this when he tells us:

> *Sin is not first and foremost horizontal, social (though of course it is all of that): it is vertical, the defiance of Almighty God. The sin which most consistently is said to bring down God's wrath on the heads of his people or on entire nations is idolatry – the de-godding of God. And it is the overcoming of this most fundamental sin that the cross and resurrection of Jesus achieve.*[8]

Paul points out that idolatry lies behind all human sin because he knows it is the best way *to persuade us to live as the people we now are in Jesus*. The truth is that everybody becomes like what they worship. Worship sex and you will become a drooling lecher. Worship God and you can enjoy sex as a tender lover who gives thanks to God for sex as a good thing, not as a god thing. Worship money and you will become a grasping miser. Worship God and you can enjoy money as a generous giver who gives thanks to God for providing you with everything you need. Everybody worships something. The only choice we get is what we worship. Paul shows us that living as children of darkness will harm and destroy us, but that living as children of light through Jesus will free us to enjoy life as it was always meant to be.

It's your choice: light or darkness; freedom or folly; partnership with Jesus or partnership with Demetrius and his trinket idols, which have long since been destroyed.

---

[7] Paul tells us literally in 5:3 that sexual immorality and greed *should not even be named* among believers. We should reject these idols as firmly as any graven image, rooting out even the slightest hint of idolatry.

[8] D. A. Carson wrote this in a blog entry entitled "Three Books on the Bible: A Critical Review" for the website *Reformation 21* (April 2006).

Filled Is Not Full (5:18–20)

Do not get drunk on wine, which leads to debauchery. Instead, be filled with the Spirit.

(Ephesians 5:18)

Two hundred miles along the coast from Ephesus lay the ruins of Troy. Every Ephesian schoolboy knew the story. Agamemnon had gathered a Greek armada of a thousand ships to sail across the Aegean Sea in order to recapture Helen of Troy. There was just one problem. His magnificent fleet could not set sail because there wasn't any wind.

The Ephesians knew their Greek mythology, so they knew what happened next. Iphigenia, the daughter of Agamemnon, willingly offered herself as a sacrifice to appease the gods so that the wind would come. As soon as she was sacrificed, a strong wind started blowing which filled the sails of the Greek armada. They were blown to Troy and victory by the power of this god-given wind.[1]

We have nearly reached the end of Paul's long description of how the Gospel sanctifies us, so it is important that we ensure we have understood exactly what he is saying before we move on. I don't know whether Paul used this famous story about Iphigenia and a thousand windless sails to clarify his message to his pagan audiences, but I know that it helps me. So let's slow down and use it to help us understand exactly what Paul teaches about how God makes us holy.

---

[1] Euripides tells this story in his play *Iphigenia at Aulis* (c.406 BC). Interestingly, the offended goddess who sent the wind in response to her sacrifice was none other than Artemis.

First, Paul tells us in these verses that we are sanctified the same way that we were justified. We were forgiven for our sins through the death and resurrection of Jesus, and we are freed from our sins through his death and resurrection too. That's why Paul used the word "therefore" in 4:1 to assure us that living like Jesus is the natural fruit of who we have now become in Jesus. It's also why he commands us in 5:8 to adopt a lifestyle that would have been impossible for us in the past: *"You were once darkness, but now you are light in the Lord. Live as children of light."*

If you are struggling with an area of sin in your life, however, this may not be enough detail for you. It isn't enough to be told that we must live out who we are. We also need to be told what to do with stubborn areas of sin which refuse to go away.[2] Paul addresses this when he expands in 4:22–24 that *"You were taught, with regard to your former way of life, to put off your old self, which is being corrupted by its deceitful desires; to be made new in the attitude of your minds; and to put on the new self, created to be like God in true righteousness and holiness."*[3]

Paul tells us that we need to follow the example of Iphigenia. We need to make ourselves willing sacrifices to God. If we are honest, the reason we often fail to root out sin in our lives is that we simply do not want to. We can be so fond of the fruitless deeds of darkness that Paul has to urge us strongly to take active hold of the Gospel. Paul tells us to remember that our old self died with Jesus (4:22), that we were raised to new life in him (4:23) and that this new life is completely different from the old life which was crucified with him (4:24).[4] Paul

---

[2] The fact that our old self has been crucified with Jesus does not mean it is inactive. Paul uses a present participle in 4:22 to teach us that our old self still fights back and *"is being corrupted by its deceitful desires."*

[3] The Greek verbs in these verses are infinitives and not imperatives. Paul is therefore not telling us to do anything new, but simply telling us to lay hold of the same Gospel that we were taught at our conversion.

[4] Paul explains this more in Galatians 2:20, 5:16–26, Colossians 2:16–3:17, and Romans 6:1–14 and 13:12–14.

was referring to this message when he told people in Acts 26:18 that they could be *sanctified by faith in Jesus*. When we offer ourselves as willingly to God as Iphigenia offered herself to her false goddess, and when we ask him to apply to our lives what has happened to us in Jesus, then the battle is more than half won. The question is whether we are willing to die to our old desires and to embrace the holy lifestyle that Paul describes in Ephesians 4 and 5.

Second, Paul tells us that we need God's wind to blow. Believing that we can be sanctified through Jesus is not enough to change us. Like a fleet with floppy sails in a Greek harbour, it can only change us if God blows on us by his Holy Spirit to apply the Gospel to our lives. That's why Paul tells us in Romans 8:13 that *"if by the Spirit you put to death the misdeeds of the body, you will live."* Note the way in which these verses start in 4:22–24 with a reminder about the death and resurrection of Jesus but end in 5:18–20 with a command to be filled with the Holy Spirit. Paul's constant message in his letters is that we need to have God on the inside. We are not simply sanctified because we have died and been raised to new life in Jesus. We are also sanctified because his death appeased God's righteous anger towards our sin, and because he ascended to heaven to secure for us the promised Holy Spirit. He has given us the wind of God.

Third, Paul tells us that we need the Holy Spirit every day. Some people forget this and ask questions like *"Have you been filled with the Holy Spirit?"*, yet Paul's emphasis here is not *"Have you been filled?"* but *"Are you still full?"* It didn't help Agamemnon that the sails in his warships had once been full of wind, and it doesn't help you that you were once filled with the Holy Spirit in 1995 or in 2010. What matters is whether you are full of the Spirit right now! Paul reminds us that having been filled is not the same thing as being full.

To stress this, in 5:18, Paul compares being filled with the Holy Spirit to getting drunk on wine. Drunkenness soon wears off unless a person keeps on drinking. To stress this further, Paul uses a "present imperative" in 5:18, which commands us literally to *"**Go on being filled** with the Holy Spirit."*[5] In case we miss both of these clues, Paul lists some of the marks of being filled with the Holy Spirit in 5:19–20, telling us that we should do these things *"always"* and not just as part of occasional one-off experiences of God's power.[6] Peter was filled with the Spirit in Acts 2:4, yet he needed to be filled afresh in Acts 4:8 and filled yet again in Acts 4:31. Paul was filled with the Spirit in Acts 9:17, yet he needed to be filled afresh in Acts 13:9. It is no different for us. Being filled with the Holy Spirit needs to be a lifestyle, not a memory.

So don't move on from this long section of teaching about how God sanctifies us until you have surrendered yourself willingly to God, like Iphigenia, to be a living sacrifice.[7] Don't move on until you have asked the Holy Spirit to blow on you so that you can power forward into the new life that Jesus has given you. Don't move on until you have recognized that being full of the Holy Spirit every day is what enables us to live out our new lifestyle. When we dwell in Jesus and he dwells in us, nothing can stop us from sailing to victory.[8]

---

[5] Paul would have used an aorist imperative if he had wanted us to *get filled once* with the Holy Spirit. He uses a present imperative as a Greek way of telling us that having been filled isn't the same as being full.

[6] Note the involvement of the whole Trinity in the worship that Paul describes in 5:18–20. The Spirit stirs us to sing to the Lord Jesus and to give thanks to God the Father in Jesus' name.

[7] Paul uses this language in Romans 12:1 when he uses another big "therefore" to link his explanation of the Gospel in Romans 1–11 to his teaching on how to live it out in Romans 12–15.

[8] See John 15:5. Interestingly, Matthew 4:1 uses the same nautical term as Acts 27:4 to tell us literally that the Holy Spirit blew on Jesus so that he *sailed away* into the desert. Being filled with the Spirit is not to be a one-off experience, like water filling a cup. It is to be a constant experience, like wind filling a sail.

At Home with God
(5:21–6:4)

As the church submits to Christ, so also wives should submit to their husbands in everything. Husbands, love your wives, just as Christ loved the church.

(Ephesians 5:24–25)

One of my friends watched *The Lord of the Rings* on DVD and asked if anyone had ever thought of writing a book of the film. My friends and I looked at her, thinking she was joking, but she wasn't. She really was being that stupid.

We can be just as stupid when we treat God the *Father*, Jesus the *Son* and Jesus the *Bridegroom* as clever human metaphors. We get things the wrong way round when we assume that God looked at human fathers, sons, husbands and wives and decided he could use them as a picture of his character towards us. Not at all. The very reason why he made humans to be male and female, parents and children, was so that we would reflect what he is like to the world.[1] That's what Paul means when he calls God literally in 3:14–15, *"the Father from whom all fatherhood in heaven and on earth derives its name."*

This is very good news. It means that we can worship God at home. In fact, Paul spends more verses teaching us how to walk out our new identity in Jesus in our family life than he does in any other area of our lives. Singing loudly on Sundays about God the Father, Jesus the Son and Jesus the Bridegroom is

---

[1] Genesis 1:26–27 tells us God created humans male and female so that they would reflect his character. The Devil naturally loves to blur these gender distinctions, which is partly why these verses are so unpopular.

easy. Far more costly worship is reflecting those aspects of his character in the way we live throughout the week as parents, children, husbands and wives.

Paul begins in 5:21 by telling everybody in Christian families to submit to one another. It is clear from what follows that he isn't saying that husbands are the same as wives or that parents are the same as children. They are all equal before God but they have differing roles, and the extent to which they submit to Jesus as Lord can be seen from the way they submit to one another in those God-given roles.[2] Fathers should exercise their leadership for the sake of their wives and children. Mothers should exercise their leadership for the sake of their husbands and children. Children should honour their parents for the sake of Jesus. If we are self-seeking or quarrelsome in our home lives, we are still living like the children of darkness and are not like the one who laid down his life in obedience to his Father in order to save many brothers and sisters. If God has truly made his home with us, it will be obvious in our home.

Paul gets specific in 5:22–24 by telling wives to submit to their husbands. Paul says a lot of unpopular things in Ephesians, but this one has to win the prize. Some people hate it because they think it endorses male oppression of women (it doesn't, because Paul is very clear in Galatians 3:28 that men and women are equals before God). Other people hate it because they think it teaches that all women must submit to all men (it doesn't, because Paul is very clear in 5:22 that a woman need only submit to her own husband). Paul braves our reaction because he cares more about God's creation plan than he does about our approval. He insists that marriage is a pairing of equals in which the husband carries ultimate responsibility, leading his wife in the same way that Jesus leads the Church.[3] He gives her his life

---

[2] Paul tells us to submit to one another out of *phobos* for Jesus, which means *fear* or *reverence* towards him.

[3] Some people understand the Greek word *kephalē*, or *head*, in this verse to mean "source" rather than "leader". However, Paul uses the same word

and, as part of this, he also gives her a clear lead. Paul tells wives that the extent to which they follow their husband's lead is the extent to which they follow Jesus as Lord.

Paul turns to husbands in 5:25–33, telling them to love their wives with the same love that Jesus has towards the Church.[4] Christian leadership is never self-serving. It always involves sacrifice. Paul quotes from Genesis 2:24 to remind Christian husbands that they are united with their wives, so their wives should feel the benefit of their being united with Christ.[5] If they love their wives like Jesus, Paul tells husbands in 5:33, then their wives will not find it hard to honour and respect them as part of their reverence towards Jesus as Lord.[6] This teaching may not be popular in our culture, but our messy marriages and high divorce rates suggest we need it more than ever.

In 6:1–3, Paul tells children to obey their parents.[7] He does not assume that the children of Christians are all believers, but he encourages them that if they obey their parents then they are acting *"in the Lord."*[8] He points out that the Fifth Commandment was not just a divine order but a divine promise. God the Father promises to bless any child who honours their human father

elsewhere in the same verse and throughout Ephesians (1:22; 4:15) and Colossians (1:18; 2:10; 2:19) to denote leadership. There is no reason to understand it any differently here.

[4] John 4:10 suggests that when Paul says Jesus purifies his Church through *"the washing with water through the word,"* he may be referring to the Holy Spirit as "living water" rather than to water baptism.

[5] Paul's quotation from Genesis 2:24 reminds us that marriage is a divine idea rather than a human one. We cannot redefine it or dissolve it. We can only reject it or submit to it. See also Matthew 19:1–12.

[6] The Greek verb *phobeō* in 5:33 is linked to *phobos* in 5:21. It is a strong word, which means *to fear* or *to revere*.

[7] Paul uses a different Greek word for children *obeying* in 6:1 to the one he used for wives *submitting* in 5:22. He does so again in the parallel Colossians 3:18 and 20 in order to emphasize that the dynamic is very different.

[8] Paul never quotes from the Jewish Law in order to encourage Christians to obey Jesus. He quotes from Deuteronomy 5:16 here as a way of teaching children right from wrong, whether or not they believe in Jesus.

and mother. In 6:4, Paul therefore warns parents to lead their children wisely,[9] aware that it is no small thing for a man to be the only person in the world other than God that his children address as "father".[10] How parents raise their children is a major factor in how those children learn to relate to God.

Paul's teaching in these verses is controversial and he knows it. Unbelievers belittle the importance of marriage and parenting. Legalists view them as distractions from the serious stuff of religious rituals. Yet Paul tells us that following Jesus begins at home.[11] His teaching caused the nineteenth-century evangelist D. L. Moody to conclude that *"The family was established long before the church, and my duty is to my family first; I am not to neglect my family."* It is in our families that we get to share the name "father" with God, the name "son" with Jesus and the names "husband" and "wife" with Jesus and his Bride.[12] Our worship begins at home, and our home life is the bedrock of our Christian witness. The Church is uniquely placed to teach the world how to build healthy marriages and how to parent healthy children. There is nothing more attractive to a messed-up world than a family that evidently has God on the inside.

So let's not fight Paul's teaching in these verses. Let's submit to it and see it as a promise that God wants to empower us to follow him at home. He is far more passionate about your family

---

[9] The Greek word translated *fathers* was frequently used to describe a mixed-sex group of *parents*, so Paul is not simply addressing men here. Mothers have God-given authority to lead their children too.

[10] God's character is reflected through mothers as well as fathers (Isaiah 66:13), even though he only ever refers to himself in Scripture as God the Father.

[11] This is why the Devil does all he can to undermine family life. We must not be naïve about the extent to which he hates godly marriage and godly parenting because they are such a glorious reflection of God's character.

[12] When the New Testament describes the marriage between Jesus and the Church, it refers to the *"wedding of the Lamb,"* because at the heart of Jesus' marriage is self-sacrifice (Revelation 19:7; 21:9).

life displaying his glory than you are. He has lined up the whole might of heaven to help you if you call upon his name. Even if the other members of your family reject these instructions, God will empower you to make the first step towards them. For his glory and for his own sake, God will fill you with his Spirit and help you to enjoy being at home with God.

Slaves of Christ (6:5–9)

Slaves, obey your earthly masters with respect and fear, and with sincerity of heart, just as you would obey Christ.

(Ephesians 6:5)

William Knibb, a British missionary to colonial Jamaica, wrote home: *"The cursed blast of slavery has, like a pestilence, withered almost every moral bloom. I know not how any person can feel a union with such a monster, such a child of hell. I feel a burning hatred against it and look upon it as one of the most odious monsters that ever disgraced the earth."*[1]

Most of us aren't surprised that Christians led the fight against slavery in the early nineteenth century. We aren't surprised that Christians still lead the fight against human trafficking today. What is surprising, however, is that Paul tells the slaves at Ephesus to submit to their masters instead of helping the slaves to throw off their chains.[2] We clearly need to dig a little deeper into what life was like at Ephesus.

Paul does not condemn slavery outright for *historical reasons*. It is almost impossible for us to utter the word "slavery" without thinking of the appalling transfer of 3 million black Africans across the Atlantic between 1492 and 1807. Roman slavery was very different. Most slaves were prisoners of war and had they not been enslaved on the battlefield they would

---

[1] Peter Masters, *Missionary Triumph Over Slavery: William Knibb and Jamaican Emancipation* (2006).

[2] Before we rush to condemn Paul's instructions to slaves, it is worth noting that he was in chains too (6:20).

almost certainly have been slaughtered instead.[3] Whereas black slaves in the New World tended to be slaves for life, most Roman slaves could win their freedom within a decade. That doesn't mean it was right, but it does mean it is wrong for us to read these verses without being aware of our own cultural baggage.

Paul does not condemn slavery outright *for practical reasons*. Historians cannot agree on the population of first-century Ephesus, but some estimate that its 250,000 free citizens were outnumbered by anything up to 400,000 slaves. Paul is smart enough to see that calling for their immediate emancipation would actually destroy them, since Roman slavery at least ensured that the very rich had a vested interest in providing for the very poor. The Roman orator Cicero lamented that conditions for most poor workers were worse than those of slaves, and that *"the very wage they receive is a pledge of their slavery."*[4] Friedrich Engels argued something similar during the Industrial Revolution:

> *The slave is sold once and for all; the proletarian must sell himself daily and hourly. The individual slave, property of one master, is assured an existence, however miserable it may be, because of the master's interest. The individual proletarian, property as it were of the entire bourgeois class which buys his labour only when someone has need of it, has no secure existence... Thus, the slave can have a better existence than the proletarian.*[5]

Paul was smart enough to see that legal freedom might not bring the Ephesian slaves true freedom at all.

---

[3] The Roman jurist Gaius tells us this in his *Institutes*, written in 161 AD.

[4] Marcus Tullius Cicero writing in 44 BC in his essay *De Officiis* or *On Duties* (1.42).

[5] Friedrich Engels wrote this in *The Principles of Communism* (1847), which was adapted the following year by Karl Marx into *The Communist Manifesto* (1848).

Paul does not condemn slavery outright *for theological reasons*. He tells us throughout his letters that unbelievers are slaves to sin and that the Gospel frees a person from the inside out. He therefore helps the Ephesian slaves to see that they are freer than their masters if they work as willing slaves of Jesus Christ, and he helps the Ephesian masters to see that they will only know true freedom if they recognize that they have obligations towards their slaves because they are also slaves of Christ themselves. The nineteenth-century German thinker Goethe observed that *"Nobody is more hopelessly enslaved than those who falsely believe that they are free."*[6] Paul refuses to short-change the Ephesian slaves with superficial liberty. He teaches them how to be truly free on the inside.

That's why Christians shouldn't be embarrassed by these verses. We should see them as instructions that are just as relevant to employers and employees today as they were 2,000 years ago. They teach us how the Gospel transforms the daily grind of our working hours, no matter how difficult they may be. They tell us that the way we work from Monday to Friday is as much an act of worship as the way we sing on Sundays.

My good friend Nathan discovered the transforming message of these verses a few years ago. He worked for a small business that was in serious trouble. His boss responded by cutting everybody's wages while expecting them to work harder than ever. Nathan applied for other jobs but was unsuccessful in all his interviews, and he began to feel as much like a slave as any of the original recipients of Paul's letter to the Ephesians. It was a real act of sacrifice to Jesus that he guarded his heart towards his boss (6:5) and kept working hard for him even when he was not looking over his shoulder (6:6).[7] It was an act of faith for

---

[6] Johann Wolfgang von Goethe in his novel *Elective Affinities* (1809).

[7] Paul uses the same Greek word for *obeying* in 6:5 as he used in 6:1. He tells slaves literally in 6:6 not to offer "eye-slavery as man-pleasers," because Jesus is their true Master and he is watching them all the time.

him to work for Jesus as his true Employer (6:7), believing that Jesus would reward him fairly even if his boss didn't (6:8).

Then one of Nathan's work colleagues was diagnosed with cancer. Although he was not a Christian, he had been so impressed with Nathan's attitude at work that he turned to him in his hour of crisis. Nathan was able to help him to prepare for death, first at the photocopying machine and then later at the hospital. When Nathan preached at his colleague's funeral, he was able to tell the man's widow and children how he led him to repentance and faith in Jesus before he died. Shortly afterwards, Nathan found a better job, but when he looks back on that year of slavery he says he would not have been freed early for any other job in the world. Because he learned to live as a free man, even though a slave, he was able to lead a fellow slave to freedom through the Gospel.

Paul therefore taught slaves to experience true freedom while still slaves, but he also sowed the seeds for the eventual overthrow of slavery in years to come. When people saw the godly character of Christian slaves, they began to take Paul seriously when he argued that the slave trade was evil (1 Timothy 1:10), that slaves should gain their freedom if they could (1 Corinthians 7:21), that masters ought to view their slaves as equals (Ephesians 6:9; Galatians 3:28) and that they ought to set them free at the proper time (Philemon 16). Although governments resisted his teaching for many years, the historian Rodney Stark argues that Paul's teaching eventually won the day:

> *Of all the world's religions, including the three great monotheisms, only in Christianity did the idea develop that slavery was sinful and must be abolished. Although it has been fashionable to deny it, antislavery doctrines began to appear in Christian theology soon after the decline of Rome and were accompanied by the eventual*

disappearance of slavery in all but the fringes of Christian Europe. When Europeans subsequently instituted slavery in the New World, they did so over strenuous papal opposition, a fact that was conveniently "lost" from history until recently. Finally, the abolition of New World slavery was initiated and achieved by Christian activists.[8]

---

[8] Rodney Stark in *For the Glory of God: How Monotheism Led to Reformations, Science, Witch-Hunts, and the End of Slavery* (2003).

Standing Guard (6:10–17)

Put on the full armour of God, so that when the day of evil comes, you may be able to stand your ground, and after you have done everything, to stand.

(Ephesians 6:13)

Paul knew that the Christians at Ephesus were in for a fight. He had warned their elders before his arrest and imprisonment that *"after I leave, savage wolves will come in among you and will not spare the flock"* (Acts 20:29). Having taught them to sit in 1:1–3:21 and to *walk* in 4:1–6:9, he therefore closes his letter with a final section in which he teaches them to *stand* before the onslaught which is about to come.

Don't miss the obvious here. Paul doesn't tell the Ephesians to sit, walk, *advance*. Nor does he tell them to sit, walk, *take ground*. He tells them four times in these verses that they simply need to *stand* in the good of the Gospel which he described in the first three chapters of the letter. We don't have to defeat the Devil because Jesus has already defeated him. We don't have to claim new territory from him because the entire world belongs to Jesus Christ and therefore belongs to us through the Gospel too. We don't have to achieve anything ourselves. We simply have to trust in what the Gospel says is true in the face of the Devil's concerted attempts to distract us and to make us doubt it.[1]

Paul was under house arrest in Rome while he wrote this

---

[1] The Greek word which Paul uses for *struggle* in 6:12 is *palē*, which literally means *wrestling*. A Greek wrestler had to topple his opponent and hold his neck to the ground. The winner was the last man *standing*.

letter. Perhaps the Roman soldier who was standing guard nearby caught his eye.[2] He gave Paul the perfect illustration to help his readers to grasp what he means when he says we need to stand our ground through the Gospel. He looks the Roman soldier up and down, as he compares each part of his armour to an aspect of faith in the Gospel.[3]

Paul tells us that we have two basic weapons in our struggle against the Devil: the *sword* of the Spirit and the *shield* of faith.[4] Paul uses a Greek neuter pronoun in 6:17 to make it clear that the sword is not the Word of God; the Spirit is[5] – the same Holy Spirit who inspired the Bible lives inside us. So our basic weapon in the fight against Satan is to read Scripture, allowing the Spirit to apply its message to every aspect of our lives.[6] The Greek word which Paul uses in 6:16 describes the large oblong shield that Roman soldiers carried into battle, consisting of two layers of wood glued together and covered with linen and leather to extinguish any flaming arrows that were fired at them by their barbarian enemies. Genuine faith starves doubt, discouragement and temptation of the oxygen they need to wreck our lives. When we devote our attention to the Word of God, the Devil's lies have no room to breathe. Faith in the truth is a solid defence against the lie.

Roman soldiers were famous for fighting in a *testudo* or *tortoise* formation. Although their oblong shields were only 120

149

---

[2] Ephesians 6:20 appears to date this letter to the period that Luke describes in Acts 28:16 and 20.

[3] Paul was probably also inspired by the prophecy in Isaiah 59:17, where the Messiah clothes himself with *righteousness as his breastplate* and with *the helmet of salvation*. See also 1 Thessalonians 5:8 and Romans 13:12.

[4] Some modern readers struggle with Paul's frank reference to the Devil and his demons in 6:11–12. Paul tells us that this is where the true battle lies. The Devil is delighted when people doubt the activity of demons.

[5] *Spirit* is neuter and *sword* is feminine in Greek. Paul's description of the Spirit as the *rhēma theou* rather than the *logos theou* may be a deliberate broadening of the *Word of God* to include prophecy as well as Scripture.

[6] Jesus models for us how to use Scripture to drive back Satan in Matthew 4:1–11.

centimetres high by 75 centimetres wide, soldiers could band together and use their shields to create an impregnable shell of protection around their cohort as a whole. The Roman historian Cassius Dio tells us:

> *Those infantrymen who use the oblong, curved and grooved shields are drawn up around the edges, making a rectangular figure, and facing outwards with spear-points projecting they enclose the rest. The other infantrymen who have flat shields form a compact body in the centre and raise their shields above the heads of all the others so that nothing but shields can be seen in every part of the phalanx and all the men are protected from missiles by the density of the formation. It is so marvellously strong that men can walk upon it, and whenever they come to a narrow ravine even horses and vehicles can be driven over it.[7]*

Paul may have had this in mind as he wrote, because a close-knit body of believers has even stronger faith when it stands together.[8]

Paul describes three defence weapons: the *belt* of truth, the *breastplate* of righteousness and the *helmet* of salvation. Ancient writers would often refer to a soldier's belt as his source of strength, so Paul links back to Jesus' words in John 17:17 and tells us that our strength comes from believing that God's Word is true.[9] Since the Devil loves to attack our thoughts and emotions, Paul tells us to defend our head and hearts through firm belief that the Gospel has saved us and declared us fully

---

[7] Cassius Dio writing about a campaign which took place in 36 BC in his *Roman History* (49.31).

[8] The word *pistis* can mean *faithfulness* as well as *faith*. Our faith in God's Word is strengthened by our being part of a faithful community of believers who support us when we are under fire.

[9] This Hebrew metaphor is used in Job 12:21 and in Isaiah 5:27, 11:5 and 22:21.

righteous in God's sight.[10] Ancient soldiers wore a breastplate to protect their fronts but very little on their backs, which is why the fatalities were always higher for armies that tried to flee than for those that stood their ground. John Bunyan sees this as significant when he tells us in *The Pilgrim's Progress*:

> *Then did Christian begin to be afraid, and to cast in his mind whether to go back, or to stand his ground. But he considered again, that he had no armour for his back, and therefore thought that to turn the back to him, might give him greater advantage with ease to pierce him with his darts; therefore he resolved to venture, and stand his ground.*[11]

Paul only describes one attacking weapon – the *shoes* of readiness to serve God through the Gospel – but even here his emphasis seems to be on standing our ground rather than on taking ground that isn't already ours. He does not mention the *javelin*, which was the main long-range attacking weapon of the Roman legionary, although he may have it in mind when he talks about the power of prayer in 6:18–20.[12] Roman soldiers rained down a shower of javelins on their enemies in order to put them into disarray before hand-to-hand combat began, and prayer certainly does that to the Devil's forces. If we sit with Jesus in the heavenlies and he lives inside us on the earth, we can rain down heaven's power on the Devil's army before it ever gets close enough to harm us.

These verses are so rich in meaning that the Puritan theologian William Gurnall took 261 chapters and 1,472 pages

---

[10] The Greek word *dikaiosunē*, which is translated *righteousness* in 6:14, also means *justification* and *vindication*.

[11] John Bunyan in *The Pilgrim's Progress* (1678).

[12] The javelin was an indispensable weapon for any Roman soldier on the battlefield, but Paul's guard may not have carried one when dressed for jailer duty in the capital city.

to explore them when he published *The Christian in Complete Armour* in three volumes from 1655 to 1662. His work is worth reading if you want to explore these verses further but, in reading more, make sure that you don't get distracted from starting to apply these verses straightaway. Paul uses Greek present passive imperatives in 6:10 and 6:11 in order to tell us literally to *"keep on being made strong in the Lord"* and to *"keep on being clothed with the full armour of God."*[13] Jesus is the one who clothes us in this armour through the Gospel, but we need to go to his armoury every day.

He justified us so that we could sit. He sanctified us so that we could walk. Now he arms us so that we can also stand.

---

[13] Paul teaches us the balance in 6:13 between our activity and Jesus' activity, telling us to *"put on the full armour of God"* (active) in order that we *"may be empowered"* to stand (passive).

The Postman Rings More
Than Twice (6:18–24)

*Grace to all who love our Lord Jesus Christ with an
undying love.*

(Ephesians 6:24)

The postmen at Ephesus were kept very busy. Paul is about to
sign off this letter to the Ephesians but it will not be his last. In
fact, the New Testament contains more letters to Ephesus than
to any other city in the world.

In 6:18–20, Paul hints at what will happen to him after he
posts this first letter. He asks the Ephesians to pray that God
will give him words to speak and the courage to speak them
whenever he gets a chance to do so. This refers partly to the
two years he spent preaching freely to all who came to visit
him during his house arrest at Rome (Acts 28:30–31), but it
also refers to the climactic moment when he was finally able to
make his great defence before one of Caesar's judges. Paul uses
the Greek word *presbeuō* in 6:20 because it has three different
meanings: it can mean that he is *an elder* in chains, *an old man*
in chains or *an ambassador* in chains. Although he is a church
leader in his fifties, he appears to be stressing the third meaning.
He is telling the Ephesians that he is an ambassador of King
Jesus who has been sent to speak to the imperial government of
Rome on behalf of heaven's ruler.[1]

The outcome of Paul's trial would set a precedent for the
treatment of Christians all over the world. This may be one of

---

[1] Paul uses this same Greek word in 2 Corinthians 5:20 to tell us that we are
ambassadors of King Jesus too.

the reasons why he asks the Ephesians to *"pray in the Spirit... for all the Lord's people,"* and to *"be vigilant"* about what is going on around them (6:18). Only the Holy Spirit inside them could give them the wisdom they needed to pray at this turning point in Church history.[2] Paul asks them twice to pray that he will have the courage to speak fearlessly[3] about *"the mystery of the gospel"* to his Roman judges (6:19–20).[4]

The Ephesians' prayers were answered.[5] Paul's judge was won over. He accepted that Paul was innocent, that the Christian Gospel was the continuation of ancient Judaism and that it should therefore be tolerated under the terms of Julius Caesar's treaty with the Jews as a *religio licita*, or *permitted religion*.[6] There would be several crisis moments over the next three centuries when the Roman emperors chose to ignore this, but this ruling created an environment in which the Gospel could flourish. The Christians would sit, walk and stand until their message conquered the Roman Empire.

In 6:21–22, Paul hints at what will happen in the years after his release. He tells the Ephesians that he is sending them this letter by the hand of Tychicus, one of his Ephesian co-

---

[2] "Praying in the Spirit" includes praying in tongues (1 Corinthians 14:15), but it also means more than that too. It refers to any kind of prayer that is guided and empowered by God on the inside (Jude 20).

[3] It should encourage you that Paul found evangelism as scary as you do (see also 1 Corinthians 2:3). If he overcame his fear through prayer, then so can you.

[4] We saw earlier that the Greek word *mustērion* meant far more than just a *mystery*. It was the Greek word for *something kept secret by God and only revealed to his chosen initiates*. The Ephesians therefore needed to pray.

[5] The word Paul uses in 6:18 to describe the Ephesians' perseverance in vigilant prayer is linked to the word that is used to describe the early believers' persistent prayer in Acts 1:14, 2:42 and 6:4.

[6] The first-century Jewish historian Josephus records the terms of this treaty in his *Antiquities of the Jews* (14.10.17–26). For more details about Paul's trial, see *Straight to the Heart of Acts*.

workers, and that Tychicus will speak to them on his behalf.[7]
This explains why there are no personal greetings at the end of
the letter, because Paul puts the spotlight on to Tychicus as the
Christian leader who will address them further. Paul knew that
from now on he would mainly minister to the church at Ephesus
through others. He would be released at the start of 62 AD, and
would plant churches in Spain and the Western Mediterranean,
before heading back east to Crete and Ephesus and Philippi.[8]
But only five years after his release, he would be rearrested,
brought back to Rome and executed.[9]

Before his arrest, Paul would write a second letter to
Ephesus, from Philippi in 65 AD. It is known as 1 Timothy
because one of Paul's teammates was in the city overseeing the
church without him. For the same reason, Paul's third letter to
Ephesus, written from prison in Rome just before he died in 67
AD, is known as 2 Timothy. The apostle John moved to Ephesus
and took over from Timothy, keeping the Ephesian postmen
busy with letters of his own. The letters which we know as 1
John, 2 John and 3 John were all probably posted from the city.

In 6:23–24, Paul hints at what will be the final chapter in
the Ephesian story. After wishing his readers peace, love and
faith, he ends the letter with a very insightful final warning.
He wishes God's grace on those *"who love our Lord Jesus Christ
with an undying love."* That's very interesting because the early
Christian writer Jerome tells us that John was forced to keep
repeating a single sermon to the Ephesian Christians: *"Little
children, love one another."* When they complained that they had
heard him preach that message many times before, he told them,

---

[7] Acts 20:4. Colossians 4:7 tells us that when Tychicus had finished in Ephesus
he also took another letter to Colossae. Paul calls Tychicus his *diakonos*, which
means either his *servant* or his *deacon*.

[8] We can deduce this from his letters. See Romans 15:24 and 28, Titus 1:5, 1
Timothy 1:3 and Philippians 2:23–24.

[9] Paul was arrested so suddenly at Troas that he had no time to collect his
travelling cloak and scrolls (2 Timothy 4:13).

"This is what the Lord commanded, and if this one thing shall be obeyed then it shall be enough."[10] Paul has not needed to rebuke the Ephesians in this letter, but he is evidently concerned that they may lose their initial love for Jesus and, consequently, for one another. Sure enough, this theme emerges in the final letter to the Ephesians in the Bible. The book of Revelation is a long letter that Jesus dictated to John in around 95 AD for Ephesus and six other local churches.[11] In this last letter, Jesus warns the Ephesian church that *"I hold this against you: you have forsaken the love you had at first... If you do not repent, I will come to you and remove your lampstand from its place."*[12]

The Ephesian postmen were busy but, very sadly, so were the Ephesian Christians. They were too busy with things that distracted them from loving God. They forgot what it meant to sit in heavenly places through the Gospel, what it meant to walk differently through the Gospel and how to stand their ground in the Gospel. Just like the city's harbour, which became so silted up that it became unusable, the city's Christians grew increasingly shallow in their understanding of what it means to be made new on the inside through the Gospel.[13]

These final verses are therefore a sober reminder that there is nothing automatic about the message that Paul has described in this letter. We need to lay hold of these truths and let them shape the way we live our lives. We need to be active in applying the amazing message of this letter. We must allow our

---

[10] Jerome wrote this in his *Commentary on Galatians* in around 338 AD. John's three letters do not tell us that he lived in Ephesus, but we know this from Jerome and the other early Christian writers.

[11] The continued influence of the church at Ephesus is demonstrated by the fact that the other six churches are listed in the order that a messenger would travel to them by road from Ephesus.

[12] Revelation 1:11, 20; 2:1–7. "Removing their lampstand" meant shutting their church down.

[13] This silt problem was so severe that the ancient harbour of Ephesus is now three miles inland! John's disciple Ignatius also wrote to Ephesus in about 110 AD, urging the church to grow in its love for Jesus.

lives to be transformed by the fact that the Gospel makes us new on the inside.

Part Three – Colossians:

Strong on the Inside

Rosetta Stone (1:1–2)

*To God's holy people in Colossae, the faithful
brothers and sisters in Christ.*

(Colossians 1:2)

European scholars didn't know how to read the ancient writings of the Egyptians. Such knowledge had been lost to a distant world 2,000 miles and 3,000 years away. Nobody expected to be able to understand the hieroglyphics on papyrus fragments and on ancient temple walls. But all that changed one day in 1799 when a French soldier noticed something interesting while digging defences for Napoleon's army in Egypt.

He had unearthed what would later become known as the Rosetta Stone. The hieroglyphics on the stone were unspectacular, but what was unique about the stone was that it also repeated the same message in ancient Greek below. European scholars understood ancient Greek, so they could cross-reference the two languages on the stone to crack the hieroglyphic code and unlock the language of the pharaohs. Colossians is the Rosetta Stone of the New Testament. It helps us to grasp what Paul was truly thinking when he wrote each of his letters.

Paul wrote Colossians at the same time as Ephesians, while under house arrest in Rome in around 60 AD. We can tell this from the fact that he used Tychicus as postman for both letters (Ephesians 6:21; Colossians 4:7) but, even more importantly, we can tell it from the fact that Colossians bears a similar structure to Ephesians and closely parallels its teaching.[1] Where Paul's

---

[1] Colossians 1:1–2:5 closely parallels Ephesians 1–3, and Colossians 3:1–4:1 closely parallels Ephesians 4:1–6:9. Colossians 4:2–18 only very roughly

precise meaning is unclear in Ephesians, we find clarity in the parallel verses in Colossians. Where he is unclear in Colossians, we find he clarifies his meaning in Ephesians. Watching Paul express the same message in different ways to two different churches helps us to understand his thoughts more deeply, like an Egyptologist who has been given the Rosetta Stone.

The opening two verses in both letters are very similar. Paul introduces himself in exactly the same way: *"Paul, an apostle of Christ Jesus by the will of God"*. Just as he did in Ephesians, Paul then tells the Colossians that they have two addresses through the Gospel: they are *"God's holy people **in Colossae**, the faithful brothers and sisters **in Christ**"*. He ends with an identical blessing, praying over the Colossians, *"Grace and peace to you from God our Father and the Lord Jesus Christ."*[2]

But there are also many differences between these two letters, and it is these differences which make Colossians so valuable when we place it alongside Ephesians. The church at Colossae was different from the church at Ephesus in three big ways: It was different in its *past*, its *present* and its *future*.

Colossae was different from Ephesus *in the past*. Paul had spent three years in Ephesus but he had never even visited Colossae. Acts 19 tells us that he hired a lecture hall in Ephesus and discipled people from all over Asia so that he could send them back to their home cities to plant more churches like the one at Ephesus. One of these students was Epaphras, who travelled 120 miles back east to Colossae in order to plant a church in his home town, as well as in the other two main cities of the Lycus Valley, Laodicea and Hierapolis.[3] That's why Paul tells the Colossians in 2:1 that *"I want you to know how hard*

parallels Ephesians 6:10–24.

[2] Some Greek manuscripts contain a shortened version of this blessing: *"Grace and peace to you from God our Father."* Older English translations follow the longer reading, newer translations the shorter one.

[3] Paul tells us that Epaphras was a Colossian (4:12) who laboured hard for the churches he planted in the three main cities on the River Lycus (4:13).

I am contending for you and for those at Laodicea, and for all who have not met me personally." Paul wrote to the Ephesians as his children in the Lord, but he wrote to the Colossians as his grandchildren via Epaphras.

Colossae was different from Ephesus *in the present*. Paul did not need to confront false teachers in his letter to the Ephesians, but he does in his letter to the Colossians. In fact, since Colossae had been declining in importance for the past 300 years, he might not have written to the church at all had he not heard such alarming news from Epaphras.[4] False teachers were telling the Colossians that Paul's good news about Jesus was only part of the Gospel package. If they wanted to become strong Christians then they needed Jesus *plus special knowledge* (2:1–8), Jesus *plus religious rituals* (2:16–17), Jesus *plus visions of angels* (2:18–19) and Jesus *plus self-denial* (2:20–23). Paul writes to attack these false teachers head on. He tells the Colossians that they need Jesus plus nothing. Jesus alone can make them strong on the inside.

Paul's clash with the false teachers in Colossae brings new meaning to the words that he uses to start Ephesians and Colossians. Although the Greek word that is translated *apostle* can simply mean a *sent one*, Paul shows that it carries a technical meaning by describing himself as an apostle and his co-author merely as *"Timothy our brother."*[5] In case they miss this, he stresses that he is an apostle of Jesus *"by the will of God,"* and that to defy his teaching is therefore to defy God himself. This assertive introduction prepares us for the message of Colossians as a whole. Paul insists that he speaks for God when

---

[4] Paul also wrote to nearby Laodicea (4:16), probably because Epaphras had told him about similar dangers there. Revelation 3:14–22 describes the long-term fruit of the false teaching we read about in Colossians.

[5] *Apostolos* comes from the verb *apostellō*, which means *to send*. Paul tends not to start his church letters by saying he is an apostle when his authority is in no doubt (Philippians and 1 and 2 Thessalonians). He only tends to do so when his authority is contested (Galatians and 1 and 2 Corinthians) or when he does not know the people he is writing to personally (Romans and Colossians).

he tells them that Jesus is all that they need to be made strong on the inside.

Colossae would also be different from Ephesus *in the future*. After his release from prison and his successful visit to Spain, Paul would return to the Eastern Mediterranean, where he would focus his time on Ephesus, Crete and Philippi.[6] Although Paul tells the Colossians that he would like to visit them (Philemon 22), there is no record that he ever did so. Instead, he affirms the members of his team who will minister to the Colossian church without him.[7] He co-authors the letter with Timothy, the man he will leave behind at Ephesus to oversee the churches in the area.[8] He affirms Epaphras as *"our dear fellow servant"* and as *"a faithful minister on your behalf,"* who *"is always wrestling in prayer for you"* and is *"working hard for you and for those at Laodicea and Hierapolis."*[9] This letter is similar to the one Paul wrote to the Ephesians, but its differences are the thing that makes it so helpful. These different nuances make Colossians our Rosetta Stone.

Paul told the Galatians that Jesus had made them free on the inside. He told the Ephesians that Jesus had made them new on the inside. Now he confronts the false teachers who claim that Jesus alone is not enough. He tells the Colossians that, if they truly understand the Gospel, Jesus alone will make them strong on the inside.

---

[6] We can deduce this from Romans 15:24 and 28, Titus 1:5, 1 Timothy 1:3 and Philippians 2:23–24.

[7] This may also be why Colossians ends with so many more personal affirmations than Ephesians.

[8] Paul uses the pronoun *"I"* throughout this letter, so Timothy's co-authorship is simply to affirm his authority as a co-worker with Paul.

[9] 1:7; 4:12–13. A few Greek manuscripts say that Epaphras ministered on *our* behalf, but the most reliable manuscripts say he ministered on *your* behalf. Epaphras was himself imprisoned for going to tell Paul about the problems at Colossae (Philemon 23). He would oversee the church from prison until he was released.

What Paul Prayed (1:3–14)

We always thank God, the Father of our Lord Jesus Christ, when we pray for you.

(Colossians 1:3)

Prayer is like skiing. You can't learn to do it in a classroom. You can only learn by hitting the slopes and having a go with somebody who knows how. Charles Spurgeon brought revival to Victorian London by showing his church how to pray at *"prayer meetings, when I felt compelled to let you go without a word from my lips, because the Spirit of God was so awfully present that we felt bowed to the dust."*[1] William Booth sent revival out from London to the ends of the earth by modelling for his followers fervent prayer in which *"He talked with God about the outcasts of London, the poor of New York, the lost of China, the great world lying in wickedness. He opened his eyes as if he were looking into the very face of Jesus, and with sobs he prayed God's blessing upon every mission worker, every evangelist, every minister, every Christian."*[2] If we want to pray in a similar fashion, we need somebody similar to take us out on the slopes of prayer.

That's why I'm so grateful that the Colossian Christians never had a chance to pray with Paul in person. Unlike the Galatians, the Ephesians and the Philippians, they never had an opportunity to enjoy the slopes of prayer with Paul. Instead, Paul had to show them in the opening verses of this letter how

---

[1] Charles Spurgeon recalls this in his autobiography, *C.H. Spurgeon: The Early Years, 1834–1860*.

[2] Wilbur Chapman recalled this, quoted by Charles Bateman in *The Life of General Booth* (1912).

to pray. As a result, we get to witness the apostle Paul at prayer so that we can learn to pray like him.[3]

In 1:3–8, Paul shows us that we should begin our prayers with *thanksgiving for what God has done.* This is particularly striking when we consider that Paul wrote to Colossae because he was so concerned about the problems in the church there. Paul doesn't major on the lies of the false teachers; he majors on the grace of God. He tells the Colossians that whenever he prays for them he gives thanks to God for their *faith* in Jesus, for their *love* for the Church, for their *hope* in the Gospel,[4] for their understanding of God's *grace*[5] and for the *fruit* which the Holy Spirit is bearing in their lives. We all know how easy it is to major on the problems and disappointments of church life rather than on what God is doing, but Paul didn't make that mistake.[6] His prayers were full of thankfulness because he trained himself to see God at work amidst the mess. Paul's faith stayed strong because he never stopped thanking God for all that he was doing.

Paul's prayers of thanksgiving encompassed what God was doing all around the world. It is easy to grow discouraged when we home in on local challenges, but Paul shows his global perspective when he tells the Colossians he is excited about *"the love you have for all God's people."* Despite his own imprisonment and the activities of the false teachers in Colossae, Paul thanks

---

[3] In the parallel passage, Paul simply explains the Gospel to the Ephesians in 1:3–14 and 1:19b-23. He only tells them what he prays in 1:15–19a, whereas these verses to the Colossians are all about what he prays.

[4] Note the echo of Ephesians in Colossians 1:5. Paul focuses his readers on all they have in heavenly places because this knowledge will help them to live out their faith in earthly places such as Colossae.

[5] Paul refers to the Gospel as *"the true message"* (1:5) and *"the grace of God"* (1:6). Doubting that God's grace is sufficient for us doesn't make us stronger Christians. Disbelieving God's Word always makes us weaker.

[6] We can tell from 1:2 that Paul's focus was less on the subjective outward behaviour of the Colossian Christians than it was on their objective holiness and faithfulness *in Christ.*

God that *"the gospel is bearing fruit and growing throughout the whole world"*. As he does so, it stirs him to believe great things for the Colossians. He uses these same two Greek words again in 1:10 to pray that the Colossians will *bear fruit* and *grow* in their own faith too.

The London I live in is very different from the London of Charles Spurgeon and William Booth, so I need to go out on the slopes of prayer with Paul. I could be discouraged that in the past fifty years the number of people in their twenties attending church in Britain has nosedived from well over 50 per cent to only 3 per cent today.[7] But if I keep a global perspective like Paul, I am encouraged that in the past 100 years the number of people who call themselves Christian has increased from 9 million to 516 million in sub-Saharan Africa, from 8 million to 87 million in the Philippines, and from 2 million to 67 million in China.[8] If the Gospel is bearing such great fruit around the world, I can expect similar things to happen in my own backslidden city in response to my prayers.

In 1:9–10, Paul shows us that we should pray for people to *grow in their understanding of the Gospel*. As we saw in his letter to the Ephesians, Paul isn't interested in trying to change people from the outside in by making them conform to a rulebook of Christian behaviour. He places all his confidence in God's promise that he will fill his People with his Holy Spirit and change them from the inside out. He simply prays for the Spirit to give the Colossians supernatural wisdom and understanding to live in the good of who they are in Jesus. He uses the same Greek word that he used in Ephesians 4:1 in order to assure us that such knowledge will make them live a life *worthy* of the

---

[7] This data comes from the UK Evangelical Alliance report entitled *The 18–30 Mission: The Missing Generation?* (2005).

[8] This data is from a Pew Forum report in 2011. I am not claiming that all of the people who call themselves Christians are necessarily Christians. I am simply pointing out that the global trend is hugely positive.

Lord, or *in line with* their new identity in Jesus.[9] When the Spirit helps us to understand God's will, it unleashes a virtuous circle. It helps us to live out who we really are, which in turn helps us to understand God's will even better!

The key to these two verses is the Greek word *pneumatikos* in 1:9. Tom Wright helpfully points out that

> *Adjectives of this type, Greek adjectives ending in -ikos, do not describe the material out of which things are made, but the power or energy which animates them. It is the difference between asking on the one hand "is this a wooden ship or an iron ship?" (the material from which it is made) and asking on the other "is this a steam ship or a sailing ship?" (the energy which empowers it).*[10]

Paul therefore isn't talking about *spiritual* wisdom but about wisdom that is *given through the Spirit*. When God grants us wisdom by the Holy Spirit (1:9), we are able to love by the power of the Spirit (1:8) and to live godly lives by the power of the Spirit (1:10).[11]

In 1:11–14, Paul shows us that we should pray for people to *grow in strength through the Gospel*. This is particularly significant because the false teachers were telling the Colossians that they needed to add various things to the Gospel if they wanted to become stronger Christians. Paul insists that the Gospel is all we need to gain access to God's glorious might. The message that freed us from the Devil's crumbling dominion of

---

[9] Paul also uses this Greek word *axiōs* in Philippians 1:27, 1 Thessalonians 2:12 and 2 Thessalonians 1:11. Paul uses it in a normal day-to-day sense in 2 Thessalonians 1:3 to mean *that which is fitting*.

[10] Tom Wright in *Surprised By Hope* (2007).

[11] This echoes Paul's teaching in Ephesians, as well as in Galatians 5:22–23.

darkness[12] also qualifies us to inherit the full power of God's Kingdom.[13]

Paul invites us to go out on the slopes of prayer with him because this was the source of his own strength in God. As the Gospel fuels our prayers, we will become as strong as Paul on the inside.

---

[12] Verse 14 echoes Ephesians 1:7 by treating *redemption* and *forgiveness of sins* as the same thing. We were slaves to the Devil through our sin, but now we have been freed to participate in the power of the Kingdom of God.

[13] Paul uses the same Greek word *hikanoō* in verse 12 as he uses in 2 Corinthians 3:5–6 when he tells us that *"Our competence comes from God. He has made us competent."*

Jesus Plus Nothing
(1:15–23)

The Son is the image of the invisible God, the firstborn over all creation.

(Colossians 1:15)

The largest mosque in Europe is a short walk from my house. When I last met the imam, he tried to persuade me that we were working on the same team. He assured me that *"The only difference between us is that, whilst you have Jesus, we have Jesus plus Muhammad."* But that is precisely the point. It's what made Paul write to the Colossians. Faith in Jesus-Plus-Something isn't faith in Jesus at all.

Paul could not get excited without praying and nor could he pray without getting excited. As he finishes showing us how to pray, he gets so excited about the power that Jesus has unleashed for us through the Gospel that he bursts into a hymn of excited praise.[1] He declares that Jesus is completely unique and completely sufficient to meet all of our needs. The false teachers at Colossae couldn't be more wrong. True strength and maturity is only found in Jesus-Plus-Nothing.[2]

Paul tells us in 1:15 that *Jesus is the only God*. The invisible God of the universe has made himself visible to people on earth

---

[1] Whereas Paul suggests he is quoting from an early Christian chorus in Ephesians 5:14, he gives no such indication here. These are his own words, used by Christians ever since to worship Jesus.

[2] In 1:15–20, Paul tells us seven times in six verses that Jesus is supreme over *all creation*, *all things* and *everything*.

by becoming one of us.[3] Adam was created to reflect God's image to the world, but he chose to sin and to deface that image. Jesus came as the true and better Adam who reflects God's image to the world in all its fullness and forever. Jesus told his disciples in John 14:9 that *"Anyone who has seen me has seen the Father,"* and Paul tells us in 1:19 that *"God was pleased to have all his fullness dwell in him."*[4] Jesus is the greatest human being who has ever lived, because he is fully human and fully God.[5]

Paul tells us in 1:16 that *Jesus is the only Creator.* Everything was created *in him* and *through him* and *for him* because he is the architect of the universe and the key to its true meaning. There is nothing in this sin-corrupted world that Jesus did not personally create and there is nothing that he cannot re-create as a result of his victory over sin at Calvary. He created the universe as a home for the human race and then invited us to worship him. When we refused, he became a human being in order to redeem us. Paul tells us in 1:20 that God was pleased *"through him to reconcile to himself all things, whether things on earth or things in heaven, by making peace through his blood, shed on the cross."*[6] Jesus is the Creator and Re-Creator of the universe. It's got to be Jesus-Plus-Nothing because nobody else in history is anything like him.

---

[3] It is ludicrous when some scholars assert that people only started worshipping Jesus as God in the second or third century. Paul worshipped Jesus as God only thirty years after his death and resurrection.

[4] Paul uses the word *fullness* several times in this letter because the false teachers at Colossae were teaching that Jesus was only basic Christianity and that fullness needed to be found in Jesus-Plus-Something.

[5] Paul makes it clear in 1:16 that calling Jesus the *firstborn* of creation does not imply he was created. When Jehovah's Witnesses claim that it does, they simply show that they are like the false teachers at Colossae. The word *firstborn* was used throughout the Old Testament to describe a father's supreme heir, regardless of whether they were born first. See Genesis 48:13–20 and Jeremiah 31:9, or 1 Samuel 16:11 and Psalm 89:27.

[6] Paul's reference in 1:16 and 1:20 to invisible authorities in heavenly places is a deliberate attack on the false teaching at Colossae, which advocated Jesus-Plus-Angels. Paul addresses this directly in 2:18.

Paul tells us in 1:17 that *Jesus is the only Sustainer of Creation*. It may seem odd to us that the false teachers at Colossae believed that Jesus had retreated from creation when he ascended to heaven, but it is no odder than when we sing about Jesus on Sunday and then rely on science or on ourselves from Monday to Saturday. Paul says that Jesus has not created the world as an independent entity, like a cake, which carries on existing unless it is eaten, without any help from its baker. He tells us that Jesus has created the world to depend on its Creator every moment, like a musical note, which ceases the moment a musician decides not to sustain it any longer.[7]

The seventeenth-century theologian John Owen comments on a similar statement in Hebrews 1:3:

> *Such is the nature and condition of the universe, that it could not subsist a moment, nor could anything in it act regularly unto its appointed end, without the continued support, guidance, influence, and disposal of the Son of God... The things of this creation can no more support, act, and dispose themselves, than they could at first make themselves out of nothing... Neither could sun, or fire, or wind preserve themselves in their being, or retain the principles of their operations, did not the Son of God, by a continual emanation of his eternal power, uphold and preserve them.*[8]

Paul tells us in 1:18–20 that *Jesus is the only Saviour*. His blood alone has created peace between God and sinful human beings. His work alone has created the Church, which is his body, and he alone rules as its undisputed Head.[9] His resurrection alone has

---

[7] Isaiah 40:26 tells us that the universe only continues to exist *"because of his great power and mighty strength."*

[8] John Owen in his commentary on *The Epistle to the Hebrews* (1667).

[9] Again we hear an echo of the other letter which Paul sent via Tychicus. Compare 1:18 with Ephesians 5:23.

granted new life to our mortal bodies so that we can become part of his new creation forever. The firstborn over all creation (1:15) has now become the firstborn from among the dead too (1:18). His resurrection body is our first foretaste of the new creation that will be revealed when he finally comes again in glory.[10]

Paul tells us in 1:21–23 that *Jesus is the Finisher of our Salvation*. He bore our sins on the cross so that he can present us to God the Father without any blemish or legitimate grounds for accusation. He was raised from the dead so that he can strengthen us in our newfound faith if we persevere in the hope held out for us in the Gospel.[11] We do not "graduate" as Christians by adding anything extra to the finished work of Jesus. Paul tells us that we only become strong *"if you continue in your faith, established and firm, and do not move from the hope held out in the gospel."*[12] This is the Gospel message which rang out across the whole universe through Christ's resurrection, and it is the Gospel message of which Paul tells the Colossians he has become a servant.[13] He is ready to die to proclaim Jesus-Plus-Nothing to every nation of the world.

Paul ends his excited exclamation with three verses that emphasize the once-and-for-all uniqueness of Jesus. He has completely changed our past (1:21). He is completely changing our *present* (1:22). He will completely change our *future* if we continue in him (1:23). He is the only Creator and the only Saviour. He is all we can ever need. It's Jesus-Plus-Nothing or it isn't really Jesus at all.

---

[10] Paul uses similar language to teach the same thing in 1 Corinthians 15:20–28.

[11] Paul's teaching in Colossians 1:21–23 echoes his teaching in Ephesians 2. We were once enemies of God but now we have been reconciled to him through the lavish grace of God.

[12] Paul's encouragement to be rooted in *faith* in 1:23 echoes a similar encouragement to be rooted in *love* in Ephesians 3:17.

[13] The Gospel had not even spread to the whole of Europe by 60 AD, but Paul is telling us in 1:23 that the resurrection proclaimed Jesus' once-and-for-all uniqueness to creation as a whole (see Romans 1:4).

As Strong as an Old Lady
(1:24–29)

To this end I labour, struggling with all his energy,
which so powerfully works in me.

(Colossians 1:29)

Kevin Fast is not your average church leader. The Canadian pastor is included several times in the *Guinness Book of World Records* as one of the strongest men in the world. I have a photo of him which was taken in 2007, wearing his clerical collar while he uses sheer brute force to pull a 63-ton fire truck 100 yards. He is a colossus of a Christian hero and many people think that Paul was like him.

Some of the Colossians were probably guilty of this kind of hero worship. They had never met Paul, so they probably imagined him a superhuman hero. Who else could have planted churches in every major city in Cyprus, Asia Minor, Macedonia and Greece in just nine years from 48 to 57 AD? Who else could have performed the miracles that Epaphras told them Paul performed? That's why Paul ends this chapter with a warning not to think that he is strong like Kevin Fast.

Some of the Colossians had the opposite view of Paul. They believed the unkind rumours that *"His letters are weighty and forceful, but in person he is unimpressive and his speaking amounts to nothing,"* and that he was *"a man of small stature, bald-headed, bow-legged, with eyebrows which met in the middle, thick-set, and with a large crooked nose."*[1] They despised the

---

[1] These two statements come from 2 Corinthians 10:10 in 55 AD and from the apocryphal *Acts of Paul and Thecla* in about 160 AD. Both are examples of the

manual labourer whom they heard left most cities in a hurry. They were suspicious of a man who was frequently in trouble with the law and who was writing to them from prison in Rome. Although they were grateful that Paul had sent Epaphras to plant a church in their city, these Colossians looked down on Paul as a person. He wasn't like the new teachers who promised to fill up what was still lacking in Paul's simple message about Jesus.

So don't be confused when Paul writes in 1:24 that *"I fill up in my flesh what is still lacking in regard to Christ's afflictions."* Paul is deliberately dealing with both groups of Colossian Christians – those who view him as a hero and those who view him as a zero. He tells the Colossians that they do not need to be taught by a human strongman. They need to be taught how God can make us strong on the inside.

In 1:24, Paul deals with his fan club in Colossae by telling them that he is weaker than they think. He reminds them that the Gospel is a message about a crucified Messiah, and that the only thing he needs to add to Jesus' sacrifice is the suffering involved in preaching about his death in weakness all across the Roman Empire.[2] Their hero is a suffering servant who points to the true Suffering Servant.[3] This is very important if you think you could never become a Christian or that you could never be fruitful as a Christian because of your own inherent weaknesses. God isn't looking for people who are strong enough to drag sixty-three tons of Christian requirements behind them.

In 1:25–28, Paul deals with his critics in Colossae by telling them that they have fallen for a lie. He has already preached to

rumours that were circulating about Paul.

[2] Paul uses the Greek word *thlipsis* to describe Jesus' afflictions in 1:24, a word that is never used in the New Testament to refer to Jesus' suffering on the cross. Jesus' work of salvation is unique and complete (John 19:30). We get to suffer in a different way to take that message of salvation to the world.

[3] Paul uses the Greek word *diakonos* to tell us that he is both a *servant* of the Gospel (1:23) and a *servant* of the Church (1:25). If we try to be heroes instead of servants, we have misunderstood Paul's Gospel.

them *"the word of God in its fullness – the mystery that has been kept hidden for ages and generations, but is now disclosed to the Lord's people."*[4] We do not grow as Christians by chasing after smooth-talking teachers with stricter rules or more experiences of angels. We grow through Jesus alone, becoming *"fully mature in Christ"* through understanding that the Gospel is the God-given promise of *"**Christ in you**, the hope of glory."*[5] Spiritual strength comes from experiencing ever more deeply the fact that we are now in Jesus and Jesus is now in us.

The crowds were very impressed when Kevin Fast dragged a 63-ton fire truck 100 yards in 2007, but here is the ridiculous thing: If he had taken off his harness and allowed a 95-year-old lady to climb into the cab, she could have put her foot on the accelerator pedal and driven that fire truck many thousand times further than Kevin Fast had dragged it, and at many times the speed. She would not even have broken a sweat, because trucks are not built to be dragged but to be driven. God has made us exactly the same. Some of us are better at following religious rules than others, but none of us can do all that God has told us unless we have God on the inside. That's why Paul tells the Colossians in 1:29 that the secret of his fruitful ministry is very simple: *"I labour, struggling **with all his energy**, which so powerfully works in me."*

Following Jesus is not easy. It means swimming against the tide of our polluted culture. It means filling up in our flesh what is still lacking in regard to Christ's afflictions – pouring out our lives to play our part in God's unfolding plan.[6] But don't let the

---

[4] The Greek word Paul uses for this *commission* in 1:25 is *oikonomia*, a word that was commonly used for a master entrusting *stewardship* of a task to one of his slaves.

[5] Colossians 1:27 links back to Galatians 3:14. Being filled with the Holy Spirit is not an add-on to the Gospel. It lies at the very heart of the Gospel and to miss it is absolutely tragic.

[6] The Greek word Paul uses for *struggling* is *agōnizomai*, a word that was used for wrestlers *straining hard* in the Olympic Games, because working by God's power still means working hard. Working by our own strength leads to burnout,

fact that following Jesus isn't easy fool you into thinking that following Jesus is difficult. It isn't. It's absolutely impossible. You will never make it if you try to follow him by your own brute force. You will only make it if you surrender fully to the Gospel. God isn't calling you to pull the truck hard like Kevin Fast, but to put your foot down and use his power like the old lady in the cab. He invites you to let him live inside you through his Holy Spirit and empower you to follow him from the inside out.

This message could not be more important. That's why the Devil works so hard to make sure that we miss it. If he cannot stop us from understanding in Galatians and Ephesians how to be justified and sanctified by Jesus, he will try to stop us from understanding in Colossians how to be made strong by Jesus.[7] But Paul is adamant. He insists that we are made strong by grace through faith in Jesus, just as he insists on it in his other letters:

> *We preach Christ crucified: a stumbling-block to Jews and foolishness to Gentiles, but to those whom God has called, both Jews and Greeks, Christ the power of God and the wisdom of God. For the foolishness of God is wiser than human wisdom, and the weakness of God is stronger than human strength.*[8]

---

not working at all is a cop-out, but working by God's strength leads to break-out.

[7] Paul insists in 1:28 that this message is for you too. God wants *everyone* to be fully mature like this in Christ.

[8] 1 Corinthians 1:23–25. The problem is not having human strength or wisdom, since Paul commends wisdom in Colossians 1:28, but *relying* on human strength or wisdom (2 Corinthians 12:8–10).

Deep and Wide (2:1–15)

*Just as you received Christ Jesus as Lord, continue
to live your lives in him, rooted and built up in him,
strengthened in the faith.*

(Colossians 2:6–7)

Plants have to grow underground before they can reach towards
the sky. The ones that grow tallest and strongest are the ones
that go down the deepest and the widest. The roots of the
English oak tree go down deeper into the soil than its highest
branches tower above it, and they go out two or three times
wider than the radius of its leaves. That's why the English oak
can live for over 1,000 years and its wood is one of the strongest
in the world.

The Colossians, on the other hand, were very shallow.
They were far too easily impressed by the outward appearances
of the false teachers. They liked their wise-sounding arguments,
their claims that they had special knowledge, and their boasting
about angelic encounters and about experiences beyond those
of Paul.[1] He therefore directs their attention to the mighty trees
which grew throughout the Lycus Valley when he urges them
in 2:6–7: *"Just as you received Christ Jesus as Lord, continue to
live your lives in him, rooted and built up in him, strengthened in
the faith as you were taught."*[2] If they wanted God to make them
strong on the inside, they must not be distracted by the flashy

---

[1] Paul tells us in 2 Corinthians 12:1–4 that he is so in awe of his deep
experiences of God that he dares not tell anyone about them. False teachers
can be spotted by their lack of such self-restraint.

[2] Paul told us in Ephesians 3:17 to be *rooted like a tree* (*rizoō*) and *founded
like a building* (*themelioō*) in Jesus' love. He used the verb *themelioō* again in

promises of the false teachers. They needed to put down deeper roots into Jesus instead.

In 2:1–5, Paul urges the Colossians to broaden their understanding of who Jesus really is.[3] He warns them against the *"fine-sounding arguments"* of false teachers who promise to lead us into hidden wisdom and greater insight into the mysteries of God. Jesus alone is all we need because he is *"the mystery of God… in whom are hidden all the treasures of wisdom and knowledge."* We need to explore the breadth of Jesus' character and of his work so that we can draw spiritual nourishment from *"the full riches of complete understanding."* We will never exhaust the rich soil of what Jesus has to offer us.[4]

In 2:6–8, Paul urges the Colossians to deepen their understanding of what they already know about Jesus.[5] The roots of an oak tree do not merely spread out over a wide area. Its taproots delve deep into the earth and anchor it securely to the ground so that even a hurricane cannot topple it. Paul warns the Colossians not to be distracted by the human traditions and human wisdom of the false teachers, because they are nothing but *"hollow and deceptive philosophy."*[6] It cannot rival the strength that comes through a deep understanding of what it truly means to receive Christ Jesus as our Lord.

Colossians 1:23, and now he tells us to be *rooted like a tree* (*rizoō*) and *built up like a building* (*epoikodomeō*) in Jesus himself.

[3] Paul models for us in 2:5 that we are at our most persuasive when we believe the best of our listeners.

[4] Paul echoes the message of Ephesians 4:1–16 when he tells us in 2:2 that we can only get to know Jesus fully if we act as a united team. Each of us is different, so we discover Jesus more fully together than we can alone.

[5] Paul starts 2:6 with the word *therefore* because this is the natural application of his teaching about the supremacy and all-sufficiency of Jesus. He uses the same Greek word for *walking* in the light of who we are in 2:6 as he does in Ephesians 4:1.

[6] The Greek word that Paul uses in 2:8 for *the basic principles* of this world is the same word that he uses in Galatians 4:3 and 9. He also uses it again in Colossians 2:20.

In 2:9–15, Paul spells it out for us. He tells us that "Jesus is Lord" means that Jesus is the flesh-and-blood incarnation of the God who, throughout the Old Testament, called himself *Yahweh* in Hebrew and *Kurios* in Greek (2:9). It means that he is the supreme ruler of heaven and earth, because this is the name the Father gave him when he had defeated all his enemies through his death and resurrection, when he ascended to sit on heaven's throne (2:10).[7] It means that we no longer have any need of Jewish circumcision or any of the other traditions peddled by the false teachers at Colossae. Cutting off the foreskin was an ancient expression of faith that our sinful nature would be dealt a death blow through Jesus' death and resurrection (2:11–12).[8] Now that we have seen the real thing and have been baptized into Jesus as Lord, we do not need these obscure shadows any more. We simply need to dig down deep roots of understanding into who we have become now that we are in the Lord Jesus and the Lord Jesus is in us.

Paul tells us that strength comes through understanding that our dead and sinful souls have been raised to new life in Jesus (2:13).[9] Jesus bore away the debt of our trespasses by nailing it to the cross through his crucified body (2:14).[10] He was defeated and disgraced for our sake on the cross, but he turned the tables on the Devil and his demons by using this

---

[7] The Roman emperor called himself the *Kurios*, the ultimate ruler (Acts 25:26), but God proclaimed that Jesus is the true *Kurios* when he raised him from the dead and up to heaven (Acts 2:36; Philippians 2:9–11).

[8] God told the Hebrews that circumcision was an outward symbol of deep change on the inside (Deuteronomy 10:16; Jeremiah 4:4; 9:25). In 2:11, Paul refers literally to *"the circumcision of Christ"* because this has not simply been fulfilled *by* Jesus but by the fact we are *in* Jesus.

[9] This verse strongly echoes Ephesians 2:1–10.

[10] *Cheirographon* means *a handwritten note* so it cannot refer to Moses' Law which was written by God himself (Exodus 31:18; 32:16). It was the common Greek word for a debtor's note, so it refers to the debt we accrued through our rebellion against God (Matthew 6:12). The Greek word *exaleiphō* can be translated that Jesus *cancelled*, *erased* or *blotted out* this debt. He did away with it completely (John 19:30).

seeming defeat to strip them of all their weapons and their armour.[11] He put them to public shame and he ascended to heaven like a Roman general riding back from war at the head of a triumphal procession of prisoners and plunder taken from the hands of his defeated enemies.[12] The false teachers show how clueless they are when they tell the Colossians to honour angels and demons, because Jesus is more powerful than all of those celestial beings put together.[13] Jesus is the undisputed Lord of the universe and, the more we grasp the scale of his massive triumph, the stronger we become.[14]

In the opening scene of the movie *Gladiator*, Russell Crowe leads a Roman legion to victory over a large barbarian army. When he manages to outflank them, he knows that the battle is won and so he starts shouting *"Roma Victor!"*, which is Latin for *"Rome is the Winner!"* It's an impressive opening scene, but it's not as impressive as what Paul says to the Colossians. Theologians tend to summarize the message of these verses as *"Christus Victor,"* the once-for-all announcement that *"Christ is the Winner."*

So don't settle for a shallow view of Jesus, which celebrates his compassion but not his conquest. Don't see him as our deliverer from sin but not as the destroyer of Satan and of all our other enemies. Dig down roots into Jesus that are deep and wide enough to grasp all that he has done for you through the Gospel. When we know Jesus and when we understand the

[11] The Greek word *apekduomai* was used to describe soldiers stripping the corpses of their foes after a battle. The word *thriambeuō* described victorious Roman generals returning to celebrate a triumphal procession.

[12] The Devil and his demons have no weapons, since Jesus broke the power of sin and sickness and death. Their only hope is to keep us ignorant of the full extent of Jesus' victory over them.

[13] Verse 18 explains why Paul emphasizes Jesus' supremacy over angels and demons so strongly in verses 10 and 15.

[14] The Greek pronoun Paul uses in verse 15 is deliberately ambiguous. It can mean that God triumphed either through Jesus or through Jesus' *cross*. Both are true.

depth and breadth of his work of salvation, then and only then does God makes us truly strong on the inside.

Four Dummies (2:16–23)

Such regulations indeed have an appearance of wisdom... but they lack any value.

(Colossians 2:23)

During the spring of 1944, the British built a massive army base near Dover. The Germans readily believed that an invasion army was gathering at the narrowest point of the English Channel to mount an assault on the European mainland at Calais. German spies sent back information: the port was full of landing craft, the land around it had been turned into airfields, the airwaves were full of radio traffic and the great General Patton had arrived to conduct troop exercises on the beaches. But what looked like an army base was not an army base at all. The landing craft were dummies, the airfields were dummies, the radio messages were dummies and the army exercises were dummies too. It was all an elaborate deception which tricked the Germans into moving their troops away from Normandy, where the D-Day landings would actually take place a few weeks later.

We have an enemy and he wants to deceive us in the same way. The word *Devil* comes from the Greek word for *Liar*, and Jesus tells us in John 8:44 that *"when he lies, he speaks his native language."* Because the Christians at Colossae had failed to dig deep roots into Jesus, they had fallen easy prey to the Devil's deceptions. Paul mentions four dummies that had fooled the Colossians, and it appears that the false teachers in the city were teaching a mishmash of all four. These dummies still fool many believers today and we still need to be on our guard against them.

The first dummy fooled the Colossians into relying on *Jesus-Plus-Special-Knowledge*. Paul warns them against this in 2:1–8, saying that they are in grave danger of falling for *"hollow and deceptive philosophy, which depends on human tradition and the basic principles of this world rather than on Christ."* Perhaps the Colossians were so influenced by their Greek worldview that they made some subtle changes to the Gospel in order to make it fit a little better with the presuppositions of their culture. We can be just as tempted to change the Gospel to fit better with our commitment to human reason and to modern science. When we are tempted to deny the divine inspiration of Scripture, the reality of miracles or God's active work in creation, we need to listen to Blaise Pascal. The French philosopher warned against the limits of our worldview by observing that *"The supreme function of reason is to show man that some things are beyond reason."*[1]

The second dummy fooled the Colossians into relying on *Jesus-Plus-Religious-Rituals*. Colossae was not a very Jewish city, which is why Paul never quotes from the Old Testament in this letter, but its citizens were very attracted by the antiquity of many Jewish traditions. We can tell from 2:11–12 that the false teachers were advocating circumcision, just like their counterparts a decade earlier in nearby Galatia. We can also tell from 2:16 that they were advocating Jewish food laws, Jewish Sabbath-observance and Jewish feast days as ways to deepen their walk with the Lord.

The Devil wants us to believe that we would never fall for these four dummies, so let me illustrate how this might look in modern clothes. When the official Roman Catholic catechism teaches that *"through baptism we are freed from sin and reborn as sons of God,"* it falls for the deception that Paul addresses in 2:11–12.[2] It views water baptism in the same way that the false

---

[1] This is the 267th of Blaise Pascal's *Pensées* (1670).

[2] Article 1213 of the *Catechism of the Catholic Church*, taken directly from the Vatican website.

teachers viewed circumcision, as an outward ritual through which human hands achieve something which only Jesus can do in response to our faith through the power of his Holy Spirit.[3] Protestants can be just as susceptible to this deception, as was demonstrated by the American Puritans who founded the New Haven Colony. They fell into the trap Paul warns against in 2:16 when they passed a law in 1656 which ruled that *"profanation of the Lord's Day shall be punished by fine, imprisonment, or corporeal punishment; and if proudly, and with a high hand against the authority of God – with death."*[4]

Paul warns us in 2:17 that the Jewish rituals in the Old Testament were merely shadows of the Messiah who was to come. Shadows may look bigger and more impressive than the real object, but that doesn't make them real. However impressive our religious rituals may appear, they are toxic if they stop us from trusting in Jesus alone.

The third dummy fooled the Colossians into relying on *Jesus-Plus-Visions-of-Angels*. Paul tells us in 2:18–20 that the false teachers pretended to be humble and yet boasted about their deep experiences of angelic beings.[5] They appear to have argued that, since Jesus had now ascended into heaven, he was too far away to help them and they needed mediators to connect them with their far-off Saviour.[6] This may sound odd to us, but we can easily fall into the same deception ourselves. Archaeologists have found a Roman amulet not too far from Colossae which invokes the names of four angels: *"Michael,*

---

[3] Paul does not link Old Testament circumcision to Christian baptism in order to teach us to baptize babies. He does so to teach us how different Christian baptism is from Old Testament circumcision! It is only true Christian baptism if a person has *"faith in the working of God, who raised him from the dead."*

[4] Quoted by Alice Morse Earle in *Sabbath in Puritan New England* (2007).

[5] Paul tells us in 2:18 that a person who boasts in spiritual experiences is very fleshly.

[6] This is why Paul states so firmly in 1:16, 1:20, 2:10 and 2:15 that Jesus is superior to these celestial beings.

Gabriel, Ouriel, Raphael – protect the wearer!"[7] It isn't difficult to imagine a Catholic going to Mary and the saints for similar help. Nor is it hard to imagine a Protestant going to his pastor or to members of his midweek Bible study group instead of directly to the Lord. We can all turn to mediators instead of pursuing a deeper walk with Jesus as the only Mediator between human beings and God the Father (1 Timothy 2:5).

The fourth dummy fooled the Colossians into relying on *Jesus-Plus-Self-Denial.* Paul tells us in 2:20–23 that the false teachers gave the Christians lots of rules, telling them that they could make themselves godlier by refusing to touch, taste and handle certain things. We can easily fall for this lie ourselves, which is why Paul warns us that asceticism looks wise on the outside but such *"self-imposed worship"* has no power to change anyone.[8] Fasting doesn't make desires go away – it actually makes them stronger![9] We cannot become godlier by relying on rules to change us from the outside in, but only by relying on the power of Jesus' death and resurrection to change us from the inside out.[10]

Paul uses very strong language in these verses to stop us falling for these four dummies of the Devil. He uses a technical word from the athletic games when he tells us in 2:18 that we must not allow the Devil to *disqualify us from our prize.* Make no doubt about it, the stakes are high and the Devil is trying to hoodwink you. He wants to fool you with one of these four dummies into forgetting that Jesus Christ alone is everything you need.

---

[7] Clinton E. Arnold describes this amulet in *The Colossian Syncretism* (1995).

[8] The Greek word for *self-imposed worship* in 2:23 is *ethelothrēskeia.* It means literally *worship-of-what-we-want.* Asceticism isn't an aid to godliness. It is an act of rebellion in disguise.

[9] Paul argues in 1 Corinthians 7:5–9 that fasting from sex makes us more, not less, likely to fall into sexual sin.

[10] Paul uses a Greek aorist tense in 2:20 to tell us that *we have died* with Jesus through the Gospel. He will go on to explain how Jesus sanctifies us from the inside out at the start of the next chapter.

What Not to Wear (3:1–14)

Since you have taken off your old self with its practices and have put on the new self... clothe yourselves with compassion, kindness, humility, gentleness and patience.

(Colossians 3:9–12)

A week before my wife and I got married, we gave each other permission to throw out any of each other's clothes we didn't like instead of moving them into our new married home. If I remember rightly, I got the raw end of the deal. I threw out three items of my wife's clothing. She threw out three bin bags of mine. And the most painful item that went in the rubbish bag was my precious orange fleece.

It wasn't just that I loved my orange sleeveless fleece, although I did. It was the sheer irony of my wife telling me that she hated it, because I had gone out and bought it in order to look good for our first date together. I thought it looked amazing, but my wife told me it belonged to my bachelor days. When she wasn't looking, I took it out of the bin bag. It's still hanging on a hook on the back of my office door as I write this chapter.

Hold that thought, because it will help you to understand one of the most important passages in Colossians. Paul starts chapter 3 with the Greek word *"therefore,"* just like Ephesians 4:1, because this is the turning point between his outline of the Gospel in the first two chapters of this letter and his application of the Gospel in the final two chapters of the letter. Having warned us that none of the Devil's dummies can sanctify us, but only Jesus, he explains himself a little further. He tells the

Colossians that it is a bit like the orange fleece that is hanging on my door.

In 3:1–4, Paul reminds the Colossians that their life has changed. He doesn't need to give them a series of commands to help them become like Jesus – he has just told them in 2:16–23 that external commands are powerless to sanctify. He simply needs to encourage them, as he did the Ephesians, to live in the good of who they are. Their faith in the Gospel means that they are now in Jesus, so it follows that they have died with him (2:20),[1] been raised to new life with him (3:1), been hidden in God with him (3:3) and been primed for glory with him (3:4).[2] They do not need to strive after godliness as if it were not already in their possession. They simply need to be on earth who they are in heaven (3:2). They are in Jesus and Jesus is in them. They simply need to live out who they already are.[3]

In 3:5–8, Paul reminds the Colossians how ugly their old way of living used to be. They fooled themselves that they looked good – a bit like me with my orange fleece – but none of these things has any beauty next to what they now know of Jesus' character.[4] *"Because of these, the wrath of God is coming,"* Paul warns us, so we cannot live in them any longer.[5] We need to wave goodbye to our *"earthly nature."* God doesn't sanctify us by reforming our flesh; he sanctifies us by killing it.

---

[1] In Romans 6:6 and Galatians 2:20, Paul says we were crucified with Jesus. We have no more reason to doubt this than John 19:32 when it uses the same Greek word to tell us two robbers were crucified with him too.

[2] Note the massive contrast between the two fates that are open to people in 3:4 and 3:6.

[3] Paul uses present imperatives to tell us in 3:1 and 3:2 to set our hearts on things above. He is therefore saying literally, *"go on setting your hearts"* on what has happened to you in Jesus every day.

[4] Colossians 3 contains an abbreviated version of the list in Ephesians 4:17–5:20. Note the clear echo in 3:5 of Paul's statement in Ephesians 5:5 that such sins are a form of idolatry.

[5] A few Greek manuscripts read that *"The wrath of God is coming on the sons of disobedience,"* but this is almost certainly a later corruption of the text by scribes who had the words of Ephesians 5:6 in their heads.

In 3:9–11, Paul tells us that we have already waved goodbye to this way of living. He uses Greek words that were normally used for taking off and putting on clothes when he tells us that we *have taken off* our old self with all its evil practices[6] and *have put on* the new self, which is becoming more and more like Jesus as we come to know him more.[7] He uses both of these Greek words in the aorist tense, which means that they refer to something that has already happened in the past. We don't need to take off our old wicked lifestyle because we took it off when we were crucified with Jesus – whether we are Jew or Greek, educated or uneducated, slave or free. Jesus is all that any of us needs.[8]

In 3:12–14, Paul deals with a very natural objection. If we have taken off our old self and if it has been crucified with Jesus, why does it often still seem so alive?! Paul answers our question, but we need to watch his tenses closely to catch his meaning. He says it's like the orange fleece hanging on the back my door.[9] We still face a daily battle over what to wear and what not to wear.

Our old sinful self has been dealt with once and for all through the fact that we are in Jesus. It died with us on the cross with Jesus, and it stayed dead when we were buried and raised to new life in Jesus (3:1–4). Our faith in Jesus means that we have taken off our old self and have put on our new self (3:9–10). That's what it means to have repented and been counted into Jesus by God's grace. There is no such thing as a person who has been justified by God but who is not sanctified in Jesus.

---

[6] Paul uses the Greek phrase *palaios anthrōpos* in 3:9 to refer to our *old man*. This is the same phrase that he also uses in Romans 6:6 and Ephesians 4:22.

[7] Paul told us in 1:15 that Jesus is the *eikōn*, the exact *image*, of God. Now he uses the same word to tell us in 3:10 that we are also being transformed into the image of God through our faith in Jesus.

[8] 3:11 echoes Paul's teaching in Galatians 3:28 and Ephesians 4:6. See also 1 Corinthians 1:30.

[9] This same mixture of tenses is used in Romans 13:12–14, Galatians 5:16–26 and Ephesians 4:17–24.

We simply need to live out our new heavenly identity in Jesus down here on the earth.[10]

But this faith isn't passive. We need to express it by letting the Holy Spirit put our old self to death daily whenever it tries to rise up from the dead like one of the zombies in Michael Jackson's *Thriller* video. That's why Paul uses an aorist imperative in 3:5 to tell us that we must count what belongs to our earthly nature dead once and for all. It's why he uses another aorist imperative in 3:8 to tell us that we need to throw away our old clothing once and for all. We need to express our active faith in the Gospel by letting the Holy Spirit clothe us every day in Jesus' way of living, which is why Paul uses a present imperative in 3:12 to tell us literally to *"go on clothing yourselves with compassion, kindness, humility, gentleness and patience."*[11] He tells us to complete our outfit with the overcoat of love in 3:14.[12]

My orange fleece belongs to my bachelor days but it is still hanging there on my office door. Sometimes when I look at it fondly and reminisce about my bachelor days, I suddenly find that it is off the hook and on my back. Paul tells us not to do the same thing and gaze back fondly on our sins. We may never be fully sinless in this life, but we should definitely sin less! We simply need to embrace the fact that our old self has died with Jesus and ask the Holy Spirit to bring our lifestyle into line with our new identity. When we set our minds on things above and not on earthly things, Jesus gives us the strength to follow through on what we know we should and shouldn't wear.

---

[10] Paul repeats this reasoning in 3:12. He tells us to live this way because we are already *"God's chosen people, holy and dearly loved."*

[11] Verses 5–8 are about putting off a wicked lifestyle of sins of commission. Verses 12–14 are about putting on a godly lifestyle, dealing with sins of omission too.

[12] Paul also describes love as the overarching feature of the Christian life in Romans 13:8–10, in Galatians 5:13–14 and 6:2, and in Ephesians 5:2.

The Emperor's New Clothes
(3:12–4:1)

Therefore, as God's chosen people, holy and dearly loved, clothe yourselves with compassion, kindness, humility, gentleness and patience.

(Colossians 3:12)

In Hans Christian Andersen's famous children's story, two swindlers trick the emperor into stripping off his royal robes and dressing in clothes made from material that is visible to everyone except for those who are hopelessly stupid. He cannot see the clothes they are selling him, but he dares not admit it for fear of appearing stupid. His courtiers and subjects dare not admit it either. Only a child who is watching the emperor's procession dares to shout out that the emperor is actually naked. As Christians, we can sometimes be like the characters in Hans Christian Andersen's story when we talk about being filled with the Holy Spirit.

You see, the early Christians *knew* that they had been clothed with the Holy Spirit as Paul describes.[1] Jesus told them in Luke 24:49 that *"I am going to send you what my Father has promised; but stay in the city until you have been clothed with power from on high,"* but they left Jerusalem because they knew for sure that they had been clothed with the Holy Spirit. They were not like the emperor in his new clothes, hoping that they were clothed but nursing secret fears of being exposed as naked.

---

[1] Paul uses similar language to Colossians 3 in Romans 13:12–14, Galatians 3:27 and Ephesians 4:24.

Paul wants us to know for sure like those early Christians, so he gives us several ways to tell if we are full of the Holy Spirit.

In 3:12–14, Paul says we can tell if we have been clothed with the Holy Spirit *by our attitude towards others*. He echoes his teaching on the fruit of the Spirit in Galatians 5:22–23 when he tells us that being filled with God's Spirit is always evidenced by the way we live our lives. The Spirit always works on the inside to make a person compassionate, kind, humble, gentle, patient and forgiving.[2] If we lack these attributes, it isn't a measure of our personality, but a measure of our experience of God. Self-centred people are more likely to be dressed in the emperor's new clothes than in the clothes of the Holy Spirit. We are not full of the Holy Spirit if we are still full of ourselves.

In 3:15, Paul says we can tell if we have been clothed with the Holy Spirit *by the way God guides us*. He used a sporting metaphor when he warned us in 2:18 not to allow the Devil to *disqualify us from our prize*, and now he uses the same word again to tell us to *"let the peace of Christ be your umpire."*[3] People who rush around aimlessly in search of external signs from God are seldom full of the Holy Spirit. Spirit-filled Christians can read Christ's mind as the Spirit gives them peace or lack of peace about each course of action.[4]

In 3:16–17, Paul says we can tell if we have been clothed with the Holy Spirit *by the way in which we worship*. These verses echo Ephesians 5:18–20 so closely that it is clear Paul views *the message of Christ dwelling in us richly* as the same thing as our *being filled with the Spirit*.[5] One of the signs that

---

[2] People who know that God has forgiven them forgive others. That's why Jesus repeatedly says we have not been forgiven if we refuse to forgive others (Matthew 6:12, 14–15; 18:21–35; Mark 11:25; Luke 6:37).

[3] The word in 2:18 was *katabrabeuō*. The word in 3:15 is simply *brabeuō*.

[4] This is the promise of 1 Corinthians 2:10–16, Galatians 5:22 and Philippians 4:7.

[5] This is a great example of why Colossians is the Rosetta Stone that unlocks much of Paul's teaching. Word and Spirit are not opposites. God's Word promises that he will fill us with his Holy Spirit.

we are full of God's Spirit is that we get excited about gathering with likeminded people to sing worship songs.[6] 1 Chronicles 12:18 tells us literally that *"the Spirit clothed Amasai,"* one of David's soldiers, and that as a result he sang impromptu praises to his king. Paul tells us that Spirit-filled Christians will also love singing psalms and hymns with one another, as well as launching into similar impromptu *"songs inspired by the Spirit"* in praise of their heavenly King.[7]

In 3:17, Paul says we can tell if we have been clothed with the Holy Spirit *by the way we go about our daily lives.* 2 Chronicles 24:20 tells us literally that *"the Spirit of God clothed Zechariah,"* and that as a result he refused to conform to the backslidden lifestyle of the rest of Judah. He became so passionate to see God glorified that he was willing to die rather than put up with his nation's half-heartedness any longer. One of the signs we have been filled with the Holy Spirit is that we refuse to compartmentalize our lives; we proclaim Jesus as Lord over every single thing we do. Are you living as Paul expects when he tells you, *"Whatever you do, whether in words or deed, do it all in the name of the Lord Jesus, giving thanks to God the Father through him"*?

In 3:18–21, Paul says we can tell if we have been clothed with the Holy Spirit *by the way we relate to the other people in our home.* Paul condenses seventeen verses in Ephesians into just four verses here, but his point is very simple. If we are home to the Holy Spirit, the people in our home will be the first to notice. Spirit-filled wives submit to their husbands,[8] and Spirit-filled husbands are loving and forgiving towards their wives. Spirit-

---

[6] Paul is as Trinitarian in his language here as he was in the parallel passage in Ephesians 5:18–20. Father, Son and Holy Spirit are all involved in Christian worship.

[7] We saw earlier that the word *pneumatikos* means more than *spiritual.* It means *empowered-by-the-Spirit.*

[8] As in Ephesians 5, Paul uses different Greek words for wives *submitting* and for children and slaves *obeying.* Paul also says wives should submit to their own husbands, not women submit to men in general.

filled children obey their parents,[9] and Spirit-filled parents are gentle with their children because they know that how they treat them shapes the way in which they relate to God as their Father.[10] It was a child who pointed out to the emperor that he was naked. It is very often family members who do us a similar favour.

In 3:22–4:1, Paul says we can tell if we have been clothed with the Holy Spirit *by the way we act at work*. He tells us that Spirit-filled workers are always cheerful and hardworking because they know their work is an act of worship towards Jesus their true Master. He tells us that Spirit-filled bosses never mistreat their workers because they know that they will stand before a heavenly Master of their own. Ray Kroc, the founder of the McDonald's chain of fast-food restaurants joked that *"I believe in God, family, and McDonald's – and in the office, that order is reversed."*[11] Paul tells us that the people we work with are often the best placed to tell us if we are truly full of the Holy Spirit.

You may find these verses encouraging, reassuring you that you have indeed experienced the fullness of the Holy Spirit which Paul describes throughout his letters. Alternatively, they may convince you that you have not yet been clothed with the Holy Spirit after all. Do not be discouraged. It is a sign of progress to confess that you are naked. Paul invites you to get on your knees and to ask Jesus to fill you with his Spirit as he has promised. Paul encourages you not to settle, like many Christians, for a theoretical experience of the Holy Spirit. He tells you that it's time to step out of the emperor's new clothes.

---

[9] As in Ephesians 6:1, Paul tells children to obey their *parents* and not just their fathers. Mothers have their own authority over their children and do not simply wield the delegated authority of the children's father.

[10] Verse 21 emphasizes even more strongly than Ephesians 6:4 that poor parenting can crush a child's spirit.

[11] Ray Kroc in his book *Grinding It Out: The Making of McDonald's* (1977).

Five Simple Steps (4:2–6)

Be wise in the way you act towards outsiders; make the most of every opportunity.

Colossians 4:2–6 is very unusual. It's unusual compared to the rest of Colossians, and it's even more unusual compared to Paul's letters as a whole. The fact that these verses are so unusual is what makes them so insightful.

These five verses spoil the closeness of the parallel between Paul's two letters to Ephesus and Colossae. We have seen that Colossians 1:1–2:5 closely parallels Paul's explanation of the Gospel in Ephesians 1–3, and that Colossians 3:1–4:1 closely parallels his application of how to live in view of the Gospel in Ephesians 4:1–6:9. But these five verses do not parallel Paul's teaching in Ephesians 6:10–20 on how to do battle with demons. The Colossians were already far too focused on angels and demons, so Paul keeps their gaze on Jesus by only paralleling Ephesians 6:18–20. But this isn't the main thing that is unusual in these five verses. Paul does something here that he does not do anywhere else in his New Testament letters.

Paul gives us some practical teaching on how to share the Gospel with unbelievers. It may sound odd, but nowhere else in any of Paul's letters does he give us similar training in personal evangelism. Elsewhere he describes the Gospel, defends the Gospel and tells us that the Gospel is not tied to any race or culture, but he never gets this practical about how we should actually share the Gospel. He just assumes it will come easily to people who are heirs to Jesus' promise that *"You will receive power when the Holy Spirit comes on you; and you will be my witnesses"* (Acts 1:8). These verses are very valuable because here, like nowhere else, Paul tells us how to share the Gospel as Spirit-filled witnesses of Jesus.

Step One is to *allow the Holy Spirit to help us pray* (4:2). Paul uses the same Greek word that Luke uses in Acts 1:14 and 2:42 to describe the early believers *devoting themselves* to steadfast prayer, because if we want to be as fruitful as the early Christians, we need the Holy Spirit to help us pray as they did.[1] We need to pray doggedly and determinedly for unbelievers, looking out for what God is doing in their lives and thanking God for any sign of progress. James Fraser, the British missionary to the Lisu people of China at the start of the twentieth century, discovered the power of evangelistic prayer. Treacherous conditions prevented him from reaching the mountain villages for eight months of the year, so he decided to devote the time he would have spent travelling back and forth to concerted prayer for them instead. He found to his surprise that he saw more fruit from his four months a year in the mountains than he did from his twelve months a year in the lowland villages. He concluded that *"Solid, lasting missionary work is done on our knees... I used to think that prayer should have the first place and teaching the second. I now feel that it would be truer to give prayer the first, second and third place, and teaching the fourth."*[2]

Step Two is to *ask God to open up great doors of opportunity* (4:3). Paul reminds us that he is a prisoner under house arrest and in chains, because he wants us to grasp that he is too weak to step out of his front door without God's help. It's exactly the same for us when it comes to sharing the Gospel. Paul wants us to pray for God-given opportunities to share the mystery of

---

[1] Zechariah 12:10 describes the Holy Spirit as *"the Spirit of grace and supplication."* Paul tells us in Romans 8:26–27 that the Holy Spirit therefore helps us in our praying.

[2] Quoted by Geraldine Taylor in *Behind the Ranges: The Life-Changing Story of J.O. Fraser* (1944).

Christ with unbelievers.[3] The more we pray, the more the doors of opportunity will open.

Step Three is to *ask God to help us speak clearly* (4:4). Paul does not ask the Colossians to pray for a list of individuals in Rome, because successful evangelism refuses to restrict its sights to a handful of friends. Most Christians spend too much time on too few people, which is why Jesus warned us in Matthew 13:1–23 that we need to scatter our seed widely if we want to see lasting fruit anywhere. We must not downsize the Great Commission to go and make disciples of all nations by treating it as a command to create a prayer list of a dozen non-Christian friends. Of course we should pray for individuals, but our main prayers should be for ourselves: that we will proclaim the Gospel clearly, anytime and anywhere.

This leads into Step Four, which is *to share the Gospel at any and every opportunity* (4:5).[4] We must guard against the idea that we need to build bridges of friendship in order to earn the right to share the Gospel with people. Paul tells us to be wise in the way we act towards outsiders because it is true that people respond better when they hear the Gospel from somebody they trust,[5] but this is only part of the story. Paul believed that God had entrusted him with a message that belonged to unbelievers and that he needed to steward this commission faithfully (1:25–26). When he tells us to make the most of every opportunity to share, with both friends and strangers, he is telling us we do not need to earn the right to speak. He is telling us we have no right to remain silent.

---

[3] Paul also calls the Gospel the *mustērion*, the *secret revelation*, of God in the parallel Ephesians 6:19. He wants to emphasize that evangelism is not difficult. It is absolutely impossible without the Holy Spirit's power.

[4] As in Ephesians 5:16, Paul tells us literally to *"redeem the time."* Time is running out but we can redeem lost time by making sure we milk it of every opportunity to speak for the Lord.

[5] This comment also shows us that Paul expects us to live our daily lives among unbelievers. He cannot conceive that anybody who is clothed with the Holy Spirit might want to withdraw into a Christian ghetto.

Step Five is to remember that *how we share is just as important as what we share* (4:6). Paul tells us to speak graciously and attractively because it is possible to win an argument but lose a person.[6] Paul Jones, the lead singer of the 1960s' pop group Manfred Mann, dates his Christian conversion to a television debate in which he argued over faith with the newly converted Cliff Richard. He recalls humiliating the more famous singer by rubbishing his faith, but he also remembers being overwhelmed by Cliff Richard's gracious response to his point-scoring. If we are concerned about scoring points against unbelievers, we will only score own goals. But if we share in a manner that shows we have been clothed with the Holy Spirit, we will win people to Christ even if we lose the argument.

Paul confesses in the parallel verses in Ephesians that he finds evangelism scary. He identifies with all the reasons we don't take these five steps more often. But being clothed with the Holy Spirit is what enables him to overcome his fears, like Gideon. Judges 6:14 and 34 tell us literally that the Lord told Gideon to *"Go in the strength you have"* and then *"the Spirit of the Lord clothed Gideon with himself"*, enabling him to go out and win a mighty victory in battle. Paul promises us that we can do the same if we have God on the inside. Jesus has clothed us with the Holy Spirit and empowered us to take these five simple steps to share the Gospel.

---

[6] Paul refers to seasoning our speech with *salt* because salt was used to prevent decay and to make bland food more attractive.

Meandering into Trouble (4:7–18)

He is always wrestling in prayer for you, that you may stand firm in all the will of God, mature and fully assured.

(Colossians 4:12)

Not many people have heard of the River Lycus, which flowed past the Phrygian cities of Colossae, Laodicea and Hierapolis, but it was a tributary into a much more famous river. When the Roman travel writer Strabo describes the River Meander, which dominated the geography of the region, he tells us that *"Its course is so exceedingly winding that everything else which is winding is referred to as meandering because of the course of this river."*[1] As Paul draws his letter to the Colossians to a close, he is still concerned that they are meandering into trouble.

In 4:7–8, Paul tells the Colossians that he is sending Tychicus to look out for them. He was more than just a postman. Acts 20:4 tells us that he was a leading member of Paul's team. Paul commends his spiritual authority to the Colossians by telling them that he is *"a dear brother, a faithful minister and fellow servant in the Lord."*[2] Paul says this to prepare them for the fact that Tychicus will need to take a firm grip on the church when he arrives in their city. Some Greek manuscripts tell us he is coming *"that you may know about our circumstances,"* but

---

[1] Strabo wrote this in about 20 AD in his *Geography* (12.8.15).

[2] Paul refers to Tychicus literally as a *fellow slave* in the Lord, possibly to prepare the Colossians for the return of Philemon's runaway slave Onesimus. They needed to remember that we are all slaves of Christ too.

many others tell us more ominously that he is coming *"that he may know about **your** circumstances."* Tychicus would soon discover whether they were strong on the inside or whether their faith had been weakened by the false teachers. If they were meandering through life like the river that dominated their region, Tychicus would make them run faster and stronger through the Gospel.

In 4:9, Paul prepares the Colossians for another letter in Tychicus' postbag. He mentions a runaway slave named Onesimus who is the subject of Paul's letter to Philemon. As we will see shortly, the return of Onesimus would shake the Colossians out of complacent Christianity. Roman law decreed that runaway slaves like him must die, but Paul calls him *"our faithful and dear brother, who is one of you."* The Colossians would not be able to respond half-heartedly when Onesimus walked in through their door. It would force them to sit up and show their whole city just how deep and powerfully the river of grace ran throughout their congregation.

In 4:10–11, Paul reminds the Colossians that following Jesus will cost them everything. He mentions Aristarchus, who came from Thessalonica and who is mentioned in Acts 20:4 as another leading member of Paul's team.[3] He tells the Colossians that Aristarchus is now in a Roman prison, and that he finds this so distressing that he needs to be comforted by his friends Justus and Mark. Everybody knew that Mark used to be a half-hearted meanderer himself and that Paul had fallen out with Mark's cousin Barnabas over the fact that Mark gave up when things got tough among the churches of Galatia.[4] The news that even Mark had now learned to be strong on the inside through the Gospel would encourage them to stop meandering half-heartedly themselves.

---

[3] Having barely survived a riot at Ephesus (Acts 19:29), Aristarchus sailed with Paul to Rome (Acts 27:2).

[4] Acts 13:13 and 15:36–40. This is the same John Mark who wrote Mark's gospel and who later went on to serve as part of Peter's team (1 Peter 5:13).

In 4:12–14, Paul reminds the Colossians that they need to be strong against the false teachers. He is at pains to emphasize that his team in Rome is very much a non-Jewish affair, and that they therefore fully understand the challenges of converting to Christ from a pagan background. Paul is working with Luke, a Gentile doctor from Antioch who is busy chronicling Paul's missionary journeys among the pagans, and he is working with Greeks such as Demas and Tychicus and Aristarchus.[5] Most importantly of all, he is working with Epaphras, *"who is one of you"* – a Colossian Christian who knows how important it is not to fall for the superstitions which are popular in their region. Paul tells the Colossians that Epaphras is praying that they will stop their meandering: *"He is always wrestling in prayer for you, that you may stand firm in all the will of God, mature and fully assured."*

In 4:15–16, Paul reminds the Colossians that the churches in nearby Laodicea and Hierapolis are engaged in the same struggle against false teaching and compromise.[6] He tells them to pass on their letter to the Laodiceans when they have read it,[7] and to read his recent letter to the Laodiceans so that they can draw strength for the fight together.[8]

We do not know how the Colossians responded to Paul's letter, but we do know how the Laodiceans responded. Jesus dictated a follow-up letter to Laodicea thirty-five years later in Revelation 3:14–22 to confront their continued spiritual meandering. *"Because you are lukewarm – neither hot nor cold –*

---

[5] Although Paul did not know it at the time, Demas would tragically abandon him later because he looked back fondly at the sinful world (2 Timothy 4:10). None of us can afford to ignore Paul's warnings.

[6] Laodicea was 12 miles from Colossae and Hierapolis was 14 miles from Colossae.

[7] The name Nympha was used for both men and women. Some Greek manuscripts read that the church met in *his* house, while others read that it met in *her* house.

[8] This letter has not survived. The New Testament only preserves a fraction of Paul's letters.

I am about to spit you out of my mouth," he warned them. They had not listened to Paul's teaching about how to be strong on the inside through the Gospel, so Jesus told them, *"You do not realise that you are wretched, pitiful, poor, blind and naked. I counsel you to buy from me gold refined in the fire, so that you can become rich; and white clothes to wear, so that you can cover your shameful nakedness."*

So much for Laodicea. Paul hopes for a far better response from the Colossians. When he tells one of their young men in 4:17 to *"See to it that you complete the ministry you have received in the Lord,"* he might as well have been talking to the entire congregation.[9] As he takes the pen from his scribe in 4:18 and signs off the letter in his own handwriting as a mark of its authenticity, he reminds the Colossians that his words carry authority.[10] He expects them to take his teaching seriously because, as he told them in the first verse of this letter, he is *"an apostle of Christ Jesus by the will of God."*

Paul is in chains but he has been made strong through God's grace. Now he invites the Colossians to be strong like him. If they stop their meandering, get radical in dealing with the false teachers and lay hold of the Gospel fully, then their fate will not be like that of the Laodiceans. God will see their faith and make them strong on the inside.

---

[9] Philemon 2 suggests that Archippus was the son of Philemon, one of the leading Christians in Colossae.

[10] Paul used scribes to write his letters (Romans 16:22), but always signed them personally because he knew that some false letters were circulating in his name (2 Thessalonians 2:2; 3:17).

Colossians Chapter Five
(Philemon 1–25)

To Philemon our dear friend and fellow worker... and
to the church that meets in your home.

(Philemon 1–2)

I can see why the early Christians placed the twenty-seven books of the New Testament in the order they did, but it isn't always terribly helpful. They grouped together Paul's nine letters to churches, the longest to the shortest, and then they grouped together his four letters to individuals in the same way. Unfortunately, this means that five books come between Colossians and Philemon. That's quite unhelpful because Philemon is Colossians chapter five.

Tychicus did not just leave Rome with two letters in his postbag, or even three if he was also carrying the letter to the Laodiceans. He was also carrying in his postbag another letter to the church at Colossae, which asked one of its leaders to make a very practical response to the Gospel which makes us strong on the inside.

In verses 1–3, Paul links this letter to Philemon very closely with the one that he sent to the church as a whole. He names Timothy as his co-author and yet uses the pronoun *"I"* throughout the letter, which is exactly what he did throughout Colossians. He names one of its recipients as Archippus, the same young man he addressed in the penultimate verse of Colossians. Archippus was probably Philemon's son and Apphia was probably Philemon's wife. We can tell they were a leading family in the church from the way Paul calls Philemon his *"fellow worker"* and Archippus his *"fellow soldier,"* as well as from the fact that the church met in their home.[1] Paul addresses the letter to the church as a whole and not just to their family, beginning with the same blessing that began his letter to the Colossians.[2] These are all clues which inform us that we are not reading a letter to an isolated individual. We are reading Colossians chapter five.

In verses 4–7, Paul builds a good rapport with Philemon before making his request. He is not simply trying to charm him into saying yes – the echo of Colossians 1:3–14 confirms that he really did pray for Christian leaders in the same way that he prayed for churches. He genuinely thanked God whenever he prayed for Philemon because Epaphras had told him that Philemon had the kind of *love* and *faith* and *partnership* in the Gospel that Paul wanted to see in all of the Colossians. Paul tells Philemon that he is very encouraged to hear that one of the key leaders in Colossae has been made strong on the inside through the Holy Spirit and that he is strengthening the rest of the church through his example.

In verses 8–9, Paul prepares the ground for the big request he is about to make of Philemon. Whereas he started his letter to the Colossians by emphasizing that he was *"an apostle of Christ Jesus,"* he starts his letter to Philemon by emphasizing that he is *"a prisoner of Christ Jesus"* instead. He is looking for sympathy, so he reminds Philemon that he is writing to him as *"an old man and now also a prisoner of Christ Jesus."*[3] Paul uses

[1] Paul uses Greek singular pronouns to refer to *"your"* home and to Philemon as *"you"* throughout the letter, because Philemon was the legal owner of his house and slaves. Paul uses Greek plural pronouns for *"you"* in verses 3, 22 and 25 in order to include Philemon's family and friends in what he is saying.

[2] We saw in Colossians 1:2 that some Greek manuscripts have a shortened version of this blessing, but Paul essentially begins both letters in the exact same way.

[3] The Greek word *presbutēs* could mean that Paul is either an *old man* or an *ambassador*. Unlike the verb in Ephesians 6:20, it could not mean that he is an *elder* because that would be *presbuteros* instead.

all of his people skills to build up to his big request in a way which will be very hard to refuse. With Philemon's wife and son and the entire church looking on, Paul is finally ready to make his appeal.

In verses 10–16, Paul pleads for Philemon to have mercy on his runaway slave.[4] Paul has already commended Onesimus to the whole church as a *"faithful and dear brother"* in Colossians 4:9, but he is much coyer now and does not speak his name until the very final Greek word of verse 10.[5] The name Onesimus means *Useful*, so Paul plays on this meaning when he admits freely that until now Onesimus has proved anything but useful to his master.[6] To crown it all, he has run away and travelled over 1,000 miles to try and lose himself in the crowded streets of the imperial capital. But in Rome he met Paul. He heard the Gospel and he surrendered his life to Jesus. As a result, he has been made strong and very useful through the Holy Spirit. Paul feels genuine love for his new convert, calling him *"my son"* and *"my very heart."* Although Philemon has the right to have him executed under Roman law, Paul begs him to view his runaway slave *"as a dear brother"* who is *"very dear to me but even dearer to you."* This is where the rubber of the Gospel hits the road. What will Philemon do with his new *"brother in the Lord"*?

In verses 17–21, Paul does more than preach the Gospel. He embodies it. He imitates the way that Jesus laid down his life so that all of God's runaways could be brought home. He asks Philemon to charge him for all of his slave's transgressions, including all of the money that he stole from him when he ran

---

[4] The letter does not actually state clearly that Onesimus ran away – he could have just been in Rome on an errand – but verses 17–19 suggest strongly that he did.

[5] The Holy Spirit does not empower us so that we can grow lazy in our people skills. Paul shows the importance of interpersonal skills by praising Philemon for refreshing people's hearts (verse 7) as a prelude to urging him to refresh his own heart too (verse 20)!

[6] Paul also uses the verb at the root of the name Onesimus when he says in verse 20 that he wants to *benefit* from Philemon.

away. He asks Philemon to shower his slave with all of the honour and affection that he owes to Paul for sharing with him the message of salvation.[7] He fully expects that Philemon will respond well to this act of substitutionary intercession, because Philemon can plainly see that it is the very same prayer that Jesus prayed to God the Father when he saved him.

In verses 22–25, Paul signs off the letter, having laid out his request for Philemon to consider. He tells him that he would love to visit his house if he ever gets to make a trip to Colossae,[8] and he tells him the sad news that Epaphras has now become a fellow prisoner in Rome too. Visiting Paul with news about the false teachers at Colossae marked him out to the authorities as a dangerous collaborator with their prisoner. Paul did not mention this imprisonment in Colossians 1–4, but he does so now in order to put Philemon's own problems in stark perspective at the end of Colossians chapter five.

Tychicus carried this extra letter in his postbag to help Onesimus, but he also carried it in order to help you and me. It gives us a window into one of the real-life situations in the church at Colossae and it sheds light on how we are to live out the Gospel in our daily lives. Understanding what Jesus has done for us has to shape all of our actions, which is why Paul ends this letter with a prayer that God will strengthen our spirit through the grace of the Lord.[9] Only Jesus can change us from the inside out. Only he can fill us with his Spirit and make us strong on the inside.

---

[7] As a wealthy homeowner, Philemon must have travelled frequently to Ephesus. Paul's warm affection towards him suggests that they knew each other well, despite Paul never having been to Colossae.

[8] Paul would be in prison for another year and a half, and there is no record that he ever made it to Colossae.

[9] When Paul refers to *"your spirit"* in verse 25, the word for *your* is plural and the word for *spirit* is singular. He views Philemon, his wife, his son and the rest of the church as so united in their faith that they share one *spirit* together. Paul says something similar in Galatians 6:18, Philippians 4:23 and 1 Thessalonians 5:23.

Give Away Your Faith
(Philemon 6)

I pray that you may be active in sharing your faith, so that you will have a full understanding of every good thing we have in Christ.

(Philemon 6)

At the moment, my young children are fascinated by riddles. Here is their latest one:

Question: What is the one thing you get more of, the more you leave behind?

Answer: Footprints.

Paul throws out a similar riddle in his letter to Philemon. It is so surprising that most people miss it and many English Bibles translate it incorrectly.[1] Paul says that he prays Philemon will be active in sharing his faith with other people *"so that you will have a full understanding of every good thing we have in Christ."* He doesn't pray it so that unbelievers will understand the Gospel, although of course it means they will. Rather, he prays it because he knows that the more we give away our faith the more we come to understand it fully ourselves.

When we think about what Paul says in Philemon 6, his

---

[1] The job of translators is made difficult by the ambiguity of *hē koinōnia tēs pisteōs sou*: does it mean *the sharing of your faith* with Christians or with non-Christians? Since Philemon was already sharing his faith actively with Christians (he hosted a church in his home!), I believe it refers to his sharing his faith with non-Christians.

riddle makes perfect sense. The Gospel is the only thing that you get more of the more you give it away. The more we share with unbelievers, the more we get challenged by what we share. I am very grateful to the Christians who have discipled me over the years, but I am also very grateful to the hostile unbelievers whose questions have discipled me too. Their challenging questions have often felt like punches, but those punches have pushed me back against the ropes of Jesus and forced me to dig deeper into the Gospel so that I could come back out fighting. Even in this short letter to Philemon, Paul demonstrates for us how Christian maturity means recognizing that we need to share the Gospel with unbelievers for our own sake as much as for theirs. Yes, they need to be told the Gospel so that they can be saved, but we also need to tell them the Gospel so that they can point out all the ways in which we haven't yet fully understood it. Our continuing spiritual growth and well-being depends on our willingness to give our faith away.

Paul shows us that sharing the Gospel helps us *to understand the true depth of our sin*. He told us in Ephesians and Colossians that we were dead in our sins before Jesus saved us, but he understood this in a fresh new way when he started to share it with Onesimus. Archaeologists have found a collar worn by a slave in Ancient Rome that reads, *"I have run away. Catch me. If you take me back to my master Zininus, you'll be rewarded."*[2] The person who returned a slave would be paid cash, but the poor slave would be whipped and branded on his forehead with the letters *F-U-G*, short for *fugitivus*, the Latin word for *runaway*. Slaves with particularly strict masters would be executed. As Paul opened up his life to Onesimus and explained the Gospel to him, he understood more deeply than ever what it means to be a rebel under the sentence of sin.

Paul shows us that sharing the Gospel helps us *to understand the true depth of Jesus' sacrifice*. Roman laws were just as harsh

---

[2] Mary Johnston describes this collar in her book *Roman Life* (1957).

towards citizens who harboured runaway slaves. Paul quickly realized that there was no way to save Onesimus unless he was willing to step into his shoes. He had used the language of the slave-market when he told us in Ephesians and Colossians that Jesus *redeemed* us from our sins through his own blood,[3] but now those words took on a whole new meaning. Paul had to risk his life by meeting with Onesimus under the noses of his Roman guards. He had to sacrifice his bank balance by repaying all of the money that the slave had stolen. He had to humble himself when he asked Philemon to penalize him like a slave and to treat Onesimus as he would his beloved apostle. We can read about Jesus' act of redemption in the comforts of a library, but we can only experience what it meant for him by laying down our own lives to help the people in the streets outside.

Paul shows us that sharing the Gospel helps us *to understand the true meaning of repentance.* Saying sorry is easy, but it isn't repentance. Paul tells us in Acts 26:20 that the Gospel calls people to *"repent and turn to God and demonstrate their repentance by their deeds."* He grew in his understanding of this message as he helped new believers like Onesimus to process their conversion. As he sent Onesimus back to Colossae in order to make restitution with Philemon for the past, knowing that it might mean death, Paul gained fresh insight into what Jesus meant when he said in Luke 9:23 that *"Whoever wants to be my disciple must deny themselves and take up their cross daily and follow me."*

Paul shows us that sharing the Gospel helps us *to understand the true meaning of God's grace.* The landscape picture of our salvation is beautiful in Ephesians 2, describing how the one who reconciled us back to God has also reconciled us back to one another, but it is never more beautiful than when it is played out in relationships right before our eyes. As

---

[3] It should go without saying that Jesus did not pay Satan to free us. He defeated and plundered Satan! This redemption price was what it cost him to satisfy God's justice and to overturn our just enslavement to sin.

Philemon embraces his rebellious slave, *"no longer as a slave, but better than a slave, as a dear brother... a brother in the Lord,"* the landscape picture of salvation lights up with glory. Ignatius of Antioch tells us just how glorious the Gospel is in his letter to the Ephesians in around 110 AD. He tells us that Onesimus went on to become one of the elders of the church at Ephesus.

God has not finished Colossians chapter five. It just gets better. Paul's willingness to share his faith with Onesimus eventually sounded the death knell for slavery as a whole. Miroslav Volf points out that, the moment masters start treating slaves as their brothers, *"slavery has been abolished even if its outer institutional shell remains as an oppressive reality."*[4] Slavery was abolished in the British Empire at the start of the nineteenth century partly through Christians who wore medallions made by Josiah Wedgwood and inspired by Paul's words to Philemon. Under a picture of a black slave in chains were the words: *"Am I not a man and a brother?"*

So give away your faith. Share the Gospel with others because they need to hear it, but also share it because you know you need to discover it more deeply by sharing it with others. It doesn't matter if your evangelism yields eager converts or hostile enemies; it has been successful if it has helped you to understand the Gospel a little more. People's responses do not change the answer to Paul's amazing riddle: the Gospel is the only thing that you get more of the more you give it away.

---

[4] Miroslav Volf in *A Public Faith* (2011).

Part Four – Philippians:

Joyful on the Inside

A Year Is a Long Time
(1:1–2)

To all God's holy people in Christ Jesus at Philippi,
together with the overseers and deacons.

(Philippians 1:1)

A year is a very long time. It is when you are languishing in prison, anyway.

Paul had plenty of reasons to be cheerful when he wrote Ephesians and Colossians in 60 AD. He had just arrived in Rome and was getting used to life under house arrest while awaiting trial before Caesar. He had survived the death threats and the shipwreck, and he had even been permitted to receive visitors and to carry on his evangelistic ministry in chains. Paul must have been excited to be finally in the imperial capital. He even entertained high hopes that he would soon be released and started making travel plans about where he would go as soon as he was free.[1]

But a year is a very long time. By the time Paul wrote his letter to the Philippians, it was late in 61 or early in 62 AD, and his case had still not come to trial.[2] If we include his two years in prison at Caesarea and his journey as a prisoner to Rome, he had been in jail now for almost five years. He had been in chains for so long that he was starting to imagine he was going to die

---

[1] Philemon 22. As far as we know, Paul would never make it to Philemon's house at all.

[2] We can tell Paul wrote this letter towards the end of his imprisonment in Rome because he refers to his influence over *the palace guard* and *Caesar's household* in 1:13 and 4:22.

in jail. His friends at Philippi had grown so concerned that they sent one of their key church leaders to comfort him while his lonely wait went on.[3] The more we consider Paul's worsening situation when he wrote his letter to the Philippians, the more we expect depression and frustration to fill its pages.

That is what is so amazing about Paul's letter to the Philippians. He isn't depressed and discouraged at all. The big theme of Philippians is that he is joyful on the inside. He uses the word *joy* or *rejoice* sixteen times in these four short chapters because he is more aware of who he is in Jesus than he is of all the disappointments along the way. The Philippians saw this in the early days of his public ministry, when he sang for joy in their city's prison in Acts 16 and converted many jailbirds through his smiling faith in God. But that was eleven years ago. A bigger gap exists between Paul planting the church at Philippi and his writing to it than exists for any of his other church letters. He amazes the Philippians by still exhibiting that same joy under pressure, even after all the intervening years. The Gospel doesn't just make us free on the inside, new on the inside and strong on the inside – it makes us joyful on the inside too.

The Gospel has helped Paul to remember that *it isn't about him*. The opening verses of Philippians, more than the opening verses of any other letter, emphasize that Paul knew he was part of God's much bigger team. He writes with Timothy and, even though he uses the personal pronoun *"I"* rather than *"we"* throughout this letter, he includes Timothy when he talks in 3:17 about the lead that *"we"* gave to the church in Philippi. He wrote all of his other church letters direct to congregations, so Philippians is unique in the fact that he writes to the congregation *"together with the overseers and deacons."*[4] If our plans and priorities revolve around ourselves, it is very easy for

---

[3] Paul tells us that they sent Epaphroditus to comfort him in 2:25–30.

[4] Acts 20:17 and 28 tells us that *overseer* is simply another word for *elder*. Acts 6:1–6 uses the sister word of *deacon* to show us that deacons are men and women who lead ministries on behalf of the elders.

us to lose our joy. But if we remember that the Gospel tells us life isn't about us at all, this perspective changes everything. As times got harder for Paul, he began to turn his focus more and more onto God's plans for other people. This would be the last letter that he wrote to a church in the New Testament. From now on he would only write to equip and release emerging leaders such as Timothy and Titus.

The Gospel has helped Paul to remember that *he deserves nothing*. Most of our depression and discouragement stems from a thwarted sense of pride. It is easy to blame God for our circumstances when we think that he owes us something and has failed to deliver. Paul shows us that he doesn't think that way by introducing himself in a strikingly different manner to his other letters. Instead of reminding his readers that he is an apostle, he says literally that he and Timothy are *"slaves of Christ Jesus."* That's the same word that he used to describe Onesimus to Philemon, because he has not forgotten what sharing his faith with a runaway slave taught him about himself. The things he has suffered are nowhere near as bad as he deserves. He counts it an enormous privilege to have been forgiven through Jesus and to have become a slave to the best Master in the world. He uses the same blessing to begin his letter in 1:2 that he used to begin Galatians, Ephesians and Colossians, but this time his talk of grace and peace is more profound than ever. He is happy to let Jesus choose his circumstances, so he still enjoys God's grace and peace in the midst of suffering. He recognizes that "Jesus is Lord" means that we are slaves and that Jesus is our Master.[5]

The Gospel has helped Paul to remember that *God does not change*. In these two opening verses, he rejoices once that God is Father, once that Jesus is the Lord, and three times that Jesus is the Christ or Messiah. He isn't joyful because he has mastered the art of positive thinking. His joy is grounded in a proper

---

[5] The Greek word *kurios* or *Lord* is the same word that Paul uses for slave-masters in Ephesians 6:5–9 and Colossians 3:22–4:1.

knowledge of the Lord. *"Rejoice in the Lord!... Rejoice in the Lord always!"* he commands us in 3:1 and 4:4. How we react during difficult times says less about how we view our circumstances than it does about how we view God. *"I rejoiced greatly in the Lord,"* Paul tells us in 4:10. So must we.

The Gospel has helped Paul to remember that *being in Jesus changes everything.* Despite the fact that he has heard there is quarrelling and false teaching in the church at Philippi, he is still confident that they are all *"God's holy people."* He reminds them that they live in two locations: they are both *"in Philippi"* and *"in Christ Jesus."* Paul is not confined to his prison lodgings in Rome because he lives with Jesus in heaven through the Gospel. It is difficult to be miserable when you remember that you are sitting at the right hand of God the Father.

Billy Sunday, who gave up his major-league baseball career to preach the Gospel, used to argue that *"If you have no joy, there's a leak in your Christianity somewhere."* Paul tells us in his final church letter that Billy Sunday was right. Paul wants to teach us how to rediscover the Gospel as the firm foundation of our Christian joy. So get ready to read the letter that Paul penned during some of the darkest days of his life. Get ready to rejoice with him as he teaches us how to be joyful on the inside.

Three Anchors (1:3–11)

In all my prayers for all of you, I always pray with joy.

(Philippians 1:4)

There is a famous story about one of the students at a naval academy in England. An admiral who was visiting the academy barked questions at the students in order to discover whether they were ready for the challenges of commanding a ship at sea.

Admiral:	*"What would you do if a storm blew up?"*
Student:	*"Lower the anchor, sir!"*
Admiral:	*"What would you do if the anchor broke away and another storm blew up?"*
Student:	*"Lower another anchor, sir!"*
Admiral:	*"What would you do if that anchor broke away and a third storm blew up?"*
Student:	*"Lower another anchor, sir!"*
Admiral:	*"Where are you getting all these anchors from?"*
Student:	*"Same place that you're getting all the storms from, sir!"*

Paul had been enduring storm after storm of disappointment in his prison lodgings in Rome. Although Epaphroditus had come from Philippi to comfort him, he had actually made things worse by telling him about the stormy troubles in the church at Philippi. False teachers were gaining ground and two of the leading women in the church had fallen out with each other.[1] It isn't surprising that Paul tells us he responded by praying (his prayer list in 1:3–11 echoes similar prayer lists in Ephesians 1:15–23 and Colossians 1:3–14), but it is surprising that he tells the Philippians that *"In all my prayers for all of you, I always pray* **with joy***"*. For every storm that was thrown at him, Paul always seemed to have an anchor that kept him joyful through the pain. He describes three of the most important anchors in these opening verses of Philippians.

In 1:3–6, Paul's first anchor is his belief in *the faithfulness of God.* He thanks God for the Philippians' partnership with him in the Gospel because he recognizes that it has all been a miracle from the very start.[2] Luke tells us in Acts 16:12 that he and Paul *"travelled to Philippi, a Roman colony and the leading city of that district of Macedonia. And we stayed there several days."* Paul was only there for a few days and yet he saw remarkable conversions. A wealthy Jewish lady was converted and she offered them her home as the venue for a church plant. A demonized slave girl at the other end of the social scale was set free and added to the church through a single authoritative command in the name of Jesus. The suicidal local jailer was dramatically saved and Luke tells us *"he was filled with joy because he had come to believe in God."* When fierce storms beat against Paul's soul, he drew on all of this as an anchor. The church at Philippi had only come into being in the first place because of the faithfulness of God.

How you think people have been saved determines how you think they must stay saved. If you think you won them

---

[1] We will read about the false teaching in 3:1–21 and about the bickering women in 4:1–3.

[2] Paul used this Greek word *koinōnia* in Philemon 6 to describe *"the sharing of your faith"* with unbelievers, but he uses it here to describe *"your sharing in the Gospel"* through partnership with believers. We see practical examples of the Philippian church's partnership with Paul in 4:18 and 2 Corinthians 8:1–5.

by your caring heart or your clever sermons, you are in for a really rough ride. Paul's only anchor when he heard the church in Philippi was in trouble was to remember that the church had been planted through the faithfulness of God. If you are in Christian leadership or if you are concerned for those you have led to salvation, you should take 1:6 and frame it and hang it on your wall. Paul says he is *"confident of this, that he who began a good work in you will carry it on to completion until the day of Christ Jesus."* God is not a quitter. He finishes everything he starts.[3] That's a mighty anchor which keeps us smiling when the stormy winds begin to howl.

In 1:7–8, Paul's second anchor is his experience of *the love and compassion of Jesus*. Not everybody in the church at Philippi was very easy for Paul to love. He must have felt quite cross about the two bickering women because they were his co-workers of old and really ought to have known better. Every church has people who are harder to love than others and, when the storms of life start raging, loving those difficult people can get harder than ever. That's why we need to read these verses slowly, because Paul is telling us his secret. He says that God can testify that he loves every single Christian at Philippi with the supernatural love that Jesus gives him. Our mistake is to strain hard to love *like* Jesus, because doing this doesn't work. Paul tells the Philippians that he doesn't love them like Jesus; he loves them with Jesus' own love. He considers his old self to be dead and his new self to be clothed with the Holy Spirit. Because he has God on the inside, he asks the Spirit of Jesus to fill his heart with the love of Jesus for everyone. As a result, he is able

---

[3] This confidence in God's faithfulness is sometimes referred to as "the perseverance of the saints". If God truly saves somebody, he will also keep them saved until the Last Day. See also John 10.28–29.

to tell the Philippians that he loves them all *"with the affection of Christ Jesus."*[4]

In 1:9–11, Paul's third anchor is his expectation of *fruitfulness in Jesus*. If his joy were based on wishful thinking or on mushy sentiment, it would be quickly blown away in a storm; but it isn't. He tells the Philippians that they will share his confidence too if they deepen their understanding of the Gospel. The normal Greek word for *knowledge* is *gnōsis*, but the word he uses in 1:9 is **epignōsis**, which means **complete** *knowledge*. The more the Philippians understand the Gospel, the more they will share Paul's confidence that Jesus will make them fruitful.[5] The more they let their lifestyle be shaped by the fact that they are in Jesus and he is in them, the more they will grasp God's will for them and the more they will bear righteous fruit in Jesus.[6] Although Paul has personally suffered many setbacks, and although the news from Philippi is not good, he is still confident that Jesus meant it when he said in John 15:16, *"You did not choose me, but I chose you and appointed you so that you might go and bear fruit – fruit that will last."*[7]

Storms will keep on coming, right up until the end of time. Paul mentions the second coming of Jesus in 1:6 and 10 because his troubles make him long for Jesus to return, but he also mentions it because it reminds him that his suffering is all part of God's eternal plan. God is completely faithful in fulfilling

---

[4] Philippians 1:8 is simply Paul's own outworking of Galatians 5:22. See also Romans 5:5.

[5] Colossians 1:9–10 tells us that this is a virtuous circle. God gives us wisdom to understand the Gospel better so that we can bear more fruit, and bearing fruit helps us to understand the Gospel even better!

[6] The word Paul uses for *blameless* in 1:10 is *aproskopos*, which means literally *without stumbling block*. It means that they will neither stumble nor do anything that causes other people to stumble.

[7] Paul is also affirming John 15:5 when he tells us that all lasting fruit in the Christian life *"comes through Jesus Christ."* Having justified and sanctified us by his grace, Jesus also makes us fruitful by his grace too.

his purposes. He fills our hearts with his love and makes us very fruitful. This knowledge anchors Paul and it gives him joy in fierce storm after fierce storm.

Backfire (1:12–26)

*Now I want you to know, brothers and sisters, that
what has happened to me has actually served to
advance the gospel.*

(Philippians 1:12)

One of the greatest backfires in military history occurred in 466 BC. The Athenian fleet was anchored unsuspectingly off the coast of Cyprus, so an enterprising Persian commander thought he had found the perfect chance to sink his enemies and secure complete control of the Mediterranean Sea.

He hadn't reckoned on the cunning of the Athenian admiral Cimon. He was ready for the Persian ships and, having defeated them, he dressed his sailors up in captured armour and sailed the captured ships back to where the Persian army was gathered. Since they recognized the ships and thought they recognized the sailors in them, the Persian lookouts welcomed them ashore and were caught completely off guard when thousands of Athenians suddenly leapt onto the beach and started attacking them. The original attack had completely backfired. By the end of the Battle of the Eurymedon River, the entire Persian fleet had been destroyed and the entire Persian army had been either slaughtered or routed.[1]

One of the reasons why Paul was so joyful in prison in Rome was that he could see the Devil's strategy was completely backfiring too. As he viewed his sufferings with the wisdom given him by the Holy Spirit, he saw the Devil on the run like

[1] The late-first-century Roman writer Frontinus tells us about this colossal backfire in his book of military tactics entitled *Stratagems* (2.9.10).

the Persian army and Jesus claiming a victory more stunning than the one on the banks of the Eurymedon River. He tells the Philippians that *"I want you to know, brothers and sisters, that what has happened to me has actually served to advance the gospel."*

In 1:13, Paul rejoices that his sufferings have enabled him to preach the Gospel to some of the world's most influential people. His two years in jail at Caesarea had not been wasted because Luke tells us in Acts 25:23 that the Roman governor gathered all *"the high-ranking military officers and the prominent men of the city"* so that Paul could share the message of Jesus with them.[2] He could never have gained access to those individuals on his own, but they all gathered to him when the governor put him on trial. Even now, his sufferings had gained him access to many of the leading men in Rome. Being chained to a succession of Roman guards had not prevented him from sharing the Gospel; it had simply given him a captive audience! He had shared with so many soldiers from the Praetorian Guard and with so many palace officials that he writes in 4:22 that *"All God's people here send you greetings, especially those who belong to Caesar's household."* Paul was shut up in jail but it had opened a mighty door for the Gospel in Emperor Nero's palace.[3]

In 1:14, Paul rejoices that his sufferings have made the Christians in Rome far braver in their own evangelism. Paul's letter to the Romans had helped them to understand the glories of the Gospel, but it had not stirred them to share the Gospel as much as when they saw its writer prevented from carrying on his missionary journeys. Far from being browbeaten into silence, they had become so active in sharing their faith that the historian Tacitus complained that the mass Christian

---

[2] In 1:13 in the Greek text, Paul does not say he is in chains *for* Christ, but *in* Christ.

[3] The Greek word *praitōrion* is a transliteration of the Latin word *praetorium*. It meant the *palace of the governor* and in Rome it referred to the barracks of Caesar's private bodyguards.

conversions proved, in his view, that *"all degraded and shameful practices collect and flourish in the capital."*[4]

In 1:15–18, Paul rejoices that his sufferings have mobilized an army of missionary preachers. He isn't as concerned as the Philippians that some of these preachers (their names now forgotten) are only preaching because they see this as a chance to become better known than he is.[5] If his being out of action means that an army of preachers arises, whatever their mixed motives, he is happy to stay in jail for even longer!

We need to remember this, because spreading the Gospel always involves being hated and suffering temporary setbacks. When James Chalmers, the British missionary to the cannibals on the island of Goaribari in the Pacific Ocean, was murdered and eaten in 1901 by those he preached to, many Christians were angry with God. But when a Christian newspaperman in London printed the defiant headline, *"James Chalmers is dead, but others will carry on his work,"* thousands of men and women enlisted. When Jim Elliot, the American missionary to the Huaorani Indians of Ecuador, was murdered by those he preached to in 1956, many more thousands of missionaries and many more millions of dollars were mobilized to reach the nations of the world.

In 1:19–26, Paul rejoices that his sufferings have deepened his own walk with God. We must not become so focused on advancing the Kingdom of God in the world that we neglect the advance of the Kingdom of God in our own hearts. Some of our biggest moments of personal growth come, not in the quiet of a spiritual retreat, but in the turmoil of a spiritual attack. Paul tells us in 1:21 that his sufferings have taught him what it really

---

[4] Tacitus says this describing Christianity in Rome three years after Paul wrote this letter. See *Annals* (15.44).

[5] God always thwarts those who want to promote their own name (Genesis 11:1–9), but he is always eager to promote those who are willing to die to themselves and live only to promote his name (Genesis 12:1–4).

means to die with Jesus,[6] and he tells us in 1:22–26 that he has also learned what it truly means to live for Jesus' cause. He tells us in 1:19 that his sufferings have taught him to rely more on *"God's provision of the Spirit of Jesus Christ."*[7] In times of ease, we are too easily satisfied with past experiences of the Holy Spirit. In times of trouble, it is not enough to have been filled yesterday. We know that our only hope is to be full today.

I love the way that God always makes the Devil's plans backfire. I love the way he takes the chains that bind us and uses them as his weapons of war. I love the way my friend who used to be a gay prostitute is able to use his past to lead his many gay friends to Jesus. I love the way another friend who was in and out of jail as a gang member is able to use his testimony to help many teenagers on the wrong side of the law. I love the way another friend is able to use the way God helped him during his traumatic divorce to help other hurting people. I love it when God outwits the Devil and makes his evil strategies backfire. I love it when we are able to rejoice along with Paul: *"What has happened to me has actually served to advance the gospel."*

---

[6] Paul is clear that Christians go to be with Jesus the moment that they die. They are with him straight away (Luke 23:43), even while they await their resurrection bodies on the Final Day (1 Thessalonians 4:13–18).

[7] Paul also tells us in 1:19 that it taught the Philippians to do so. It drove them to fervent prayer.

Outpost of Heaven
(1:27–30)

This is a sign to them that they will be destroyed, but that you will be saved.

(Philippians 1:28)

There is a lot of talk nowadays in Christian circles about how we can take our cities for God. Churches long to achieve citywide influence and to effect citywide transformation. But unless our plans are grounded in the Gospel, our triumphant talk is simply setting us up for disappointment. Paul tells the Philippians that we shouldn't focus on *taking* our cities at all. We should focus on *being* the city we already are.

Paul has finished the introduction to this letter. He has come to the end of all his greetings and prayers and reassurances. Now, in 1:27 to 2:30, he turns to a series of exhortations for God's People to be united in love and humble in the way they act towards one another. He probably has the conflict within the church at Philippi in mind, but his teaching is much more far-reaching than the case of these two bickering ladies. Paul teaches us how to make our cities sit up and listen to the Gospel. He says the most effective way to change our cities is to show them Christian unity.

Philippi was not the full name of the city to which Paul was writing. It was known in Latin as the *Colonia Iulia Augusta Philippensis*, meaning The-Roman-Colony-of-Philippi-Which-Is-Dedicated-to-Julius-and-Augustus-Caesar. It was a bit of a mouthful but it proclaimed that the city had been colonized as a little foreign outpost of Rome. It was a little piece of Rome in a faraway land, as different from the region around it as an ex-pat compound of Westerners in Saudi Arabia. In Acts 16, the magistrates of Philippi were scared to discover that they had flogged two Roman citizens without a trial, because they knew what Roman citizenship meant. Philippi was fiercely proud that its citizens were Roman citizens, living under Roman law and enjoying the same legal rights as those who lived in Italy. Roman citizenship had become a kind of idol throughout Philippi, so Paul redeems the concept and applies it to the Gospel.

Paul's main point is lost in many English translations, so make sure that it isn't lost on you. He doesn't tell the Philippians to *"live a life worthy"* of their calling, as he did the Ephesians and Colossians and Thessalonians. Instead, he tells them literally in 1:27 to ***"behave as citizens*** *in a manner which is worthy of the gospel of Christ."*[1] This change is intentional because he uses a sister word again in 3:20 to teach the Philippians that *"our citizenship is in heaven."* He takes the concept of Roman citizenship, so precious to his readers, and uses it to teach them how they can win their entire region to Christ.

Paul says converting a city is actually very easy. We simply have to live in the good of the fact that we are citizens of heaven. Most well-born Philippians would describe themselves as "Roman citizens living in Macedonia", so he tells the Christians to view themselves as "heavenly citizens living in Philippi." They are an outpost of heaven on the earth. They are *"God's holy people **in** Christ Jesus **in** Philippi."* All they need to do is live out their new identity in Jesus in Philippi and they will find that the city sits up and listens to what they have to say.

The only striving we need to do in order to change our cities is to remember who we are in Jesus. In 1:27, Paul uses the Greek word *sunathleō*, from which we get our own word "athletics", in order to tell the Philippians that there is a race for them to run.

---

[1] Ephesians 4:1; Colossians 1:10; 1 Thessalonians 2:12; 2 Thessalonians 1:11. *Politeuomai* means *to act like a politēs*, or *citizen*. Paul also uses the word *politeuma* to mean *citizenship* in 3:20.

Athleō means *to compete in the games*, but **sun**athleō means *to compete in the games **together***.[2] We need to strive together as a united team, as in a relay race, if we want to win the prize that God has set before us. We need to share *one spirit* and *one mind* if we want people to recognize that we are a heavenly city at the heart of their earthly city.[3] Paul assures the Philippians in 1:27 that, if they do this, it matters little that he is absent from Philippi. Ongoing unity is a much more powerful force to change a city than any visiting speaker.

The Philippian Christians were being persecuted for their faith in Jesus, so Paul takes the idea of citizenship still further. He reminds them that refusing to surrender is part and parcel of being a citizen. Augustus had established their colony after the Battle of Philippi in 42 BC because he expected the region to be hostile and unruly. He parcelled out land to his veteran soldiers so that whenever there was trouble in the region they would stand firm for his rule. The Philippians knew full well that whenever unrest was brewing in the region, their city grew more united, spoke more Latin and talked more than ever about the supremacy of Rome. In the same way, Paul encourages his readers to stand firm for Jesus in the midst of persecution. He tells them in 1:29–30 that living in Jesus means sharing in his sufferings as well as in his salvation. If they follow in Paul's footsteps, bearing in mind that he was imprisoned in their city long before them, their persecution will only make their witness stronger.

In 1:28, Paul tells us that when churches display unity as fellow citizens of heaven in the face of persecution, it is a prophetic sign to unbelievers that the Gospel is true. Anyone

---

[2] The only other place this word is used anywhere in the New Testament is in 4:3, where Paul uses it again to urge the two bickering women to run as a united team together.

[3] This emphasis on unity is lost in some English translations. Also, since ancient Greek originally had only capital letters, it is ambiguous whether Paul is telling them to stand firm in *one spirit* or in *one Spirit*.

who sees them senses, deep down, that such unity and love and joy and faith under pressure can only come from God. Philippi might be dedicated to Julius and Augustus Caesar, deified posthumously by the Roman Senate, but a church united under pressure would convict the rest of the city that theirs was the real God.

Paul is right. This is precisely how the early Christians won the Roman Empire to Christ. At the end of his comprehensive study of the remarkable growth of the Early Church, Michael Green concludes that

> *Neither the strategy nor the tactics of the first Christians were particularly remarkable. What was remarkable was their conviction, their passion, and their determination to act as Christ's embassy to a rebel world whatever the consequences... They might be slighted, laughed at, disenfranchised, robbed of their possessions, their homes, even their families, but this would not stop them. They might be reported to the authorities as dangerous atheists, and required to sacrifice to the imperial gods: but they refused to comply... They were not prepared to deny Christ even in order to preserve their own lives; and in the manner of their dying they made converts to their faith.*[4]

That's what Paul promises will always happen if we unite together as citizens of the heavenly city. The world will be saved when it sees a church that looks like an outpost of heaven living very differently in its own backyard.

---

[4] Michael Green in *Evangelism in the Early Church* (1970).

Dirty Word? (2:1–11)

Have the same mindset as Christ Jesus.

(Philippians 2:5)

Humility was a dirty word across the Roman Empire. It has always been a dirty word to sinful men and women. We all like to be thought of as humble, but very few of us actually want to be so. We are like Uriah Heep in the Charles Dickens novel *David Copperfield*, who is always telling people *"I'm a very 'umble person,"* while secretly conniving for self-promotion behind their backs.

Yet Paul tells the Philippians that pride is a far greater enemy to their church than persecution. He starts chapter 2 with the word *"therefore"* because this teaching on humility is closely linked to his teaching on unity in 1:27–30. The reason two women were bickering in the church at Philippi was that neither of them was humble. The fact that false teachers had tricked them into relying on man-made rules and lusting after self-indulgent pleasures proved that the rest of them were just as bad. The biggest reason why their city ignored the Gospel was that the people called to be an outpost of heaven were in fact as proud as hell. Put more positively, Paul says that we can quickly make a city sit up and take us seriously if we deal with this issue. Christian humility is so rare in the world that it always draws a crowd.

In 2:1–4, Paul gives us two great reasons to be humble. He reminds us in 2:1 that we are united with Jesus and that Jesus is inside us through his Holy Spirit.[1] If this is true, we cannot persist in those two great enemies of unity: *selfish ambition* and *vain conceit*.[2] People who dwell in Jesus, the one who left heaven's throne to become a crucified carpenter for their sake, must also value others above themselves and look to other people's needs before their own. If unbelievers see a church that shares the *same thoughts*, the *same love*, the *same desires*[3] and the *same mind* as one another, they will take more note of this sign than any other miracle performed by the Holy Spirit.

In 2:5, Paul promises us that Jesus will help us to be humble. He chooses his words carefully in Greek so that he is deliberately ambiguous. They can be translated as a command to *"have this mind in you, which was also in Christ Jesus,"* but they can also be translated as a promise: *"have this mind in you, which is yours in Christ Jesus."*[4] Just like unity, humility isn't something that we need to strive to possess because it isn't ours. It is something that we already have because we are in Jesus and he is in us.

In 2:6–8, Paul encourages us by describing the staggering humility of Jesus' character.[5] Many scholars believe that Paul is quoting from an early Christian hymn in 2:6–11 and, whether or not they are right, these verses have inspired Christian worship ever since. Paul points out that Jesus is as much God as the Father is, and yet he did not use force to be recognized as such by

---

[1] Although 2:1 could technically refer to Christians being united in their *spirit*, almost all English translations agree Paul is saying that we share in the one Holy *Spirit*.

[2] The Greek word *eritheia* means *selfish ambition*, *factionalism* or *manoeuvring for office*. The word *kenodoxia* means *vainglory* or *vain conceit* about ourselves.

[3] Some English translations are misleading by rendering this *"one in spirit."* Paul does not use the Greek word that he normally uses to refer to human spirits or to God's Spirit.

[4] The Revised Standard Version and English Standard Version both translate it as a promise.

[5] Peter met Jesus as a man and marvelled that God exalted him (Acts 2:32–36). Paul met Jesus as God and marvelled that he had humbled himself.

the world.[6] He made himself nothing and was willing to become as lowly as a slave.[7] If we want to know how this Greek word *doulos* – the same word that Paul used to describe Onesimus to Philemon – sounded to Philippian ears when applied to Jesus, we can tell from the histories of Tacitus. Whenever he wants to insult a person, he simply tells his readers that they had *"the mind of a slave"*.[8] Paul is telling us that Jesus looked like the most despised person in the Roman Empire, and that he wants us to be willing to be despised alongside him too.[9]

It gets worse. Paul tells us that Jesus sank even lower than a slave. He was humble enough to obey his Father by dying on a cross like a runaway slave.[10] Peter Lewis reminds us that

> *In polite Roman society the word "cross" was an obscenity, not to be uttered in conversation. It is understandable, therefore, that the style of the hymn becomes abrupt at this point, the additional phrase "even death on a cross" being inserted like an exclamation mark to signal emphasis or astonishment... It took Christ as far beneath his original incarnation as the incarnation was beneath his heavenly glory. In his coming he made himself a*

---

[6] The Greek word *harpagmos* usually means *robbery* or *seizure*. Since Jesus is and always has been God, it must in this context mean either that he refused to *hang onto* his glory or that he refused to *seize* recognition for his glory.

[7] Paul uses the Greek word *kenoō* to tell us literally that Jesus *emptied* himself. The "kenotic heresy" uses this verse to argue that Jesus divested himself of his divinity, but Paul does not say this at all. He is not so much teaching us about Christ's divinity as about Christ's humility. He is telling us that Jesus so emptied himself of his own desires that he was willing to become like a slave while remaining God.

[8] Tacitus says this as much about noblemen (*Histories*, 5.9) as about former slaves (*Annals*, 15.54).

[9] The Greek word *morphē* in 2:6–7 means the *form* or *external appearance* of something. Jesus is the perfect image of God (Colossians 1:15–19), but he became the perfect image of a human slave.

[10] Unlike the animal sacrifices in the Temple, the humble Jesus was a willing sacrifice (John 10:18).

beggar; in his dying he made himself a curse. In the one he
descended to earth; in the other he descended to hell.[11]

Nobody in Philippi wore a cross around their neck. It was too offensive. The orator Cicero said that *"the very mention of the cross should be far removed not only from a Roman citizen's body, but from his mind and his eyes and his ears"*.[12] Paul says that Jesus stooped this low for us and that he wants to help us stoop this low for others too.

In 2:9–11, Paul points out the amazing results of Jesus' humility. Because he refused to assert his own cause, God the Father *"therefore"* asserted his cause for him by exalting him to the highest place and decreeing that every human being, every angel and every demon must now bow down and recognize he is the *Kurios* – the God who is known throughout the Old Testament as *the Lord*.[13] Jesus was Yahweh already, but Acts 2:36 and Hebrews 2:9 concur with Paul that it was only because he was willing to humble himself by dying on the cross that he has now been revealed to the world as Yahweh and become the object of the world's worship alongside the Father. Because he was willing to become like a slave, God the Father has revealed him to be the ultimate Master.

Paul's *"therefore"* in 2:9 is absolutely crucial. He is offering us a choice. Will we treat humility as a dirty word and therefore refuse the benefits of travelling the way of the cross? Or will we get dirty with Jesus and therefore allow God to promote us as those who refuse to promote ourselves? Will we make this song our own because we live in Jesus and he lives in us? If we do so as churches, then our cities will see that humility is not a dirty

233

---

[11] Peter Lewis in *The Glory of Christ* (1992).

[12] The orator Cicero in his legal defence of Gaius Rabirius in 63 BC (section 16).

[13] Paul is not simply talking about the Final Day in 2:10–11, since he uses Greek aorist subjunctives rather than future tenses. Jesus' name has this complete authority now, and we get to speak commands in his name.

word. They will be convicted that we are beautiful outposts of heaven.

Stars (2:12–18)

Then you will shine among them like stars in the sky
as you hold firmly to the word of life.

(Philippians 2:15–16)

People will go to absurd lengths to become a star. If you don't believe me, you obviously haven't watched enough reality TV. People will do just about anything to become a star. Anything, that is, except the one thing God says we actually have to do.

The words of Paul's song about Jesus in 2:6–11 are so awe-inspiring that it's very easy to forget why he actually wrote them. He didn't write them as a treatise in theology (that's worth remembering when you see scholars wrangling over what it means for Jesus to "empty" himself or to "seize" equality with God). He wrote them as an invitation for us to become more like Jesus and as a promise that we can live this way because we are in Jesus and Jesus is in us. Paul moves on from the song with another *"therefore"* at the start of 2:12, which is meant to remind us that his song serves a particular purpose. Paul takes us back to the message that he began in 2:1–4. He tells us in 2:12–18 that, if we are humble like Jesus, God will turn us into stars.

Paul tells us in 2:13 that we do not need to work hard to become humble. Remember what he has taught us throughout his letters about sanctification: we can only become more like Jesus by believing that we live in him and that he lives in us. *"It is God who works in you to will and to act in order to fulfil his good purpose."* Only God can change us from the inside out, giving us a desire to be humble. Only God can empower us to follow through on that desire, demonstrating to the world around us that we have God on the inside. Paul tells us that humility begins with an admission that we cannot make ourselves humble. Submission to others always begins with submission to God.

Got that? Good. Now Paul tells us in 2:12 that we must work very hard to become humble! He sees no contradiction in his instructions when he tells us to *"continue to work out your salvation with fear and trembling."* He expects us to understand the detailed message of Colossians 3. God has poured out his Spirit into our hearts to do the hard work for us, so we must work out our salvation by cooperating hard with him. Our old self is dead through the Gospel, so we need to consider it dead every single day. Nothing makes our old self try to reassert its broken power quite so much as following the way of the cross. Being humble is hard work. It's a daily battle, standing shoulder to shoulder with the Holy Spirit.[1]

Now for some more encouragement to help us in the battle. Paul tells the Philippians that, if they win this battle, God will make them shine like bright stars in the darkness of their self-centred city. This was Israel's calling, but Israel failed (Paul makes this clear in 2:15 by linking back to Deuteronomy 32:5, just as Peter did when addressing the failure of the Jewish nation in Acts 2:40). Now Paul promises that the church at Philippi need not fail. They have God on the inside to help them succeed.

Moses wrote his worship song in Deuteronomy 32 in order to help the Israelites who had grumbled and argued and sinned their way through forty years in the desert. Paul quotes from this song in order to warn the Philippians that they are currently acting in the same way. They must be alert to the dangers of

---

[1] Paul strikes the perfect balance here between reliance on God and taking personal responsibility before him. See also 1 Corinthians 15:10: *"I worked harder than all of them – yet not I, but the grace of God that was with me."* We do not need to work *for* our salvation, but we do need to work *out* our salvation.

pride and hold firmly to the Gospel which he preached to them.[2] They need to learn from him as he pours out his life as a prisoner in Rome as a humble act of worship. Paul uses words from the Temple, such as *drink offering* and *sacrifice* and *priestly service*, in order to tell the Philippians that he is very happy to "waste" his life by pouring it out as a libation on God's altar.[3] In all his sufferings he knows that he is imitating the humble lifestyle of Jesus, and it makes him joyful on the inside. He encourages them to imitate this humble lifestyle instead of the grumble lifestyle of the Israelites in the desert.

The Philippians did not know it yet, but the backdrop in their city was about to get even darker. Three years after Paul wrote this letter, the Emperor Nero blamed the Christians for the great fire of Rome in 64 AD. He launched a murderous campaign of persecution against the church in Rome, which quickly spread to Roman colonies such as Philippi. The Philippians would need to hang onto Paul's promise that their loving unity under pressure would be a prophetic message to their city that they were an outpost of heaven on earth (1:27–30). They would need to remember his promise that their Christ-like humility under pressure made them shine like stars in their ever-darkening city (2:12–18). They would need to believe that their witness shone more beautifully than ever as things got darker. Stars always shine brightest in the darkest sky.[4]

The Greek word that Paul uses in 2:15 is *phōstēr*, which means a *luminary*. It can just as easily mean a *sun* as it does a *star*.

---

[2] The Greek phrase that Paul uses in 2:16 is deliberately ambiguous. It can mean either *holding firmly onto the word of life* or *holding out the word of life*. Paul wants us to do both: continually applying the Gospel to our own lives and continually sharing it with other people.

[3] All of these Greek words were used for worship at the Lord's Temple in Jerusalem and for the worship of pagan idols in the temples throughout Philippi.

[4] Paul refers to Jesus' return in 2:16, just as he did in 1:6 and 1:10. As the persecution got harder, Paul kept himself joyful by meditating on the return of Jesus for his faithful people on the Final Day.

Perhaps he is linking back to the prophecy in Malachi 4:2 that the Messiah would be *"the Sun of Righteousness"* and promising us that the Messiah's glory will shine out through his People too. Stars are so bright that they can be seen millions of miles away, and true humility is so rare that it has a long-distance impact too. Think for a moment about Mother Theresa and her work in the slums of Calcutta, which became famous all around the world. Paul reassures us that convincing unbelievers that the Gospel is true is not difficult. We simply have to live out who we truly are, as a bright colony of heaven against the night sky of a sinful world.

Leader Means Like Jesus
(2:19–30)

Welcome him in the Lord with great joy, and honour people like him.

(Philippians 2:29)

They say a picture paints a thousand words. In that case, a real-life example must paint a million words. Having told the Philippians to be united and humble like Jesus, Paul ends this chapter by modelling for them what that means. He draws their attention to two of his teammates, Timothy and Epaphroditus, and he demonstrates what his teaching means in practice.

If you are a Christian leader, then you should find these two examples very challenging. They make us reflect on our own humility and Christ-like character, and they make us think very carefully about the team members we raise up to lead with us. What is embodied by church leaders soon becomes the norm throughout the body, so who we recognize as leaders is a very important decision. If you are not yet a Christian leader but would like to be, you should also find these two examples very challenging. The world grants stardom to people based on their gifting or ambition, but God says that the stars in his Kingdom shine brightly through their godly character instead.

First, Paul tells us that true Christian leaders *are humble like Jesus*. Paul deliberately matches the character of his team members to his teaching in 2:1–4. He uses a very similar word in 2:20 to the one he used in 2:2 when he tells us that Timothy is *"likeminded."*[1] He uses similar language to 2:4 when he tells us in 2:21 that Timothy has sacrificed his own interests in order to seek the interests of Jesus and of the Philippians. Timothy did not have too much going for him in terms of gifting. We are told in Paul's other letters that he was young and in poor health.[2] But he had one big thing going for him, which made him a star player in Paul's team: he exhibited the Christ-like humility that Paul describes throughout this chapter.

Epaphroditus was humble like Jesus too. Paul tells us that he was an apostle (there is no reason for us to translate the Greek word *apostolos* any differently in 2:25 than in the rest of the New Testament[3]), but he did not see himself as too important to run errands on behalf of the believers. He was willing to be sent by the church at Philippi to care for Paul's practical needs, playing postman for their financial gift to him and for Paul's thank-you letter back to them.[4] When describing Epaphroditus' willingness to serve, Paul deliberately uses Greek words in 2:25 and 30 which echo his teaching on sacrificial *service* in 2:17. Somewhere on his travels or in the dirty backstreets of Rome, Epaphroditus had contracted an illness from which he almost died, but he doesn't resent getting his hands dirty in the service of his Lord. He understands that humility means becoming like Jesus, and he refuses to view it as a dirty word.

Paul's own humility shines out of these few short verses too. Even though he is the foremost Christian leader of his generation, he spends more time honouring his teammates than he does talking about his own very pressing needs. He compares his relationship with Timothy to that of *"a son with*

---

[1] Paul is not just saying that he has nobody *like* Timothy. He uses a similar word to the one he uses in 2:2 in order to tell us that nobody else is so *likeminded*.

[2] 1 Timothy 4:12; 5:23.

[3] Paul tells the Philippians that he is *"your apostle."* He was a home-grown apostle from Philippi.

[4] Paul says thank you in 4:18 for the financial gift that they sent him via Epaphroditus.

his father," and he calls Epaphroditus "my brother, co-worker and fellow soldier." They are more than work colleagues. They are people with whom he models what he taught us in 2:1–4: "In humility value others above yourselves."

Second, Paul tells us that true Christian leaders *are obedient like Jesus*. He deliberately echoes his teaching in 2:5–11 by telling us literally that Timothy "has slaved with me in the gospel." Timothy followed the example of Jesus by sacrificing his own rights to obey the Lord. He does not mind the fact that Paul names him as co-author of this letter but then talks throughout as "I", and he appears to be happy for Paul to decide whether he should go to Philippi or stay in Rome. Timothy might not have the greatest gifting going for him, but his character was what mattered. A Christian leader who simply does whatever Jesus tells him is worth his weight in gold.

Paul also echoes his teaching in 2:5–11 when he says that Epaphroditus almost died out of obedience to the call of God upon his life. When he contracted a near-fatal illness, he did not complain that God had let him down by not healing him straightaway.[5] He was simply distressed that the news of his illness would worry his friends in Philippi and that his illness would make him an additional burden to Paul.[6] He is happy to smile through whatever comes his way as he lives his life in obedience to God's every command. Leaders like Epaphroditus shine like stars next to the darkly self-assertive leaders of the world.

Third, Paul tells us that true Christian leaders *are joyful like Jesus*. He personally models his teaching in 2:12–18 by refusing to grumble in prison. He tells the Philippians in 2:19

---

[5] We cannot argue from 2:25 that it is wrong always to expect God to heal people. After all, Epaphroditus was healed! However, it is a helpful reminder that even Paul did not see everybody healed straightaway.

[6] Paul uses a strong Greek word to describe how much Epaphroditus was distressed. It is only used elsewhere in the New Testament to describe Jesus' distress in the Garden of Gethsemane (Matthew 26:37; Mark 14:33).

and 24 that he is happy to wait in Rome because any plans he makes are always *"in the Lord."* He is more concerned for Epaphroditus' health and for the church at Philippi than he is about cataloguing his own sufferings. He demonstrates in every way that humble obedience to the Lord is the only pathway to experiencing true joy.

When Jim Elliot went to preach to the Huaorani Indians of Ecuador and they murdered him in cold blood, his widow Elisabeth was forced to put Philippians 2 into practice. She refused to blame God for her husband's death, and she inspired millions through her example of humble obedience. She became a significant Christian leader herself, inspiring many people to carry on her dead husband's mission. She explained her secret in words which echo Paul: *"The world looks for happiness through self-assertion, The Christian knows that joy is found in self-abandonment. 'If a man will let himself be lost for My sake,' Jesus said, 'he will find his true self.'"*[7]

Paul has reached the end of the second section of Philippians. He has taught us about unity, humility and obedience. He has also gone one step further by modelling it together with his team. The question now is whether we will follow his example. Are you willing to tread the painful path of humility? Are you willing to sacrifice your pride and your priorities, like Jesus? Only if you do so will you discover how the Gospel makes believers joyful on the inside.

---

[7] Elisabeth Elliot writing in John Piper and Wayne Grudem, *Recovering Biblical Manhood and Womanhood* (1991).

Dog Dirt (3:1–16)

I consider them dog dirt, that I may gain Christ.

(Philippians 3:8)

If you want to know how seriously Paul viewed legalism, look no further than the language he used when dealing with anyone who taught it. When he warned the Galatians against the Judaizers who taught that we can achieve forgiveness from God and acceptance by God through our obedience to God, he got so angry that he wished out loud that these advocates of circumcision would go the whole hog and castrate themselves.[1] Now, as we start the third section of Philippians, Paul addresses similar false teachers in Philippi. He calls them *"dogs"*[2] and *"evildoers"* and *"mutilators of the flesh."*[3] Then his language gets even bolder. He says their teaching is a pile of dog dirt.

I don't want to offend you, but I do want you to understand what Paul is saying in Philippians 3. Most English translations tone down Paul's language for the sake of our sensibilities, but Paul chooses his words carefully in order to make us sit up and listen. Legalism really is that serious.

When a man named Gemellus wrote to his son Sabinus to complain about his donkey driver in 103 AD, he used the same

---

[1] Galatians 5:12. If God is impressed by our cutting off our foreskins, then why stop there?!

[2] Strict Jews referred to Gentiles as *"dogs,"* so Paul is using the false teachers' own word back against them.

[3] The false teachers called themselves the *peritomē*, or the *circumcision group*. Paul makes a parody of their name in 3:2 by calling them the *katatomē* – the *mutilation group*. He repeats in 3:3 what he taught in Colossians 2:11–12: those who have died and been raised with Jesus are the true *peritomē*.

Greek word that Paul uses in Philippians 3:8 to describe his frustration. His papyrus letter has survived so we know that he told his son: *"Aunes the donkey driver has bought a rotten bundle of hay for 12 drachmas, a little bundle of rotten hay, the whole of which is so decayed it is like dog dirt."*[4] Paul uses the same word to describe the legalism that is being taught in the church at Philippi. Although most modern English Bibles translate the Greek word *skubalon* as *"rubbish"* or *"garbage"*, it means literally *"what dogs eject"*. The old Geneva Bible tries to capture this when it tells us in sixteenth-century English that Paul says: *"I doe iudge them to bee dongue."*

Paul tells us in 3:1–4 why legalism is so serious. Rejoicing in God is a safeguard against legalism because one of the first signs we have fallen into legalism is that we lose our joy. Paul reminds us in 3:3 that the Gospel contains the amazing truth that we are in Jesus, that Jesus is in us and that God will work inside us to enable us to serve him through his Spirit.[5] The Gospel makes us joyful because it tells us we have nothing at all to prove to God – he does it all and he gets all the glory. Legalism is the exact opposite of the Gospel. It tells us to strive for God's approval and it makes us miserable, because none of us has got what it takes to score any points on God's righteous scorecard. That's why Paul uses such a strong word in his warning. He wants to shock us into seeing that legalism isn't a hybrid of Christianity. It isn't Christianity at all.

Paul tells us in 3:5–6 why legalism is so foolish. He reminds the Philippians of his own pre-conversion history. If anyone could impress God through legalistic rule-keeping then it was Paul. He wasn't just circumcised; he was circumcised on the eighth day in accordance with the Law of Moses. He wasn't just an Israelite; he was descended from the tribe of Benjamin, the offspring of

---

[4] This is known as "Papyrus Fayum 119".

[5] Paul tells us in 3:1 that it is just as important to remind people of what they know as it is to teach them fresh things. Christian maturity is as much about not forgetting as it is about learning more.

Jacob's beloved wife Rachel rather than the ugly Leah or either of his two concubines. He wasn't just a law-keeper; he was a Pharisee, part of the sect which exaggerated the commands of the Law to ludicrous proportions. He wasn't just a zealous Jew; he had led the charge against the early Christians. The false teachers are obviously deluded. If they were right, then Jesus would not have needed to save Paul by appearing to him on the Damascus Road!

Paul tells us in 3:7–8 that, when he met Jesus, he didn't just need to repent of his rebellion. He needed to repent of his reliance on man-made religion as well. He tells us in 3:7 that he needed to treat his religious achievements as *zēmia* – the Greek word for a *loss* or *liability*. They hadn't just failed to set him right with God; they had become a liability by giving him false confidence that God was pleased with him without his needing Jesus to be his Saviour. This is so important that Paul repeats himself in 3:8. He needed to consider everything except for Jesus to be a liability. Now for the shock effect. He says he has come to view such things as *skubalon* – they are a steaming pile of dog dirt compared to the amazing beauty of the Gospel.

God really wants you to take this message seriously, so he isn't embarrassed about Paul's language. He hopes that it will wake you up to smell the stench of legalism in your own life. He inspired Isaiah to say something similar in the Old Testament in a verse that is also sanitized in most English translations. Isaiah 64:6 tells us literally that *"We have all become like an unclean person; all of our 'righteous acts' are like a menstrual rag."* God tells us that he is as offended when we try to gain forgiveness, acceptance and approval from him through our own religious efforts as he would be if we offered him a used tampon or sanitary towel. It's a horrible image, but God uses it because we need to grasp that legalism really is that horrible.

By way of contrast, Paul reminds us in 3:9–16 of the beauty of the Gospel. It means that we are now in Jesus and that all of his righteousness is counted as if it were ours (3:9).[6] It means that we have died with him and that he lives inside us through the power of the same Holy Spirit who raised him from the dead (3:10–11).[7] It means that Jesus has done all the hard work for us – he has taken hold of us and we merely need to take hold of him and keep tight hold of the Gospel as we run towards the goal (3:12). It means that God has given us first prize in the race of life, if we just keep running like the people we are in heaven, instead of looking back at the people we once were (3:13–14).[8] Read these words slowly and breathe them in deeply. Unlike legalism, they smell like sweet perfume.

Like the false teachers at Colossae, the troublemakers at Philippi were claiming that the Gospel was just kindergarten Christianity. They were telling the Philippians that if they wanted to be mature in Christ then they needed to add a bit of legalism to their walk with God. But Paul tells the Philippians that anyone who is truly mature will take the same view on this as him.

They will ditch the dog dirt and keep to the Gospel.

---

[6] Paul echoes 1:29 when he reminds us in 3:10 that being in Jesus means sharing in his sufferings as well as in his blessings.

[7] Many people find 3:10–11 confusing, but it isn't if we understand it as a direct parallel of Paul's teaching in Colossians 2:11–12.

[8] The Greek word *brabeion* means a *prize in the athletic games*, and it is linked to the words which Paul uses in Colossians 2:18 and 3:15. Paul uses other athletics metaphors in Philippians 1:27, 2:16, 4:1 and 4:3.

Civil War (3:17–21)

But our citizenship is in heaven. And we eagerly await a Saviour from there, the Lord Jesus Christ.

(Philippians 3:20)

The people of Philippi knew all about civil war. Their city had been founded as a Roman colony as a result of it. Even its name, *Colonia Iulia Augusta Philippensis*, spoke about the terrible events that surrounded the Battle of Philippi in 42 BC. The future Emperor Augustus had led an army against Brutus and the other senators who had assassinated Julius Caesar. Augustus won and re-founded the old Greek city as a colony of Rome.

It helps to know this as Paul returns to his theme of the church at Philippi being a colony of heaven. He warns the Philippians that their colony is at civil war because they have opened its gates to false teachers and to an army of earthly thinking. Having tackled the teachers of legalism in 3:1–16, Paul now tackles the teachers of licence in 3:17–21. He tells the Philippians that pagan pleasure-seeking will destroy their church just as easily as Jewish rule-keeping. They need to take the threat of these false teachers seriously and to face up to the fact that their colony of heaven is at civil war.

In 3:17–19, Paul exposes how sinful the teachers of licence actually are. They are just as much enemies of the cross of Jesus as the legalists. The legalists claim that good deeds can atone for sin without the cross, but the teachers of licence claim that sin isn't serious enough to require atonement at all. Paul feels so upset about the eternal fate of the teachers that he tells the

Philippians it brings him to tears.[1] They are not simply bringing a wrong emphasis into the church. They are proving they are not Christians at all. Their destiny is *apōleia*, the same word that Paul used in 1:28 for the *destruction* of the pagans at Philippi when he talked earlier about the church being citizens of heaven. The false teachers worship their fleshly appetites (*stomachs* is probably shorthand for pleasure-seeking in general), and they honour things which God calls shameful and vile. They have not died with Jesus. They have simply commandeered the Gospel as a way to indulge their love of earthly things while fooling their consciences that they are clean.

In the first half of 3:20, Paul reminds the believers of their new identity in Jesus. He uses the Greek word *politeuma*, or *citizenship*, which was one of the most highly prized words in the Philippian vocabulary, to remind them that they are citizens of heaven. Philippi was an outpost of Rome in a sea of Greeks and barbarians; the Philippian church was an outpost of heaven, which could not live by this earth's rules. The false teachers were no more Christian than a man was Roman if he walked into the forum, threw Caesar's emblems on the ground and trampled them under his barbarian shoes.

In the rest of 3:20–21, Paul explains what this means in practice. We need to read these verses slowly because we often get it wrong. He is not saying that we are citizens of heaven and that we therefore need to hold on tight until Jesus comes back to earth to whisk us away with him to our heavenly home. Augustus had not established a Roman colony at Philippi so that its citizens could hold on tightly until he came back and escorted them back to Rome.[2] He had established the colony

---

[1] Paul teaches about hell frequently but never flippantly. The manner in which we proclaim the Bible's teaching about hell is as important in convincing our hearers as the words we say.

[2] When Paul talks about our "heavenly hope" in verses such as Colossians 1:5, he isn't saying that history will end with us leaving the earth and going to heaven. He is saying that heaven will come down to earth.

with a mandate to Romanize the entire region and to bring it under his rule. Paul therefore tells the Philippians that they are a foretaste of heaven on the earth, operating by the power of Jesus to bring everything under his rule until he returns.[3] On that day he will transform our earthly bodies to be like his own glorious heavenly body, and he will make the rest of the earth like our own outpost of heaven.[4] We are here to stay. We are a prophetic demonstration of what the rest of the world will one day become.

The rest of the New Testament sheds more light on what Paul is teaching here. It tells us that we are to pray *"Your kingdom come, your will be done, on earth as it is in heaven"* (Matthew 6:10). Instead of longing for an airlift to heaven, we are to download the power of heaven through our prayers, confident that history will not end with us going up to heaven but with heaven coming down to earth (Revelation 21:1–4). Heaven and earth will be united together as a new heaven and earth in which we will dwell with Jesus forever. On that day we will sing, *"The kingdom of the world has become the kingdom of our Lord and of his Messiah, and he will reign for ever and ever"* (Revelation 11:15). With that in mind, we now live as a colony of heaven with our eyes fixed on our coming Master. He is coming back to destroy his enemies and to reward those who have gladly received his rule before his army arrives.

We already know who will win this civil war, but still it rages fiercely. The teachers of licence have infiltrated our colonies of heaven too. Christians fight for their rights and indulge sin

---

[3] This is one of several references to Jesus' second coming in Philippians. The more Paul suffered on earth, the more he learned to rejoice in the fact that Jesus is coming back to restore his creation.

[4] The Greek word that Paul uses in 3:21 for our bodies being *transformed* to be like Jesus' body is linked to the word he used in 2:8 to describe Jesus being willing to take the *form* of a man. The Greek word he uses for the *nature* of Jesus' body in 3:21 links to the word he used for Jesus' *nature* as God and man in 2:6–7.

today just as much as the Philippians in the days of Paul. Eugene Peterson, writing as a Western Christian, comments that

> *It is useful to listen to people who come into our culture from other cultures, to pay attention to what they hear and what they see. In my experience, they... see a Christian community that has almost none of the virtues of the biblical Christian community, which have to do with a sacrificial life and conspicuous love. Rather, they see indulgence in feelings and emotions, and an avaricious quest for gratification.*[5]

The way to win this civil war is to become more like Jesus. It is to fix our eyes on our citizenship in heaven and to cooperate with the Holy Spirit as he works in our hearts. It is to think like heaven, to pursue the goals of heaven and to wear the righteous clothes of heaven. It is to follow the path of Jesus, through humble obedience to the Father, and to share in his glory on earth while we wait for the full arrival of his glory from heaven. Paul encourages us in 3:17 to *"Join together in following my example, brothers and sisters, and just as you have us as a model, keep your eyes on those who live as we do."*

We are citizens of heaven and we await the imminent return of heaven's King. Let's not succumb while we wait to either rule-keeping or pleasure-seeking. We are at civil war but, because we live in Jesus and he lives in us, we are on the winning side.

---

[5] Eugene Peterson in *The Contemplative Pastor* (1989).

Therefore (4:1–7)

*Therefore, my brothers and sisters, you whom I love
and long for, my joy and crown, stand firm in the Lord
in this way, dear friends!*

(Philippians 4:1)

One of Paul's favourite words in his letters is "therefore". It's
not just that he uses the word a lot in his letters. He also uses
it to signpost the chain of his logic throughout his letters. He
uses the word "therefore" to help us follow his arguments and
to ensure that we understand what it truly means to live out
the Gospel. So we mustn't miss the significance of the fact that
Paul begins chapter 4 with the word "therefore". He is letting us
know that he has started his conclusion. In these seven verses,
he encourages us to respond to his teaching in the previous
three chapters.[1]

In 4:1, Paul encourages us to live out the teaching of chapter
3. He uses a soldier's word when he tells us to *"stand firm in the
Lord in this way"* – the same word that he used when telling us
to stand firm against false teaching in 1:27 and Galatians 5:1.
He wants us to stand firm against the siren voices of legalism
and licence ringing in our ears. He wants us to be like one of the
strong soldiers who guarded the door while he wrote this letter.
To help us further, he also uses a sporting word when he tells us
he is running for a *stephanos*, the Greek word that was used for
the laurel crowns that were awarded to victors in the Olympic

---

[1] Paul actually uses three Greek words for "therefore" in his letters. He uses
the word *hōste* in 2:12 and 4:1, the word *dio* in 2:9 and the word *oun* in 2:1,
2:23, 28–29 and 3:15.

Games. If we drift out of our lane, we will be disqualified, but if we run with our eyes fixed on the Gospel, we will win the eternal prize.[2]

When Paul tells the Philippians that they have become his joy through the Gospel, he brings us back to the overarching theme of Philippians. Christians who allow legalism to infect their faith in Jesus exchange joy on the inside for guilt instead. If God's approval can be won through our obedience, it can also be lost through our disobedience, so legalistic Christians tend to sink into a downward spiral of inward focus and despair. Their church services become more like funerals than celebrations of a risen Saviour. In the same way, Christians who allow licence to infect their faith in Jesus exchange joy on the inside for mere fun on the outside. Their fun does not last. Their pleasure-seeking brings them misery, as C. S. Lewis observes:

> *If we consider the unblushing promises of reward and the staggering nature of the rewards promised in the Gospels, it would seem that Our Lord finds our desires not too strong, but too weak. We are half-hearted creatures, fooling about with drink and sex and ambition when infinite joy is offered us, like an ignorant child who wants to go on making mud pies in a slum because he cannot imagine what is meant by the offer of a holiday at the sea. We are far too easily pleased.*[3]

In 4:2–5, Paul encourages us to live out the teaching of chapter 2.[4] He names the two bickering women in the church at Philippi and pleads with them personally to apply the teaching

---

[2] Paul also uses athletic metaphors in 1:27, 2:16, 3:13–14 and 4:3. See also 1 Corinthians 9:24–27, Galatians 2:2 and 5:7, Colossians 2:18 and Hebrews 12:1.

[3] C. S. Lewis in *The Weight of Glory* (1949).

[4] The Greek phrase Paul uses for *being likeminded* in 4:2 is very similar to the phrase he uses in 2:2.

in his chapter on unity and humility.[5] He knows it will not be easy, so he asks Syzygus[6] (presumably one of the church elders he addressed in 1:1) to help both of them to repent of their pride.[7] Paul tries to encourage them with another sporting metaphor, reminding them literally that in the past they joined with him to *compete as athletes* for the sake of the Gospel.[8] They were members of his relay team along with Clement and the other leaders in Philippi.[9] They are seasoned runners who ought not to be tripped up by pride like clumsy members of the junior team.

Once again, Paul motivates us to apply his teaching by telling us that this is the only way that we can know true joy on the inside. Gentle humility produces joy because people who are secure in Jesus have nothing left to prove (4:4). Whether they are promoted or not, they know they already have everything. Gentle humility produces joy because it makes us shine like stars and convinces unbelievers that the Lord Jesus is truly near (4:5). Gentle humility produces joy by gaining us an eternal reward (4:3). Fighting for fame in this world is like running for school president on graduation day. Earthly fame evaporates more quickly than it can be enjoyed. But surrendering our lust

[5] Euodia means either *Enjoying Good Journeys* or *Sweet-Smelling*. Syntyche means *Arrived By Accident*. Paul addresses them by name to make it very difficult for them to refuse – a similar strategy to Colossians 4:9.

[6] The Greek name *Syzygus* means *Yoke-Fellow*, so it is not clear whether Paul is addressing an elder named Syzygus or simply a faithful co-worker. English translations take different views.

[7] Paul is convinced that they will repent because they are both *"in the Lord"*. He always believed the best for the people in his churches through the Gospel, and they usually lived up to his expectations.

[8] The only other place where this Greek word *sunathleō* is used in the New Testament is in 1:27.

[9] Some people believe that this Clement is the same man who served as Bishop of Rome (92–99 AD) and wrote a non-biblical letter to the church at Corinth, although there is no concrete evidence to support this.

for fame in order to make Jesus famous instead gains our names an entry in the Lamb's Book of Life for all eternity.[10]

In 4:6–7, Paul encourages us to live out the teaching of chapter 1. He uses another military metaphor, encouraging us literally that if we share his prayerful faith then the peace of God will *mount an armed guard* over our hearts.[11] Perhaps he is looking at the Roman sentries barring his door when he tells us that if we go to God with our anxious thoughts and feelings, he will protect our hearts and minds. If we thank God in every circumstance, just as Paul did in chapter 1, he will fill us with peace through his Holy Spirit, a peace that the world can neither give nor understand.[12] While worry robs today of its strength, God's peace guards our hearts and minds forever, guiding us at every fork in the road of our walk with Jesus. If we truly understand Paul's Gospel – that we are in Jesus and that Jesus is in us through his Holy Spirit – we will know true joy on the inside.

Athletes, soldiers, runners, guards – Paul loves to use these sporting and military metaphors. He hopes that they will help us to understand his little word "therefore", and that we will live in the good of all that he has taught us. If we allow Paul's teaching to strengthen us through the Gospel, we will inherit the ancient promise in Nehemiah 8:10:

"*Do not grieve, for the joy of the Lord is your strength.*"

---

[10] This Book of Life is also mentioned in Luke 10:20 and in Revelation 3:5, 13:8, 17:8, 20:12, 15 and 21:27.

[11] Paul also uses this Greek word *phroureō* to describe a king's soldiers guarding Damascus in 2 Corinthians 11:32 and to describe armed prison guards protecting the Jewish nation in Galatians 3:23.

[12] John 14:27; Galatians 5:22.

What Goes in Is What
Comes Out (4:8–9)

*Whatever is true, whatever is noble, whatever is right,
whatever is pure, whatever is lovely, whatever is
admirable… think about such things.*

(Philippians 4:8)

What goes in is what comes out. Everybody knows that, but
nobody knew it better than the Philippians. Their city lay on
the great Roman road known as the Egnatian Way, which linked
the Adriatic Sea to the Black Sea and to Asia.[1] They knew that
if precious cargo arrived at the western gate from Thessalonica
then precious cargo would set out on the eastern road to
Byzantium, but if rotten cargo came in through the western gate
then rotten cargo would set out. What goes in is what comes
out. It's really very simple.

    It therefore shouldn't surprise us that it is the same with
our eyes and ears. If we watch violent movies, we will think
violent thoughts. If we listen to music that demeans women,
we will start to demean women ourselves. If we look lustfully
at somebody who is not our wife or husband, our marriage
will start to go sour. It should be pretty obvious, but we can
be as foolish as the ancient alchemists. We feed our minds on
base things yet seem curiously surprised when our character
emerges rather less than golden.

    Last year, one of the girls at my local secondary school was
abused and murdered by one of her relatives. The man who did

---

[1] This explains why Paul and his team, coming from Asia, planted their first
European church at Philippi.

it was arrested in the park behind my house. When the police investigated what might have caused him to abuse and murder his twelve-year-old step-granddaughter, they discovered violent child pornography on his computer. Yet when a newspaper reporter pointed this out to Feona Attwood, professor of cultural studies at Middlesex University, she refused to accept that there is any link at all: *"Porn is important to people on all kinds of levels... People who look at porn are not all lizard people."*[2] Of course they're not, but Paul argues that their hearts are being polluted by a great snake called the Devil. Satan knows that what goes in is what comes out, even if we deny it, which is why Paul addresses our thought life so strongly after promising that the Holy Spirit will set a military guard around our hearts if we let him.

Paul's teaching here is nothing new. Genesis 3:6 tells us that Eve feasted her eyes on the forbidden fruit before she took a mouthful. Proverbs 4:23 tells us to make guarding our thought life our biggest priority. *"Above all else, guard your heart,"* Solomon pleads, *"for everything you do flows from it."* The Hebrew word that Solomon uses likens the human heart to the source of a well. If it is pure then everything we do will be pure, but if it is poisoned then everything we do will be contaminated. He may have been thinking of his parents' own example, since David feasted his eyes on the naked Bathsheba from his rooftop while she bathed and within two short verses was in bed with her.[3] Solomon is simply repeating the consistent message of the Old Testament: what you look at with your eyes affects how you think in your heart, which affects what you do.

Jesus affirms this Old Testament teaching. He tells us that *"The eye is the lamp of the body. If your eyes are healthy, your whole body will be full of light. But if your eyes are unhealthy,*

[2] Dr Feona Attwood speaking in *The Guardian* newspaper on 16th June 2013 in an article entitled "Porn Wars: The debate that's dividing academia".

[3] 2 Samuel 11:2–5. Contrast David's sin with Joseph's commitment to purity in Genesis 39:6–10.

your whole body will be full of darkness" (Matthew 6:22–23). He warns that *"A good man brings good things out of the good stored up in his heart, and an evil man brings evil things out of the evil stored up in his heart. For the mouth speaks what the heart is full of"* (Luke 6:45). He had personal experience of the Devil tempting us by directing our eyes towards forbidden pleasures.[4] He did not simply refuse to look. He feasted his eyes on Scripture so diligently that he was quicker on the draw with a verse in reply than Clint Eastwood in a spaghetti western. Few people succumb to temptation in a moment. When we succumb to temptation it simply reveals what we have been allowing our hearts to feed upon.

Paul picks up on this and repeats this teaching in a very positive way. He does not tell us to avoid looking at what is base and vulgar and filthy and impure. He has already warned us against such things in Galatians 5:19–21, in Ephesians 4:17–19 and 5:3–18, and in Colossians 3:5–10. Instead, he tells us to feast our eyes so eagerly on what is good that we leave no room for what is evil! The nineteenth-century Scottish preacher Thomas Chalmers understood this principle when he urged his hearers to rid their minds of sinful thoughts by filling them with pure thoughts of Jesus Christ instead: *"Such is the grasping tendency of the human heart that it must have a something to lay hold of... The only way to dispossess it of an old affection is by the expulsive power of a new one."*[5]

To help the Philippians, Paul reminds them in 4:9 that they have seen his lifestyle. He isn't simply remonstrating with them; he has demonstrated it to them too. He has lived among them as a single man who was completely pure in his treatment of women. He has lived among them as a poor manual labourer

---

[4] Luke 4:1–13. See also 2 Chronicles 12:14; Matthew 12:34; 18:9; 2 Peter 2:14.

[5] He said this in a sermon on 1 John 2:15 entitled "The Expulsive Power of a New Affection." Paul's command in 4:8 is a Greek present imperative. It therefore carries the sense of *"keep on thinking about such things."*

who was completely admirable in his treatment of money and possessions. He has lived among them as a miracle-working apostle who might have abused his God-entrusted power and yet was excellent and praiseworthy in everything he did. He was able to tell them in 3:17 to *"Join together in following my example."* He was able to encourage all of his converts to follow *"my way of life in Christ Jesus, which agrees with what I teach everywhere in every church."*[6]

How about you? Can you say with Paul that you only feast your eyes and ears and heart on *"whatever is true, whatever is noble, whatever is lovely, whatever is admirable – whatever is excellent or praiseworthy"*? Can you say with Thomas Chalmers that you have fed your heart on such good things that there is no ground left for any evil sins to grow?

Stuart Hazell, the man who was arrested in the park behind my house for abusing and murdering his step-granddaughter, wrote to his father from prison: *"You know I'm not a bad person... One mistake and my whole world has collapsed... It was an accident."*[7] But it wasn't an accident. He was jailed for thirty-eight years because of a single action, but that action was the result of many years of bad decisions. The Devil does not mind how long he has to wait to destroy us, just so long as we are foolish enough to give him room in our hearts to destroy us in the end.

So let's listen to Paul when he warns us that we need the Holy Spirit to set a guard around our hearts. Let's cooperate with the Holy Spirit by focusing our minds on what is pure. As we do so, Jesus gives us an amazing promise in Matthew 5:8:

"Blessed are the pure in heart, for they will see God."

---

[6] 1 Corinthians 4:17.

[7] A transcript of this letter was printed in *The Independent* newspaper on 10th May 2013.

Kill the Python (4:10–20)

I have learned the secret of being content in any and every situation, whether well fed or hungry, whether living in plenty or in want.

Paul hasn't finished teaching us how to guard our eyes and hearts. A lot of what we look at isn't bad; it just isn't ours. That's why Paul finishes off with some teaching about contentment. He wants to show us how to have joy on the inside when our eyes want what we don't have.

Pythons are very dangerous snakes. They wrap their coils around their prey and they refuse to let go. Every time their prey breathes and cedes a little ground, their coils wrap a little tighter. Paul wants us to understand that our eyes can no more be appeased than a hungry python. Desires need to be put to death, as Philippian history had proved.

The city of Philippi owed its very existence to human greed. King Philip of Macedon had founded the city because he wanted to mine gold in the nearby hills. He became one of the richest men in history, but he didn't become content. Instead, he used the gold to conquer other kingdoms. After his death, his son Alexander the Great conquered most of the known world, but he was not content. It is said that he wept that there were no other worlds to conquer. It was appropriate that the future of the Roman Empire was decided in battle outside the walls of Philippi in 42 BC. Philippian history was a catalogue of greed and dissatisfaction.

That's one of the reasons why Paul was so delighted with

the church at Philippi. He tells us in these closing verses that the believers were not at all like Philip or Alexander. They had been the only church to fund his early church planting into Europe, sending gifts along the Egnatian Way to his new base in Thessalonica.[1] They had just sent a fresh financial gift through Epaphroditus to pay for his rented accommodation in Rome.[2] They had been as generous as their unbelieving rulers had been grasping.[3] Now Paul teaches them the secret of his own contentment so that they too can experience complete joy on the inside.

Luke tells us in Acts 16 that when Paul planted the church at Philippi he was forced to confront *"a slave girl with a python spirit."* Most English translations recognize this as a reference to the famous Oracle at Delphi, where it was believed the Greek god Apollo empowered priestesses to prophesy, so they simply tell us that the slave girl *"had a spirit by which she predicted the future."* I find it significant, however, that Luke calls the demon a python spirit. It reminds us that the Devil loves to crush our hearts with desires that rob us of our joy.[4] The legend did not claim that Apollo defeated the massive python snake at Delphi by appeasing it. He shot it through the head with his bow and arrow, dealing with its crushing coils once and for all.

Most people do not understand this. They try to appease their desires. Oscar Wilde was only half-joking when he said

---

[1] Paul tells us in 2 Corinthians 11:9 that some of their gifts also funded his church plants in Corinth and Achaia. The Philippians also gave very generously to the poor believers in Jerusalem in 2 Corinthians 8:1–5.

[2] We are told in Acts 28:30 that Paul was permitted to live as a prisoner in his house rather than in prison, just so long as he paid the rent on the property himself.

[3] Interestingly, the Greek word which Paul uses for their *sweet-smelling* sacrifice in 4:18 is *euōdia*, the name of one of the two women he was forced to rebuke for bickering in 4:2!

[4] The slave girl told people to listen to Paul. The Devil is happy with the externals of Christianity. What he cannot stand is genuine Christianity which produces joy on the inside.

that *"The only way to get rid of a temptation is to yield to it. Resist it, and your soul grows sick with longing."*[5] But the whole of Scripture tells us that we can no more appease our desires than appease a crushing python. Solomon warns us in the book of Proverbs that *"The unfaithful are trapped by evil desires... The greedy bring ruin to their households... A heart at peace gives life to the body, but envy rots the bones"*[6] Jeremiah 5:8 tells us that every sinful man thinks there are better-looking women than his wife, as was demonstrated by the Chelsea footballer Ashley Cole when he was caught having an affair in the same year that his wife Cheryl was voted *FHM*'s "sexiest woman of the year". Habakkuk 2:5 warns that success and promotion can never satisfy, and Jesus warns in Matthew 13:22 that *"the deceitfulness of wealth"* will choke us to death if we allow it to. James 3:14–15 tells us that the constant desire for more is an *"earthly, unspiritual, demonic"* emotion.

So what is the solution? Paul tells us in 4:11 that he has *"learned to be content,"* because contentment does not come naturally. He tells us in 4:12 that God has initiated him into the secret of contentment,[7] because contentment and dissatisfaction are not simply character traits; contentment comes from understanding the mystery of the Gospel.[8] Paul tells us in 4:10 that he can only rejoice because he knows he is *in the Lord Jesus*, and he tells us in 4:13 that he is only able to overcome the python's coils because he is in Jesus and Jesus is in him.[9] He tells us in 4:19 that he is only able to be content

---

[5] Oscar Wilde in *The Picture of Dorian Gray* (1891).

[6] Proverbs 11:6; 14:30; 15:27. He also says in 27:20 that the eyes of a man are as likely to be satisfied as hell is of souls.

[7] The Greek verb *mueō* only occurs in the New Testament in 4:12, but it is the root of the word *mustērion*, which means *a secret revealed by God*.

[8] Although Paul borrows the word *autarkēs*, or *self-satisfied*, from the Stoic philosophers, he is not saying he is *contented* through their wishful thinking. He is saying that Jesus alone is enough for him.

[9] 4:13 reads literally, *"I am strong enough to do everything in him who empowers me."*

because he knows that God is his providing Father and that he has made him heir to all he needs through the Gospel of his victorious Son.[10]

Paul does not expect the Gospel to bring him non-stop prosperity. Having the Lord as his Shepherd means he will never lack anything he needs (Psalm 23:1), but sometimes his needs will only be met in the Lord. He tells us up front in 4:12 that he has often been content in spite of hunger and deprivation. Even now he is writing this letter from prison.[11] Paul simply tells us that God enables him on the inside to follow Jesus – the one who fasted for forty days and nights in the desert before telling his disciples that *"I have food to eat that you know nothing about... My food is to do the will of him who sent me"* (John 4:32–34). People who feed their desires will never find contentment, but people who let Jesus fulfil all their desires will find contentment even in affliction. In a world that is being crushed by the python coils of dissatisfaction, Paul has learned to deliver the python a fatal wound with the words: *"I can do all things through him who strengthens me."*

The actress Ingrid Bergman observed that *"Success is getting what you want; happiness is wanting what you get."* That's easier said than done, but Paul tells us that it is possible through the Gospel. Our outward circumstances may fluctuate between plenty and want, but our hearts need not fluctuate with them. We know how to kill the python. Because Jesus is enough for us in every circumstance, we can always know true joy on the inside.

---

[10] Note that Paul promises us in 4:19 that God will meet all of our *needs*, not all of our *desires*.

[11] Paul lists some of his frequent deprivations in 2 Corinthians 11:23–30.

What Paul Did Next
(4:21-23)

The grace of the Lord Jesus Christ be with your spirit. Amen.

(Philippians 4:23)

We have reached the end of these four letters which Paul wrote to the churches in Galatia, Ephesus, Colossae and Philippi. It only remains for him to sign off and let us carry on the work he started. He has taught us that the Gospel means that we have God on the inside and that this one fact changes everything. Now, as we get ready to continue his work in our own generation, he makes some comments that help us piece together what he did next before he died.

In the first half of 4:21, Paul talks about *"God's people in Christ Jesus."* He longed to be free to gather more people for God, and shortly after Epaphroditus left for Philippi his dream came true. He finally stood on trial in Rome, he was acquitted and he was freed to carry on with his plans. He spent over a year planting churches in the major cities of Spain and Southern Gaul before returning back east to Greece and Asia. He spent time in Crete before visiting his friends at Ephesus and Philippi.[1] He was finally back with his beloved churches. He was home with God's People in Christ Jesus.

In the second half of 4:21, Paul talks about *"the brothers and sisters who are with me."* This reminds us that Paul's final years would be spent developing his team. Philippians is the

---

[1] We can tell all this from Romans 15:24 and 28, Titus 1:5, 1 Timothy 1:3 and Philippians 2:23-24.

last of Paul's eight letters to churches in the New Testament.[2] After this, he would only write three more letters – one to Titus and two to Timothy – and all of them would be to train up a new generation of church leaders. Paul does not name the brothers and sisters who are with him, but the Philippians would immediately have thought of Luke. We can tell that Luke stayed on in Philippi from 51 to 55 AD from the fact that he uses the word *"we"* to describe Paul's missionary team until it leaves Philippi in Acts 16:40 and then refers to it as *"they"* until it comes back to Philippi in Acts 20:6. Since Luke helped lead their church in its early years, the Philippians would be excited to learn that he had used the years Paul was in prison to write a gospel and the book of Acts. Paul's imprisonment had provided Luke with time and space to record the story of Jesus and his Church, giving us the crucial background to these four letters that makes their message so challenging for us today.

In 4:22, Paul refers to *"all God's people here"* and to *"Caesar's household."* The Emperor Nero and the Christians at Rome were about to take very different sides. On the night of 18th July, 64 AD, a fire would break out near the main chariot-racing stadium and it would quickly spread right across the sun-scorched city. Rome would burn for a week and a rumour would spread that the emperor had started the fire himself in order to make way for his plans to redevelop the capital city. The Roman historian Tacitus tells us that the emperor responded to these allegations by turning on the Christians:

> *To quash this rumour, Nero fastened the guilt and inflicted the most exquisite tortures on a class hated for their abominations, called Christians by the populace. Christ, from whom the name had its origin, had suffered the death-penalty during the reign of Tiberius at the hands*

---

[2] Paul's other four letters to churches were sent in 51, 52, 55 and 57 AD. See *Straight to the Heart of Romans, Straight to the Heart of 1 and 2 Corinthians* and *Straight to the Heart of 1 Thessalonians to Titus.*

of one of our procurators, Pontius Pilate, and a most mischievous superstition, thus checked for the moment, again broke out not only in Judea, where the evil began, but even in Rome... A large number were convicted, not so much for the crime of setting fire to the city as for the fact that people hated them. Mockery of every sort was added to their deaths. Covered with the skins of beasts, they were torn by dogs and perished, or were nailed to crosses, or were doomed to the flames and burnt, to serve as nightly illumination when daylight had expired.[3]

Many of Paul's friends in Rome would burn in Nero's gardens. A warrant would go out for Paul's own arrest and he would be taken prisoner at Troas, the port city that served the route back from Philippi to Ephesus. He would be brought back to Rome and imprisoned again, but this time there would be no escape. He would be beheaded in 67 AD.[4]

In 4:23, Paul reminds us why he was not afraid to die. He did not see himself as indispensable to the future of the Church, because he knew that he was just an ordinary believer with God on the inside. He ends his letter with a blessing – *"The grace of the Lord Jesus Christ be with your spirit"* – and this prayer of blessing would be answered. The ordinary Christians in Galatia and Ephesus and Colossae and Philippi and elsewhere followed in Paul's footsteps after his martyrdom because they understood what the Gospel truly meant: that they were seated with Jesus in heavenly places, just as Paul had been; that they could walk out their faith and take a courageous stand because Jesus was in them through his Holy Spirit, just as he had been in Paul; and that they could plant churches in city after city, even in the face of persecution, because the same grace of God was with them as had been formerly with Paul.

---

[3] Tacitus in his *Annals* (15.44).

[4] 2 Timothy 4:13. Paul appears to have been arrested so suddenly that he left his cloak and scrolls behind.

These Christians believed Paul's letters. They applied his teaching to their lives. They trusted that they really did have God on the inside. As a result, they attempted great things because they believed that God was with them. Just over 150 years after Paul's death, the Christian leader Origen was able to boast that

> *If we consider how powerful the Gospel has become in just a few short years, making progress through persecution and torture, through death and confiscation – a fact made all the more surprising by the small number of Gospel preachers and their lack of skill – and if we consider that the Gospel has been preached throughout the earth so that Greeks and barbarians, the wise and foolish, surrender to worship Jesus, then there can be no doubt that human might and power have not caused the words of Jesus Christ to conquer the minds and souls of all men with faith and power. This is what Jesus predicted would happen, and it is what He has established through divine answers to prayer.*[5]

Paul's final word in these four letters is *"Amen"*. His work is over. Ours is just beginning. If we believe his teaching in these four letters and if we trust that we have God on the inside, just like him, then we will discover that these words are equally true for us today.

The successes of the early Church were never due to the apostle Paul. They were never due to any human hero. They were simply due to the fact that a generation of believers trusted in the Gospel promise that they had God on the inside. So must we.

---

[5] Origen wrote this in c.230 AD in *De Principiis* (4.2). This is a translation of Rufinus' Latin paraphrase.

Conclusion:
God on the Inside

I can do all this through him who gives me strength.
(Philippians 4:13)

Paul came from Tarsus but when he started running he was like a Kenyan. There is a reason why a third of the New Testament was either written by him or about him. He ran fast for God, very fast. He ran so fast that most people don't think that they could ever run like him.

Emmanuel Mutai is the fastest of the Kenyan runners. He set a new record at the London Marathon in 2011 by running twenty-six miles in just two hours, four minutes and forty seconds. That's a phenomenal time and it's a bit like Paul in Acts. Luke tells us that Paul planted a church in Philippi because *"we stayed there several days,"* and that he planted a church in Thessalonica because *"on three Sabbath days he reasoned with them from the Scriptures."* Paul himself concluded after nine years of planting churches in the Eastern Mediterranean that *"there is no more place for me to work in these regions."*[1] But, instead of being challenged by Paul's example to run fast ourselves, most of us offer him our admiration instead of imitation. We applaud as spectators instead running with him.

Most of us feel that we are a bit more like Lloyd Scott. The retired footballer set another record at the London Marathon in 2002 after deciding to run the entire race for charity in a deep-sea diving suit, complete with heavy lead boots. He took longer

---

[1] Acts 16:12; 17:2; Romans 15:23.

to run the twenty-six miles than any other runner in history, finally finishing five days, eight hours, twenty-nine minutes and forty-six seconds after he started – that's sixty-four times as long as Emmanuel Mutai. Vincent Donovan challenges us to take off the diving suit and run like Paul when he concludes that *"We foreign missionaries have been in East Africa for more than a hundred years... There is something definitely temporary about Paul's missionary stay in any one place. There is something of a deadly permanence in ours."[2]* Most Christians have forgotten that they can run like Paul at all.

That's why I love these four letters that Paul wrote to his churches. The New Testament is unique among the sacred Scriptures of the world for the fact it uses letters as a form of teaching. God preserved Paul's letters for us in the Bible because he wants to give us a deeply personal insight into how Paul ran.[3] God doesn't just want us to hear Paul asking his misguided admirers in Acts 14:15, *"Friends, why are you doing this? We too are only human, like you."* He wants us to grasp that Paul ministered as he did because he was a person with God on the inside. He wants us to read Paul's letters and to conclude that he ran fast because he was in Jesus and Jesus was in him through the Holy Spirit. God promises to empower us to run in exactly the same way if we let him come and live inside us too.

Paper and postage were expensive in the ancient world, so letters tended to be no more than fifty words in length. Paul is so determined that we should know how to run like him that he writes the longest letters written by anyone in the entire ancient world.[4] He wrote at length to the **Galatians** in order to teach us how to be **free on the inside**. He warned that legalism and licence are like lead diving boots, which weigh us down and

[2] Vincent Donovan in *Christianity Rediscovered* (1978).

[3] 2 Peter 3:16 tells us that these letters were treated as authoritative Scripture very early on in Church history.

[4] Paul's letter to the Romans is over 100 times longer than the average Roman letter. It is the longest surviving single letter from the ancient world.

stop us running fast for God. *"You were running a good race. Who cut in on you to keep you from obeying the truth?"* he asked us in Galatians 5:7. Now, as we come to the end of this commentary, he urges us to take off the diving boots and to run as those who have been set free on the inside.

Paul explained the Gospel in glorious detail to the **Ephesians** in order to show us that he ran fast because he had been made **new on the inside**. He hadn't received the Gospel as medicine but as a miracle, not as healing for a sick soul but as resurrection for a dead one. As a result, he was not weighed down by his former sins. He was propelled forward by who he was in Jesus. He had learned to sit, walk and stand in the Gospel, so he knew how to run. He encourages us to throw off everything that hinders us from running too. The work of evangelism, church planting and extending Jesus' rule is as urgent now as it has ever been.

Paul explained to the **Colossians** that each of us can run fast like him because the Gospel makes us **strong on the inside**. He bares his soul freely in these letters, telling us in Colossians 1:29 that *"I labour, struggling with all his energy, which so powerfully works in me."* Olympic athletes have to undergo blood tests because race umpires know that drugs can enhance their performance and make them run faster. Paul tells us that the best drugs on the market are nothing compared to the way that people run when they know that they have God to empower them on the inside.

Paul cheered on the **Philippians**, conscious that his imprisonment made it all the more crucial that other people should start running with him. He showed them how to have **joy on the inside**, convinced that hell possesses no power that can stop a Christian running. *"I can do all things through him who gives me strength,"* he rejoices in Philippians 4:13. So can we.

D. L. Moody was an uneducated shoe salesman in nineteenth-century Chicago who read Paul's letters and believed these words were true. His friend Henry Varley encouraged him to put the words into practice, challenging him that *"The world has yet to see what God can do with and for and through and in a man who is fully and wholly consecrated to him."* Moody reflected later that *"Varley meant any man! Varley didn't say he had to be educated or brilliant or anything else. Just a man! Well, by the Holy Spirit in me, I'll be that man."*[5] The ordinary shoe salesman found that Paul's words were true and he ran fast, leading hundreds of thousands of people to Christ. That's what happens when people stop applauding Paul and start running with him.

So how about you? At the end of these four letters, will you be a spectator or a runner? Paul encourages you to take off the diving boots and run fast with him. *"I plead with you, brothers and sisters, become like me,"* he implores you in Galatians 4:12. If you will take him at his word, like D. L. Moody or like the great crowd of runners who have believed these words throughout Church history, then he promises that you will run fast with him. You will run like an ordinary person who has God on the inside.

---

[5] There are many great biographies of D. L. Moody. This quotation draws from several of them.

STRAIGHT TO THE HEART SERIES

TITLES AVAILABLE: OLD TESTAMENT

TITLES AVAILABLE: NEW TESTAMENT

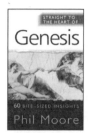

ISBN 978 0 85721 001 2

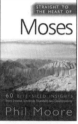

ISBN 978 0 85721 056 2

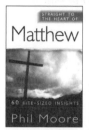

ISBN 978 1 85424 988 3

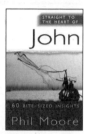

ISBN 978 0 85721 253 5

ISBN 978 0 85721 252 8

ISBN 978 0 85721 428 7

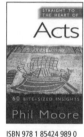

ISBN 978 1 85424 989 0

ISBN 978 0 85721 057 9

ISBN 978 0 85721 426 3

ISBN 978 0 85721 002 9

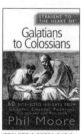

ISBN 978 0 85721 546 8

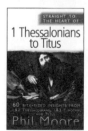

ISBN 978 0 85721 548 2

ISBN 978 1 85424 990 6

GAGGING JESUS
Things Jesus Said We Wish He Hadn't

Phil Moore

"Whether you are a believer or merely a curious sceptic, this book will help you to discover Jesus as he really is."
Sandy Millar – co-founder of The Alpha Course and former vicar of Holy Trinity Brompton

If you ever suspected that Jesus wasn't crucified for acting like a polite vicar in a pair of socks and sandals, then this book is for you. Fasten your seatbelt and get ready to discover the real Jesus in all his outrageous, ungagged glory.

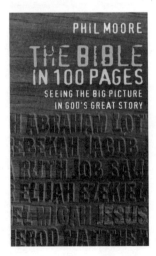

THE BIBLE IN 100 PAGES
Seeing the Big Picture in God's Great Story

Phil Moore

15 short chapters on the Bible's main narratives and the central teachings, showing how the whole relates to Christ.

Written in a punchy and engaging style, this crisp, clear summary provides a handy reference tool enabling the reader to see how the Bible fits together. Despite its many authors and vast time frame, there is a core narrative that runs throughout the text.